"Not only do the authors share stories and insights from female leaders around the world, but they turn these into actionable 'how-tos' that every one of us can take and make our own. This book reminds educators that every one of them belongs in the leadership arena and that their ideas, their voice, and their experiences matter. You will finish the book feeling inspired not only to lead, but to empower those around you to do the same."

Dr. Rania Saeb, *West Coast University & California State University, USA*

"In this insightful and honest gathering of voices, experiences, and tribulations, the authors suggest specific reflective practices to support and guide future women into leadership pathways. As a reflective experience the strategies can help women seeking leadership positions in moving forward; as a gathering space it can connect those who were interviewed to current and future leaders as a means of mentoring for success. If you are interested in these pathways, this is a book to read!"

Dr. Beverly Shaklee, *George Mason University, USA*

"What I appreciate about this book is that it acknowledges the systemic and cultural realities women face. This serves as a powerful tool in empowering women and redirecting the focus towards transforming the system, rather than placing the burden solely on women to adapt and change. By addressing these realities, the book provides a refreshing, much-needed perspective. The authors skillfully weave together the voices of inspiring leaders and the latest research, creating an inspiring and authentic connection with the reader."

Ms. Kawai Lai, *August Public, USA*

"Insightful and practical, this book engages with something for the head—a chance to reflect on evidence-based research and reframe one's current thinking; for the heart—a focus on unique stories that will resonate and connect to a leader's moral purpose; and for the hands—a call to action to make a positive difference in one's self and in the lives of others. Centered on inclusive leadership, this transformational book will serve to inspire positive changes in aspiring and established school leaders alike."

Ms. Sarah Plews, *Sarah Plews Consultancy, USA*

"With this book, Kim and Christina have created a juggernaut of a resource. Not only do these interviews validate the experiences of women everywhere aspiring to be leaders in education, but they also leverage those experiences by including relevant research to explain them. Moreover, each chapter includes pointed, sometimes provocative, prompts for even the most established leader to reflect on. This book is a call to action which will ideally result in a new generation of diverse, equitable school leadership."

Ms. Adrienne Michetti, *Ample Means Learning & Coaching, Canada*

"By allowing women leaders in education to share personal narratives in their own words, and by showcasing the experiences of women from various backgrounds, cultures, and contexts, this book establishes a sense of connection and relatability. It serves as a valuable resource for all leaders who aim to support and mentor emerging talent within their school communities, and as a roadmap for overcoming the obstacles that hinder women's progress, paving the way for a more inclusive and equitable educational landscape."

Ms. Nancy Lhoest-Squicciarini, *Educational Collaborative for International Schools, Luxembourg*

Finding Your Path as a Woman in School Leadership

Featuring the experiences of over 70 successful female leaders in international, public, and private schools around the world, *Finding Your Path as a Woman in School Leadership* brings together interconnected stories about the realities of being a woman in K–12 school leadership today. Women face distinct and unique challenges in pursuing a leadership pathway in schools; unfortunately, most of the obstacles facing women are hidden and only become visible when encountered on the journey to leadership. This book uncovers these invisible obstacles and shares the personal journeys of real women who have overcome them. Chapters feature powerful stories woven together to provide takeaway strategies and address common themes for women in leadership, including unconscious bias and daily microaggressions; physical, linguistic, and cultural expectations of leaders; perception (or reality) of lack of opportunities for women; impostor syndrome and double standards; and availability of mentorship and guidance. This impactful book provides actionable steps for both aspiring leaders and established leaders ready to support growing leaders in their school communities.

Kim Cofino is Founder and CEO of Eduro Learning and host of the #coachbetter podcast. After decades of experience at international schools in Germany, Malaysia, Thailand, and Japan, she now helps schools develop sustainable and successful instructional coaching programs. Kim is based in Bangkok, Thailand.

Christina Botbyl is an experienced teaching and learning leader in international education. She is a facilitator with the National School Reform Faculty leading Critical Friends Group coaches training and is currently the Chief Academic Director at an international school.

Other Eye On Education Books Available from Routledge
(www.routledge.com/eyeoneducation)

When Black Students Excel: How Schools Can Engage and Empower Black Students
Joseph F. Johnson, Jr., Cynthia L. Uline, and Stanley J. Munro, Jr.

Mismeasuring Schools' Vital Signs
Steve Rees and Jill Wynns

First Aid for Teacher Burnout: How You Can Find Peace and Success, 2nd Edition
Jenny Grant Rankin

Leading School Culture through Teacher Voice and Agency
Sally J. Zepeda, Philip D. Lanoue, David R. Shafer, Grant M. Rivera

Becoming an International School Educator: Stories, Tips, and Insights from Teachers and Leaders
Edited by Dana Specker Watts and Jayson W. Richardson

The Principal's Desk Reference to Professional Standards: Actionable Strategies for Your Practice
Robyn Conrad Hansen and Frank D. Davidson

Trailblazers for Whole School Sustainability: Case Studies of Educators in Action
Cynthia L. Merse, Jennifer Seydel, Lisa A.W. Kensler, and David Sobel

Get Organized Digitally!: The Educator's Guide to Time Management
Frank Buck

The Confident School Leader: 7 Keys to Influence and Implement Change
Kara Knight

Empowering Teacher Leadership: Strategies and Systems to Realize Your School's Potential
Jeremy D. Visone

Creating, Grading, and Using Virtual Assessments: Strategies for Success in the K-12 Classroom
Kate Wolfe Maxlow, Karen L. Sanzo, and James Maxlow

Building Learning Capacity in an Age of Uncertainty: Leading an Agile and Adaptive School
James A. Bailey

Leadership for Deeper Learning: Facilitating School Innovation and Transformation
Jayson W. Richardson, Justin Bathon, Scott McLeod

Finding Your Path as a Woman in School Leadership

A Guide for Educators, Allies, and Advocates

Kim Cofino and Christina Botbyl

Routledge
Taylor & Francis Group

NEW YORK AND LONDON

Designed cover image: © Getty Images

First published 2024
by Routledge
605 Third Avenue, New York, NY 10158

and by Routledge
4 Park Square, Milton Park, Abingdon, Oxon, OX14 4RN

Routledge is an imprint of the Taylor & Francis Group, an informa business

© 2024 Kim Cofino and Christina Botbyl

The right of Kim Cofino and Christina Botbyl to be identified as authors of this work has been asserted in accordance with sections 77 and 78 of the Copyright, Designs and Patents Act 1988.

All rights reserved. No part of this book may be reprinted or reproduced or utilised in any form or by any electronic, mechanical, or other means, now known or hereafter invented, including photocopying and recording, or in any information storage or retrieval system, without permission in writing from the publishers.

Trademark notice: Product or corporate names may be trademarks or registered trademarks, and are used only for identification and explanation without intent to infringe.

Library of Congress Cataloging-in-Publication Data
Names: Cofino, Kim, author. | Botbyl, Christina, author.
Title: Finding your path as a woman in school leadership : a guide for educators, allies, and advocates / Kim Cofino and Christina Botbyl.
Description: New York, NY : Routledge, 2024. | Series: Eye on education | Includes bibliographical references.
Identifiers: LCCN 2023036632 | ISBN 9781032546797 (hardback) | ISBN 9781032546780 (paperback) | ISBN 9781003426110 (ebook)
Subjects: LCSH: Educational leadership. | Women in education. | Women educators. | Women school administrators. | Educational change.
Classification: LCC LB2806 .C5266 2024 | DDC 371.2/011—dc23/eng/20230925
LC record available at https://lccn.loc.gov/2023036632

ISBN: 978-1-032-54679-7 (hbk)
ISBN: 978-1-032-54678-0 (pbk)
ISBN: 978-1-003-42611-0 (ebk)

DOI: 10.4324/9781003426110

Typeset in Optima
by Apex CoVantage, LLC

Access the Support Material: www.routledge.com/9781032546780

To all the inspiring women who participated in the Women Who Lead interviews, thank you for sharing your stories with us, and for allowing us to share them with the world.

And to the mothers who forged the pathway before us and to the daughters who continue to demand that pathways become more accessible to a diverse group of travelers—without you, this book would not be possible.

Contents

Foreword	xi
Meet the Authors	xiv
Acknowledgments	xx
Preface	xxii

PART I: SEEING YOURSELF AS A LEADER   1

1. The Path to Leadership   3
2. Recognizing Your Potential to Lead   15
3. Uncovering Essential Skills for Female Leaders   27
4. Facing Impostor Syndrome: It Happens to Successful Leaders Too!   40
5. The Power of Mentorship for Women Seeking Leadership Positions   56

PART II: FACING THE REALITIES OF LEADERSHIP FOR WOMEN   71

6. Double Standards for Women Leaders   73
7. The Old Boys' Club in School Leadership: The Elephant in the Room   88
8. Exploring Intersectionality for Women in Leadership Positions   98

| 9 | Clarifying the Lack of Opportunity for Women in Leadership | 115 |

PART III: STRATEGIES AND SKILLS FOR SUCCESS		**129**
10	Seeing the Big Picture	131
11	Lessons Learned from Head-of-School Interviews	144
12	Strategies and Skills for Handling Difficult Conversations	159
13	How Busy Leaders Prioritize and Find Focus	175
14	Finding a Space of Well-Being in a Busy Leadership Role	188
15	Shaping a Culture of Well-Being and Leading by Example	200
16	Next Steps: Moving Toward Whole-School Change	211

Appendix A: Women Who Lead Interview Participants   221
Appendix B: WWL Interview Questions   227

Foreword

Why is it so hard for women to lead? This is a question I have heard echoed through the decades, and there doesn't seem to be a reason that makes sense to me. Women are intelligent, solution-focused, hard-working, cooperative, caring, resilient, and courageous human beings, so what is the problem? Since the dawn of existence, or so we have been told, men have hunted and women have gathered. Whether or not this division really existed, I think there is something in this word *gather* that holds a key truth that is overlooked and underestimated. I truly believe that learning and growing through shared experiences is a hidden superpower that we, as women, need to leverage to make a greater impact on the lives of others. In a world where women's voices are still unheard or overlooked, it is time to raise the volume and start to use our superpower to celebrate the incredible strength of every woman who leads with intention, enthusiasm, and courage. In this remarkable book, Kim and Christina invite us to listen, learn, and grow together, so as you join this incredible journey of shared narratives, expect to find disbelief, anger, surprise, solace, and, hopefully, joy and inspiration—I did.

Leadership, for many women, is a path that unfolds in unexpected ways. Some step into it intentionally, while others stumble upon it serendipitously. Self-doubt is an all too familiar companion for almost all of us at one time or another. I still remember the day when the school director came into my classroom and asked whether I would consider stepping into a leadership role. I was too scared to disagree but couldn't understand why he had chosen me. After 25 years of attending workshops, getting an advanced degree, and thousands of professional development hours, there are still some days when I find myself asking, "Have I done enough? Am I enough?" If you have ever felt lost or alone in your leadership journey (probably most of us), these stories are a much-needed reminder that most women leaders have felt the same way at one point or another. Each story reminds us that having doubt is normal and underscores a powerful message: You are not alone; we are not alone.

Leadership skills are brought to life through practice, modeling, and support from others. The pragmatic in me loves the sections of the book in which Kim and Christina share useful, research-based tips designed to support women leaders at different stages of their leadership journey. In a practical section titled Take Action, they share differentiated strategies for developing leaders, for established leaders, and for schools and organizations. The result is that women leaders of all kinds can learn, explore, and practice key strategies and skills.

Whether you are seeking to improve your confidence or competence as a leader, hearing the voices of others who walk in similar shoes is refreshing, and you will find yourself thinking, "Yes, OMG, absolutely!" This book is a powerful combination of insightful stories, compelling research, and useful strategies, all woven together in an inspiring storybook. One of my favorite quotes in the book is shared by Lola Aneke: "As female leaders, we need to focus on both personal and collective growth. Let's stand as one, even in the same field. The sky is wide enough for all of us to fly." This message gets at the heart of the matter for me: Together we are stronger, and my wish is for every woman who reads this book to think of someone in your life or community who can benefit from your superpower.

To all the extraordinary women leaders out there (yes, you!), let's remember to celebrate who we are and find ways to support and cheer each other on. As you immerse yourself in the pages of this book, consider what role you are playing in the theater of leadership. How are you using your voice to reshape leadership for yourself? How are you empowering others to do the same? Let this book be your guide, inspiring you to identify, create, and celebrate your own leadership manifesto.

Amanda Palmer says, "Just letting someone speak their truth can sometimes be the biggest gift you can give them, to just hold the space for them." Thanks to Kim and Christina for holding the space for us to hear truths from others and our own hearts. I hope you are able to experience many "aha!" moments as a first step in reshaping your thinking about your own leadership, knowing full well that for every story in this book, there are countless more to be heard and told. Join us in this conversation, and share your story with us or someone else. It's helpful, it's special, it's necessary.

Women have always been told that we are good at gathering, but my hope is that by reading the stories in this book, we realize that whatever else we are, we are leaders. With gratitude to all the past, present, and future amazing women leaders, let's lead together.

Ji Han
Senior Partner, Orchard Learning Partners

Meet the Authors

Kim's Story

In the winter of 2020, I began to notice a disconcerting trend among the women educators I was speaking to for my podcast (http://coachbetter.tv/), in casual conversation, and in client consultations. These successful educators consistently described feeling a reluctance to identify themselves as leaders, as well as other clear symptoms of impostor syndrome.

Realizing that this issue seemed to be affecting women educators at all experience levels in many countries around the world, I wondered if I could use my podcast platform to shine a light on these challenges. There are many rarely discussed and often seemingly insurmountable obstacles to women's career advancement, and for aspiring female leaders in education, the pathway forward is often hazy. Navigating the world of international schools, with its often-exclusionary networking and recruiting practices, can be particularly difficult. When reflecting on these challenges, I wondered if personal anecdotes and stories from women education leaders would help others to recognize shared struggles and the variety of possible pathways to leadership.

As I designed the questions that eventually guided the Women Who Lead (WWL) interviews, my goal was to clarify and document the celebrations and struggles women face when pursuing leadership in the field of education. While every participant's story was different, many common threads emerged over the course of the project. The stories revealed many hidden difficulties and harsh realities encountered on their path to leadership. The clear connections among these women's experiences, especially considering the diversity of the women interviewed, mean that these stories could resonate with any woman working toward leadership in education. This book shares the real-life experiences of women who have faced these obstacles and succeeded.

When I began the interview process, I identified eight to ten successful women leaders I knew personally (or through connections) to speak with and feature in a series on the #coachbetter podcast (http://coachbetter.tv/). However, at the end of each interview, I asked each guest to refer me to another woman who might be willing to share her story. This snowball sampling approach resulted in a participant group that became bigger and bigger, eventually leading to interviews with over 70 women leaders in the span of about six months.

As I was conducting the interviews, I prioritized both inclusivity and diversity, seeking to ensure a wide representation of female leaders. My goal was to be intentionally inclusive of women from a variety of backgrounds to ensure diversity of thought and experience. These interviews represent the voices of 34 women of color, eight non-native speakers of English, three LGBTQ+ educators, and educators working on every continent except Antarctica. The women interviewed hold (and most continue to hold) a variety of leadership roles in international, public, and private schools around the world. The roles they held at the time of their interviews included 23 heads of school, over 20 principals, 20 curriculum directors, and 15 leaders working in the field of education but not employed full-time in schools (often education consultants) (Appendix A).

After interviewing over 70 women during the spring of 2020, I realized I needed to pause and determine what to do with these remarkable conversations. I had recorded over 700 hours of video content. There were patterns emerging through the interviews, and it became clear that these conversations deserved a broader platform than just a special series on my podcast. Based on my experience creating online courses for my company, Eduro Learning, including the Certificate of Educational Technology and Information Literacy (COETAIL) and The Coach Certificate and Mentorship Program, I decided to create a new online certification course called Women Who Lead. In the time between the interviews and the publishing of this book, over 50 participants have graduated from the course and have leveraged its insights and inspirations to further their individual leadership journeys. (If you would like to dig into these conversations further and hear the stories of these remarkable women in their own words, without the

Meet the Authors

filter of the authors, please consider enrolling in the Women Who Lead online course [https://edurolearning.com/women/].)

When the project was initiated, I never considered the possibility that I would be inspired to elaborate on these leaders' experiences within the pages of a book. In fact, it was several of the women interviewed, among others, who first convinced me to embark upon this book project, and I am eternally grateful for the encouragement of these inspiring leaders in so many ways.

Many of the stories shared in this book were first shared as articles on The International Educator Online. Please note that the conversations shared in this book reflect each leader's thinking at a specific point in time. Much has changed since the spring of 2020, including several of the participants' job titles and their countries of residence, and all of the responses and details shared in this book reflect their realities at the time of each individual interview.

Once I recognized that these stories needed to be shared, I knew I wanted to bring a research lens to the book. Although the stories themselves are incredibly valuable narratives, the links to evidence-based research emphasize that these narratives are more than isolated personal anecdotes.

It was at this point that I reached out to Christina to seek her expertise. Having worked with her on a number of projects over the years, I knew she would be the perfect co-author to bring a crucial research lens to this book. Christina is an experienced school leader with relevant academic expertise as a result of her doctoral studies in education leadership. Each chapter's themes uncovered a variety of opportunities to dive into academic research on topics such as bias, gender, intersectionality, leadership, and cultures of inequality.

My Background

Born and raised in the United States, I began teaching in international schools immediately after graduating from university. I have held a variety of roles, including instructional coach, across over 15 years of full-time teaching. While working full-time, I began offering workshops at conferences and consulting with international schools, initially around technology and innovation. While working as a coach at the International School Bangkok in Thailand, I co-created COETAIL and became a founding member of the Learning2 Conference and its board. As my consulting and presenting experience expanded, I founded my own company, Eduro Learning, in 2012, while working at Yokohama International School in Japan.

Since 2015, I have been based in Bangkok, Thailand, and now work full time for Eduro Learning, where I am focused on bringing sustainable instructional coaching practices to international schools. I am passionate about helping schools and coaches #coachbetter, and to do so, I host the #coachbetter podcast and designed the Coach Certificate and Mentorship Program for instructional coaches in international schools. I am an avid content creator for YouTube and my podcast, and I write for many publications, all focused on the power of coaching to sustain change in schools. I am a frequent keynote speaker and workshop presenter, and, through Eduro Learning, offer long-term partnerships with international schools to support their goals around teacher professional learning and growth through instructional coaching.

In addition to my work in education, I am also a competitive powerlifter, and I am honored to represent Thailand at international events as a member of the Thai National Powerlifting Team.

Positionality: I am a white woman, born and raised in the United States of America. I have lived and worked in the United States and abroad. I hold a bachelor of arts in history and political science, and a master of arts in education. I have taught in international schools in Germany, Japan, Malaysia, and Thailand, primarily as an instructional coach.

Christina's Story

Kim first came to my attention around 2012 when I entered the social media education technology space. I followed her journeys leading as a technology coach, providing asynchronous professional learning certificate programs, and offering private coaching services. I began to work with Kim one-on-one in the private coaching space in the fall of 2019. I chuckle now when I reflect back on the challenge that brought me to coaching pre-global pandemic: feeling confident during timed, one-way, recorded video interviews. While I was combating a particular interview format, I now recognize that I was also trying to silence the impostor who sits on my shoulder whispering negative thoughts in my ear . . . like many highly educated and competent women do. Kim was the coach and cheerleader I needed and deserved!

Meet the Authors

I worked with Kim throughout the global pandemic, focusing on a variety of topics that included leadership skills, project development and implementation, and being interviewed as a participant in the early stages of her Women Who Lead project. I also benefited from having her as a thought partner as I approached my doctoral dissertation proposal and the eventual research that I would defend to earn my degree. Because I was learning about the qualitative research process and designing my own study, I recognized similar aspects in Kim's approach to the WWL interviews. I saw that she, too, was developing and engaging in a qualitative research study. Kim and I were both interested in making meaning of a particular experience or phenomenon, the essence of qualitative research.

As I approached the last stages of dissertation writing, Kim mentioned that once I was done with my doctoral work, she had an idea she wanted to share with me. Little did I know that her motivation to share her qualitative research for the WWL project would result in a partnership to bring forth this book.

We set out on separate research explorations that eventually converged at a shared journey to deeply understand the lived experiences of women leaders in international schools. Through the words of over 70 women leaders, we have both come to better understand their experiences through each individual interview. With each theme that emerged, I dove into related academic research in order to provide deeper insights that help to explain so many of the common experiences of women leaders.

My Background

As a career educator, I began my teaching after graduating from university. My first experiences in the United States were in independent, private, and public school settings. Over the course of 14 years in the United States, my experiences included teaching students across the K–12 continuum, at the university level, and in adult continuing education settings. In 2003, I responded to a strong desire to live abroad by accepting a job teaching English Language Arts at the middle school level in an international school in Kuwait. As I entered the international stage of my career in education, I began to take on informal and formal leadership roles.

My leadership roles highlight my passion for teaching and learning, including K–12 chief academic director, K–12 curriculum director, international facilitator, principal, school visit team member, workshop leader, and unit reviewer. I have become the leader I am today through leading and training educators to become better listeners, collaborators, and thinkers. My growth and development as a woman in education leadership have been, and continue to be, a profound part of who I am.

Positionality: I am a white woman born and raised in the United States of America. I have lived and worked in the United States and abroad. I hold a bachelor of arts in French and English, a master of science in curriculum and instruction, and a doctor of education in educational leadership. I have taught and led across the K–12 continuum in public and private schools in the United States and in private schools in Kuwait and Morocco.

As an educator and a researcher, I bring both professional experience and formal learning to this work. I acknowledge the privilege I have in being able to access certain resources, and I strive to be aware of my own biases and recognize how these might and could shape my research and thinking.

Acknowledgments

Without a doubt, a significant number of eyes and brains came together in collaboration to bring this book to life.

Kim's initial endeavor to interview a few women leaders in international schools was the seed that demanded growth, but nothing can grow without a lot of care and attention. This book received a lot of attention as it was written, edited, researched, organized, reviewed, and fine-tuned throughout the various stages of the process.

We would first like to thank the Women Who Lead interview participants. Without their willingness to share their experiences as women education leaders around the world, we would not have even had the inspiration to set out on this writing journey.

We are so grateful to all those who encouraged us to write this book. It was your belief in us that was the tap on the shoulder we needed to start writing. In particular, Kim's conversations with Rania Saeb, Joellen Killion, and Madeleine Heide moved this concept from "just an idea" to "you have to share this!" Additional thanks go to Dr. Jason Richardson, who provided much-needed advice about academic writing and wonderful connections to get us started.

The following educators were kind enough to read and review our work as it began to take shape. Their insights were invaluable and provided opportunities for improvements whether they reviewed a chapter, a series of chapters, or the entire book.

    Adrienne Michetti, Vancouver, BC
    Alex Gustad, Bombay, India
    Beverly Shaklee, Fairfax, VA
    Cary Hart, Santo Domingo, DR

Acknowledgments

Fran Prolman, McLean, VA
Ji Han, Zurich, Switzerland
Kawai Lai, Seattle, WA
Nancy Lhoest-Squicciarini, Luxembourg
Sarah Plews, Porto, Portugal
Rania Saeb, Oceanside, CA
Uzay Ashton, Singapore

The structure and organization of this book would not be what they are without the significant contributions of Alex Guenther, who read and re-read our work and provided much-needed oversight on word counts. Martine Claremont provided an extremely valuable "outside eye" and first-review copy-editing of the entire manuscript. We also appreciate the attentiveness provided to two first-time authors by the team at Routledge, including Heather Jarrow and Mari Zajac, who always had prompt and thorough answers to our every question.

We would be remiss if we did not acknowledge each other in this exciting and rewarding adventure. May we continue to elevate each other and the talented women in our field through this collaboration and many more to come.

Preface

We are honored to share this work with you. In this project, we recognize that we are the couriers of other women's stories as told through the Women Who Lead interview series, and although many of their described experiences align with our own, those stories are the focus of this work.

 ## Why Do We Need This Book?

Equity is ensuring that people have access to the same opportunities. The supports and scaffolds that individuals need to succeed will not all look the same, nor will they come from the same sources. While this book focuses on equity for all women who enter leadership, we believe that furthering equity for any group can benefit everyone.

Legal, economic, and social systems have long deprived women of equal access to freedoms and opportunities afforded to men. The systemic nature of gender discrimination has been acknowledged by the United Nations General Assembly (UNGA) in the *2030 Agenda for Sustainable Development* (UNGA, 2015), which includes 17 sustainable development goals (SDGs). The fifth SDG sets out to "achieve gender equality and empower all women and girls" (UNGA, 2015, p. 14). This SDG specifically identifies the need to ensure "women's full and effective participation and equal opportunities for leadership at all levels of decision making in political, economic and public life" (UNGA, 2015, p. 18). While the United Nations agenda calls for implementing all SDGs by 2030, gender discrimination prevents women from entering leadership roles seamlessly and comfortably. Despite the perception that more women are moving into senior leadership roles in education in recent years, data indicate that there remains much progress to make to achieve gender parity by 2030.

According to the survey *From Resistance to Sustainability and Leadership Cultivating Diverse Leaders in International Schools* (Shaklee et al., 2019), although women are making some gains in teacher leadership and middle leadership positions, this "is a trickle by the time you get to the upper end" (p. 7). During the WWL interviews, Deb Welch noted that over the last 10 years, data collected by the Association for International School Heads (AISH) indicated that 28–30% of the heads of international schools were women. This statistic (among many others) confirms the reality that women remain underrepresented among upper leadership in international schools. These statistics from international schools mirror those of American public schools: "As of January 2022, there were 141 (28%) female superintendents in the top 500 largest districts" (ILO Group, 2022, p. 5).

Although each woman's story is unique, some of the common themes throughout these interviews focused on challenges around

- unconscious bias and daily microaggressions
- physical, linguistic, and cultural expectations of people who lead
- perception (or reality) of lack of opportunities for women
- exclusionary networking practices among traditional leaders
- impostor syndrome and double standards
- new levels of leadership and the interview process
- focus and priorities in a busy leadership role
- personal wellness and wellness within a school community
- availability of mentorship and guidance

This book is designed to help provide fundamental understanding of these and other common problems, combined with specific descriptions of how some current women leaders have dealt with them, in the hope that these personal stories and strategies will help others as they navigate their own leadership journeys.

An Important Note about Systemic Inequity

While we hope this book is inspirational in terms of actions you can take on an individual level, we recognize that gender-based hierarchies

Preface

exist in K–12 education around the world. Women are impacted in many different ways as we work within systems built upon inequality. Individuals and groups who are most frequently marginalized should not bear the responsibility for changing their behaviors or solving the systemic inequities that hinder their progress. For this reason, we have included actions for schools or organizations in the *Take Action* section of each chapter. We call upon schools and organizations to examine and adjust systemic expectations, norms, and practices so that marginalized groups can receive equitable opportunities and representation. Organizational and systemic actions for equity are required in order to establish sustainable spaces that welcome women leaders, as well as leaders from other marginalized groups.

While acknowledging the limitations of individual efforts, this book is primarily intended to share optimistic and inspiring stories about what individuals can achieve within larger systems of inequality, not as a critical examination of broader issues.

As you read, we invite you to do the work of addressing systemic inequity that is within your capacity. We see this work happening on three levels:

- We encourage you to reflect on internalized patriarchy that could be stopping you from advancing your goals.
- If you're in a position of power, we encourage you to reflect on how you might be able to support greater equity within your organization.
- If you have the capacity to change systems or start conversations about changing systems, we encourage you to do so to create greater equity on a systemic level within your organization.

Who Is This Book for?

This book is primarily for women educators who are considering, or pursuing, leadership, with or without formal titles. While we use the term "leadership" and while the interviews shared feature education leaders, the themes of the book could be helpful to women in most situations seeking to develop confidence and recognize their capabilities. The lived experiences of women leaders in schools around the world can help prepare the current and next generations for the individualized ways this pathway can take shape.

By sharing real-life stories of women who lead, we hope that their challenges, experiences, learnings, and successes will reveal possibilities for women who are ready to recognize and embrace their leadership potential. Our goal is for all leaders, regardless of gender, to develop the confidence, partnerships, resilience, and strategies that will empower them to raise their voices and take actions against practices that support and encourage gender discrimination.

We hope that this work might also provide inspiration for advocates, allies, and mentors, regardless of gender, to support women around them. On that note, men absorbing some of the stories in this book might initially feel left out; many male leaders, for example, do not feel welcome in the "old boys' club" at all or have had to struggle to achieve their position. As true as this might be in individual cases, on average, there are still many more layers of difficulty involved in succeeding as a woman in leadership. Men whose own journeys were challenging should therefore be able to develop, without feeling personally defensive or diminished, an awareness of all the additional potential stereotypes and biases that the average woman leader must contend with.

Men play a crucial role in achieving gender equality. Men who work in education and education leadership are key contributors to advancing gender equality. Every choice that is made and every action that is taken by men will either maintain the status quo of the systems that perpetuate inequity or help to transform and improve gender equity. Men reading this book are invited to use the learning to actively engage as partners in support for their women colleagues.

We therefore also offer this book as a resource for all members of a school community, including those already in leadership. In this work, we aim to raise awareness of the specific and unique challenges that women face and to support developing leaders. In the *Take Action* section of each chapter, we invite you to establish practices that provide more equitable experiences for all leaders in your school community.

The interviews that underlie this book focus on the experiences of women who lead in the context of international schools, an umbrella term encompassing:

- "traditional" international schools, catering principally to globally mobile expatriates

- more ideologically focused international schools, for example the various United World Colleges, established with a particular mission and not necessarily in response to a market need
- the newer, non-traditional type of international school, aimed largely at host-country nationals and often operated on a more commercial footing than the first two types of schools

(Hayden & Thompson, 2016, p. 13)

An effort has been made to focus on research centering the international school context in the *Reflections in the Research* section of each chapter. However, it must be noted there is a paucity of academic research on these schools in general and specifically on leadership or women leaders within them. Pedagogical practices, theories, and trends that inform international school leaders around the world are often guided by proven practices borne out of the work of scholars based in Australia, Canada, the United Kingdom, and the United States.

We acknowledge that every reader's experiences and circumstances are unique; readers might discover direct comparisons and contrasts between their personal experiences and what they read here. We hope that readers will be inspired by these stories and that the research will be thought-provoking as they consider their own pathways to leadership and support women leaders around them. As you are reading, please consider sharing your learning from this book with your school community.

What You'll Find in This Book

While this book is organized into three parts, we invite readers to explore the book in their own ways. These three parts are organized as follows:

Part 1: Seeing Yourself as a Leader

In Part 1, we focus on the individual experience of the leadership journey. We explore what the path might look like, summarize how women can recognize their potential to lead, identify the essential skills needed for emerging leaders, discuss the challenge of impostor syndrome, and emphasize the value of inviting a mentor into your journey.

Part 2: Facing the Realities of Leadership for Women

In Part 2, we address the many challenges women face as school leaders, including the double standards experienced in the interviewing process, barriers to networking, and daily microaggressions. We also highlight ways women need to support each other.

Part 3: Strategies and Skills for Success

In Part 3, we look closer at the daily experiences of women leaders. We discuss the mindset shifts and skills needed to be successful in a leadership role, learning how to address confrontation and accountability, bringing a sense of wellness to a busy leader's life, and shaping a human-centered school culture.

In each chapter of the book, you'll read stories from several women, woven together around a common theme. Each chapter aligns the interconnected stories of the women interviewed with relevant research and provides actionable tasks that the reader can take and put into practice immediately.

Each chapter follows the same framework:

Setting the Stage

An introduction to the chapter topic.

Reflections in the Research

Features highlights from the authors' research about the themes shared by the WWL participants to provide academic grounding.

Stories from Women Interviewed

Key highlights from the WWL interviews, woven around the theme of the chapter. A complete list of all women interviewed, and their job titles at the time of interview, can be found in Appendix A.

Finding Her Path

To help put the stories into context, each chapter features one woman's leadership journey as a feature panel.

Take Action

An opportunity to reflect and take action based on your learning, often including real-life example scenarios based on our own experiences, stories shared from WWL interviewees, or stories from the participants in the WWL online course. These sections include tailored content for three levels of increasing scope:

- **For Developing Leaders.** As a developing leader, you are interested in designing and pursuing your own path to leadership. You might already be a leader in your classroom, you might hold an informal role, or you might be starting a formal role for the first time. The *Take Action* sections after each chapter will provide an opportunity to reflect on your experiences and identify steps to move closer to your goals.
- **For Established Leaders.** As an established leader, you are a potential mentor and champion for the women around you. You currently hold a position of leadership and have first-hand experiences that frame the lessons you have to share. The *Take Action* sections will help you identify tangible opportunities to reach out and support aspiring leaders in your organization. This is also an opportunity for men in leadership roles to explore ways they can Take Action and support non-traditional leaders on their pathway.
- **For Schools or Organizations.** These prompts are designed to give space and time to reflect on how your organization is working toward equity. While you might not have the formal power to make these changes, they can be used as conversation prompts to begin a dialogue with your school's leaders in order to begin to clear systemic obstacles and create equitable, supportive pathways for developing leaders.

Like every woman's pathway to leadership, the way you work through each chapter in this book will be unique. We do recommend documenting your thinking in one place, for example in the pages of this book, in a journal, or in a digital document, so you can keep the thread of your learning visible and accessible.

Reading This with Colleagues or a Friend?

You might want to reflect on each chapter using consistent prompts. Here are some frames to guide the conversation.

Table 0.1 Conversation Frames. Conversation frames guide group discussions and provide meaningful ways to share learning and can lead to deeper understanding.

Key points		What are we wondering?	
Group Size: up to 20 Activity Time: 30–40 mins		Group Size: up to 20 Activity Time: 25–40 mins	
5 mins	Write one statement that summarizes a key learning from your reading.	3 mins	On a post-it note, write a question you have based on the content of the reading.
5 mins	Share key learning with a partner and elaborate on implementation and impact.	2 mins	Post questions on a designated shared wall space or table surface.
5 mins × 1–2	Repeat previous step with a new partner one or two more times.	~5 mins	Silently read all questions posted.
10 mins	Share with whole group key points that resonated with you.	2 mins	Choose one post-it note question that you are also wondering about.
7 mins	Discuss: Based on what was heard and shared, what did participants notice?	1 min	A volunteer reads the question on their chosen post-it note.
Practical Application Group Size: up to 20 Activity Time: 15–45 min		7 mins	Volunteer invites the group to discuss the ideas, thoughts, and insights associated with the question.
Planning for application Brainstorm ideas learned in your reading that you could develop or implement in your current leadership practice.		7 mins × 1–2	Repeat as many times as time and/or volunteers permit.
Reflecting on application Share how ideas learned in the reading have been implemented in your context.		7 mins	Discuss: Based on the discussion and questions shared, what additional learning might the group be ready for?

(Continued)

Table 0.1 (Continued)

A-HA! Learning	
Group size: up to 20	
Activity time: 30–40 mins	
5 mins	Write one surprising realization (or a helpful reminder) you had based on your reading.
5 mins	Share your A-HA! Learning with a partner, explaining how it has affected your leadership practice.
5 mins	Find a new partner and share and explain the A-HA! Learning from your previous partner.
5 mins	Repeat the previous step if time and participant numbers permit.
10 mins	In the full group, participants share the A-HA! Learnings that were shared in dyads.
7 mins	Discuss: What similarities and differences did you notice? What additional learning might individuals or the group be ready for based on the A-HA! Learnings?

Content Advisory: This book explores workplace experiences of 70 women in education leadership. Some of these experiences contain references to misogynistic behavior, gender and racial biases, and the inequities that women are subjected to in education leadership. Please attend to your well-being as you engage and disengage with sensitive content as best suits your comfort level.

Chapter Summaries

1. The Path to Leadership

Leaders often appear to have carefully crafted their careers from the onset, always knowing leadership was their path and moving intentionally through the process. However, during the WWL interviews, it became clear there are as many different paths to leadership as there are women leaders. This chapter invites developing and established women leaders to reflect on their journeys to be agents of their own experience.

Feature panel: Elsa Donohue

2. Recognizing Your Potential to Lead

When looking at how women became the leaders we see today, it is important to keep in mind that the culmination of the journey might not have been clear from the start. During the WWL interviews, each successful woman leader was asked to describe and reflect on the moment they realized they had the capacity to lead. For some, there were clear "aha moments" when they recognized their leadership potential. For others, it was an ongoing series of moments and experiences over years.

Feature panel: Caroline Brokvam

3. Uncovering Essential Skills for Female Leaders

When we think of leadership skills, we often think of traditional stereotypes, such as commanding a room, telling people what to do, or being the key decision maker. However, over the last few years, we have seen those established norms become less effective and less desirable. One lesson learned from living through a global pandemic is that leadership can look very different from these preconceived notions—and for most people, this is a welcome change.

Feature Panel: Deb Welch

4. Facing Impostor Syndrome: It Happens to Successful Leaders Too!

Despite evidence to the contrary, many women feel they have not earned the right to apply for leadership positions or that if they do not tick all the boxes on an application, they should not apply. If you feel like you are not ready for leadership, you are not alone. Most of the women interviewed spoke about experiences with impostor syndrome. This chapter will explore some of the internal challenges of the WWL participants, as well as the strategies they have developed to overcome them.

Feature Panel: Madeleine Maceda Heide

5. *The Power of Mentorship for Women Seeking Leadership Positions*

One direct impact of women's lack of representation in leadership is that developing leaders have fewer options for mentorship from someone with similar experiences. In the WWL interviews, many interviewees described challenges that arise due to a lack of opportunities to look up to or learn from other people who look like them at the leadership level. This chapter highlights the advantages of finding this sort of support.

Feature panel: Tambi Tyler

6. *Double Standards for Women Leaders*

Gender-based double standards unfortunately still impact women at home and in the workplace. If you have sought a leadership position yourself and you do not fit the traditional middle-aged white cisgender male stereotype, you might have experienced many of these frustrating double standards yourself. This chapter shares relevant stories from the WWL interviews as well as strategies you can apply in your leadership journey.

Feature Panel: Jennifer Tickle

7. *The Old Boys' Club in School Leadership: The Elephant in the Room*

One of the most common experiences for any non-traditional leader is feeling excluded from the "old boys' club" in leadership circles. As the stories in this chapter show, most female leaders in international school communities have had similar experiences. This chapter also includes constructive approaches the WWL participants implemented to move forward despite exclusion from this network of influential connections.

Feature Panel: Nicole Schmidt

8. *Exploring Intersectionality for Women in Leadership Positions*

In addition to well-known stereotypes surrounding gender and leadership, many women experience additional layers of expectations and bias. The intersection of these stereotypes can multiply the challenges women face in their leadership journeys. A better understanding of those challenges, which include stereotypes based on language, cultural background, and appearance, is an essential first step in challenging and overcoming them.

Feature panel: Junlah Madalinski

9. *Clarifying the Lack of Opportunity for Women in Leadership*

The lack of leadership opportunities for women poses an especially complex challenge. There is often an undeniably inequitable hiring process that disadvantages women, through unconscious bias, intentional discrimination, or societal stereotypes. Unfortunately, this can lead to the false perception that there are a limited number of jobs available for women and therefore that they have to fight among themselves for these positions.

Feature Panel: Dr. Chaunté Garrett

10. *Seeing the Big Picture*

As leaders, our goals range from school-wide to divisional to small-group to individual—and we need to progress on all of them, each year. Ideally, these goals are grounded in the vision and mission of the school, but that does not always make it easy to prioritize or manage conflicting responsibilities.

Feature Panel: Clarissa Sayson

Preface

11. Lessons Learned from Head-of-School Interviews

As we move through the layers of leadership in international schools, the interview process becomes increasingly demanding. This chapter shares 10 key elements of a typical head-of-school interview. Even if you don't currently plan on becoming a school leader yourself, this chapter shines a light on the complex levels of expectation that school communities have for those at the top.
    Feature Panel: Kathleen Naglee

12. Strategies and Skills for Handling Difficult Conversations

Handling confrontation, even when it is a planned conversation, is rarely an easy task, even for experienced leaders. For most educators, conflict resolution is not part of our training, hopefully because it is a rare experience in schools, but it does happen. This chapter includes 10 strategies highlighted by the WWL participants, divided into on-the-spot strategies to help defuse a tense situation and longer-term strategies to help build comfort with accountable conversations.
    Feature Panel: Katrina Charles

13. How Busy Leaders Prioritize and Find Focus

We all know how demanding a leadership role can be. Not only are we constantly trying to make progress on our goals for ourselves and our organization, but we also have to simultaneously keep in mind the varying needs of all stakeholders. Balancing those competing priorities can quickly become overwhelming, especially without a system to deal with them.
    Feature Panel: Suzanna Jemsby

14. Finding a Space of Well-Being in a Busy Leadership Role

Finding a space of well-being in a busy leadership role is challenging. After living through two years of constant crises during the COVID-19 pandemic, making time for wellness almost seems an unfair expectation. Over the course of our interviews, the WWL participants shared a number of strategies they found effective for supporting their health and well-being.

Feature Panel: Dr. Mary Ashun

15. Shaping a Culture of Well-Being and Leading by Example

Leaders must not only manage their time and priorities to find space for their personal well-being but also model strategies of well-being for others. Building on the previous section, this penultimate chapter focuses on some of the WWL participants' more public-facing strategies for refreshing, nourishing, and recharging, describing the ways that these women are intentional in designing and sharing their priorities and routines.

Feature Panel: Nadine Richards

16. Next Steps: Moving Toward Whole-School Change

In the international school circuit, only around 28–33% of all heads of school are women. Therefore, much of the drive for more equitable hiring practices in education leadership must come from our male leaders and other key allies. This chapter identifies tangible strategies that can be shared with current leaders to support the women they work with and promote equity in their organizations. We wrap up with our closing thoughts about how writing this book has changed and shaped us as leaders.

Feature Panels: Kim and Christina

 ## Beyond This Book!

When you're ready to go beyond the book, we've provided extension materials, downloads, and other resources for your own reflection as well as conversations with others on the book website.

References

Hayden, M., & Thompson, J. (2016). *International schools: Current issues and future prospects*. Symposium Books.

ILO Group. (2022, March/April). *The superintendent research project: Assessing worsening gender disparities in K–12 education leadership*. www.ilogroup.com/wp-content/uploads/2022/04/The-Superintendent-Research-Project_-April-2022-Update.pdf

Shaklee, B., Daly, K., Duffy, L., & Watts, D. (2019). *From resistance to sustainability and leadership cultivating diverse leaders in international schools: Results of the 2019 diversity collaborative survey (DCS)*. www.iss.edu/wp-content/uploads/DC_Report_Survey2019Results.pdf

United Nations General Assembly (UNGA). (2015). *Transforming our world: The 2030 agenda for sustainable development*. https://documents-dds-ny.un.org/doc/UNDOC/GEN/N15/291/89/PDF/N1529189.pdf?OpenElement

PART 1

Seeing Yourself as a Leader

# The Path to Leadership

Every time I had the opportunity to step into a role in leadership that made my heart sing, I took it. Sometimes I was lucky, sometimes I wasn't.

—Rachel Hovington

Setting the Stage

We often view our leaders as having carefully crafted their careers from the outset, always knowing that leadership was their path and moving intentionally through the process. However, during the WWL interviews, it became clear that there is a broad spectrum of different approaches to, and ways to enter, leadership. Participants were asked, "Tell me about your leadership journey; how did you get to where you are today?" During these conversations, it emerged that each pathway to leadership is as individual as the leader on the journey. One important common thread is that while an outside observer today might see the interviewees as polished, poised, and highly successful leaders, most did not start out that way.

Reflections in the Research

From a historical perspective, women have long demonstrated their ability to lead in a variety of familial and non-familial contexts, including in business and politics (Duevel et al., 2015; Klenke, 2018). In the 21st century, women's roles in society have expanded from simply being caretakers in the home to taking on leadership roles in local and global organizations (Duevel et al., 2015; Eagly, 2020). Around the globe, the number of women attaining higher levels of education is greater than the number of men (Catalyst, 2020a, 2020b; World Economic Forum, 2021). The first quarter of the 21st century has seen an unprecedented rise of female leaders in politics (e.g., Prime Minister of New Zealand Jacinda Ardern and Vice President of the United States Kamala Harris), business (e.g., Chief Executive Officer of General Motors Mary Barra), technology (e.g., Chief Operating Officer of Facebook Sheryl Sandberg), and philanthropy (e.g., American philanthropist Melinda Gates). However, despite women's impressive gains to date, the goal of gender parity in senior leadership roles has yet to be achieved.

The field of education is no exception. Women occupy 75% of general teaching positions worldwide (Robinson et al., 2017). A Council of International Schools survey indicated that men were three times more likely than women to hold the role of head of school in international schools (Neyra, 2021). The scale of gender balance tips in favor of men in the most senior K–12 education leadership roles in international schools (Diversity Collaborative, 2021; Robinson et al., 2017). In the 21st century, several hurdles on the pathway to equality in education leadership remain for women (Cofino, 2021a; Robinson et al., 2017). Both internal and external barriers impact the ascension of women from teaching roles to senior leadership and superintendent roles (Cofino, 2021c; Robinson et al., 2017). Internal barriers exist within women including low self-image, lack of confidence, and low aspiration or motivation (Cofino, 2021c; Robinson et al., 2017). External barriers exist in systemic gender-related attitudes that more frequently associate managerial and administrative characteristics with men (Cofino, 2021b; Eagly, 2020; Grant Thornton, 2016; Koşar et al., 2014; Robinson et al., 2017). Whether the barriers that confront women are internal or external, they directly impact the pipeline for women to reach senior leadership roles (Gipson et al., 2017).

Research indicates that women often take a more divergent and often uncharted path to senior-level leadership roles in comparison with their male counterparts (Eagly, 2020; Gipson et al., 2017; Robinson et al., 2017) (Figure 1.1). The path to senior leadership roles in education for a man can be as direct as "teacher, high school principal, and then superintendent" (Robinson et al., 2017, p. 3). Sometimes the pathway for a woman can be just as direct, but it will more typically include extra stops along the way (e.g., "teacher, elementary principal, central office director, and then superintendent") (Robinson et al., 2017, p. 3).

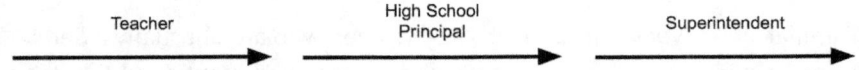

Men follow a more predictable pathway to leadership.

Teacher → High School Principal → Superintendent

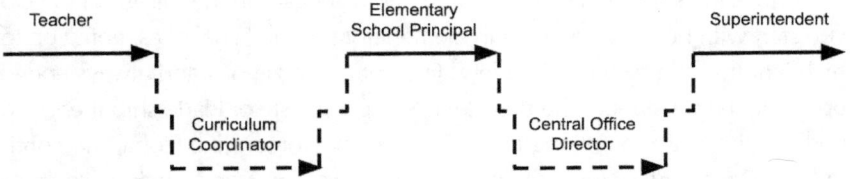

Women often follow divergent pathways to leadership.

Teacher → Curriculum Coordinator → Elementary School Principal → Central Office Director → Superintendent

Figure 1.1 Pathways to Leadership. Men and women experience different pathways in their pursuit of leadership roles in K–12 education.

Exploring the Pathways

It is important for prospective leaders to keep in mind that everyone's journey is unique, particularly given the earlier-mentioned diversity of possible pathways to women's leadership. Some of the stories presented here might resonate with you, but the fact that your path might not align explicitly does not mean that your journey will not take you where you want to go. Recognizing that we might share common elements with other women can help us feel like we are not alone. Seeing ourselves in other leaders helps us recognize that we are capable and that we can take the next step.

Although each story is unique, four general pathways to leadership emerged in these interviews:

1. growing up a leader and following a clear and natural course
2. resisting leadership and (in some ways) unwillingly stepping into the role
3. being "tapped on the shoulder" to take on additional responsibilities
4. mapping a clear and intentional path to leadership

Let's dive a little deeper into these four general pathways.

Growing Up a Leader

Familiar stereotypes surround girls and women who are unusually assertive from an early age. Many of the women interviewed mentioned that they were called "bossy" as a child. Some took charge of their younger siblings or organized their friends at school. For those women, the path to leadership seemed to grow naturally from those early experiences.

The leadership journey of Fiona Reynolds began on the playground: "Do you start with being a bossy kid in elementary school?" she jokes, going on to highlight that she "worked in a few different organizations and always ended up being the assistant to the president. So I got a taste of leadership then, and perhaps they saw something in me." For many women like Fiona, the confidence to be a leader simply seems to have always been part of their personality.

Catriona Moran describes an almost instinctive urge to step up to responsibility: "I raised my hand. I said, 'Yes, I can do that.' When I had a chance to volunteer throughout my life, I said, 'Yes I can do that,' although I never started off trying to be an administrator as a leader. My skill and experience grew; through the course of raising my hand, I became an administrator and then a leader." Early and often informal opportunities to embrace leadership skills laid the foundation for leadership later on in the lives of several female leaders.

Unexpected Leaders

Many women spoke about not having grown up expecting to be a leader at all. In fact, when presented with chances to take on a leadership role, many women turned down their first or even multiple opportunities. For those who are currently unsure if leadership is their pathway, hearing these stories of "accidental leadership" might be an eye-opening and life-changing experience.

Among these unexpected leaders, many spoke about having had a particular career goal or interest that at some point ended up guiding them into leadership. For example, some women described an earlier passion for working with students or curriculum development. Although this unexpected progression might simply demonstrate how individual the journey to leadership can be, in many cases, these circumstances might also reflect the way that societal expectations can limit the scope of women's aspirations, even the ones they formulate themselves.

Arden Tyoschin found her leadership career happening "almost organically." While she was a teacher, the way she handled an unusual situation of injustice was noticed, leading to an opportunity. She says, "I didn't have any grand dreams of having a leadership role. Within that context I was offered a small leadership role, and it grew from there and was very fulfilling, and that's how I ended up being a head of school here in Africa."

Katrina Charles similarly notes that she did not aim to be in leadership. Throughout her career, she recognized that her voice often emerged to represent the underrepresented. Katrina says, "It's not about getting into [leadership] for the sake of it, it's for making a change. Leaders lead from the back, not the front. It's your job to support everyone on the team to be the best you can be, with you at the back propelling others forward."

In spite of not having intended to become leaders, these women eventually found themselves in positions they love. This could highlight a general need for women to identify and encourage leadership capabilities both in themselves and in other women. For their part, current leaders and institutions should try to foster environments where potential leaders might be guided toward responsibilities that might suit them, which ideally might lead to the types of situations described in the next section.

An Invitation to Leadership

Many women highlighted the importance of being 'tapped on the shoulder' to lead. While some women might not have initially imagined themselves as leaders, they found they developed confidence once others pointed out their capacity.

Elsa Donahue describes her leadership path as a "journey of serendipity." When she was on a school accreditation visit, the head of school unexpectedly asked if she had ever considered leadership, and the seed was planted. She says, "It has been a journey of being in the right time, with the right person, who has seen something in me and planted a seed. Because I'm a curious person and always seeking to explore challenges, I dove in." It just took a single remark from an outside perspective to give her the confidence and curiosity to move forward.

This often-unexpected push from a single source can have the power to shape an entire career. When Carlene Hamley talks about her journey, she says "it was more of a nudge, not really something I decided." She, like many other women interviewed, mentioned Shirley Droese, who encouraged Carlene to apply for the position of curriculum director at Shekou International School. This illustrates the important effect a bit of guidance from a trusted friend, colleague, or current leader can have. Who knows where a simple word of encouragement might lead?

Mapping a Path

Perhaps the smallest percentage of women interviewed had intentionally mapped out each step on their way to leadership in advance. These women had made a conscious decision to strive for success as a leader and then worked strategically to get there.

Sanée Bell always knew she wanted to be a school leader. She followed the traditional pathway, looking for every leadership opportunity. Her philosophy is to "get ready for your next job in your current position." She stresses that "it's all about intentionality. Sometimes as women, we fall into things. I knew I wanted to be a leader, so I was always preparing for that. It wasn't by accident. I already knew that was the path I wanted to take." Sanée's clarity of vision helped keep her moving forward confidently.

Like Sanée, Sheena Nabholz always knew she wanted to be a leader. She says she likes the idea of being part of something bigger than herself, being "part of the cause." Being a leader, and using her skills and talents to benefit a group endeavor, gives her tremendous joy in her work. She is aware that this big-picture desire to make a significant impact has consistently led her to embrace leadership.

As the previous paragraphs show, it's actually not the most common way that interviewees described their path, but for some of the Women Who Lead, it was possible to see in advance where they wanted to go and successfully plan how to get there, which might be reassuring for developing leaders considering their own path.

Navigating the Journey

Whether intentional or not, all of the women interviewed had moments when they recognized their capacity to lead. For some, it happened very early in their lives or careers, while for others it came later; there is no one-size-fits-all map to follow. As you read this book, keep your eyes open so that you might recognize your next step into leadership—even if it comes when you least expect it! Stories have the power to change our behavior and our actions. Regardless of where you are in your journey, and whatever path you take, when you discover a story or moment that resonates with you, we encourage you to take a moment to reflect: What is it about this story or moment that connects to your own experience? How can you weave the thread from another woman's journey into your life story? What actions can you take based on the story?

If you're feeling like it's time to take that next step and there's no one to tap you, here: *tap, tap, tap.* We are! We're tapping you on the shoulder to take that next step in your leadership journey.

Finding Her Path: Elsa Donohue

Name: Elsa Donohue
Role: Head of School
School: Vientiane International School
Location: Laos

Elsa Donohue says that her journey to leadership is "not a glamorous story" because she had no sense of always knowing that she wanted to be a leader, or even a teacher. Elsa's is a "journey of serendipity": She was in the right place at the right time, with the right encouragement.

She remembers a moment where she recognized her own leadership ability while in high school, where at the time there was no student council and few chances for students to speak out. She realized that other students were listening to her and started more actively sharing her thinking—which, on more than a few occasions, led her and her friends right into trouble!

Her first moment of awareness of leadership possibilities in professional life came after over a decade as a teacher, when she was leading a school accreditation visit and the head of school looked at her and said, "Have you ever thought about getting into curriculum development or leadership?" After the seed had been planted by that first suggestion, she finished a degree in education leadership and moved toward a principal role. Elsa shares,

> I'm a firm believer that everyone has the potential to lead in them, but it isn't until you start feeling that responsibility that you

recognize the enormity of it. And the more responsibility you feel, the more you want to learn how to get better at it.

Looking back over her journey, she reflects that she didn't have many female role models or leaders to look up to and that it was male mentors along the way who ended up encouraging her to take the next step. She also notes that she was initially reluctant to lead because she saw teaching as her life's work and didn't want to be separated from it but that in the end, her curiosity led her to take the risk. For Elsa, her journey to leadership has consisted of being encouraged by someone who saw her capacity, which then helped her to recognize it in herself and then to take the steps to bring it into the light.

Unpacking Her Journey

- In high school, Elsa organized people or became a voice for collective ideas because people looked up to her and listened to her ideas.
- Elsa was motivated to take on new responsibilities to lead which provided opportunities to expand her practical experiences.

 ## Take Action

For Developing Leaders

Map your personal journey to leadership! Reflect on your pathway and create your own map, either here in this book, or in a blank digital document, or your journal, or in whatever way suits your learning style best.

Use the prompts in the figure (Figure 1.2) to guide your reflection.

As you think about the stories shared in this chapter,

- Do any resonate? If so, in what ways? If not, in what ways is your journey different?
- How might these stories provide insight into your own experience?
- Where and when might you have an opportunity to connect with another female leader to share your stories?

The Path to Leadership

Figure 1.2 Reflecting on Your Journey. Reflection prompts help to make sense of personal experience.

When you look ahead to the next phase of your professional growth,

- What would you like the next leg of your journey to look like?
- Where do you see specific opportunities to recognize your leadership potential?
- How might the stories shared in this chapter help you take the next step?

Taking the time to reflect on your experience, and how you might see opportunities to be intentional in your next steps, could help you begin to recognize and act on your own leadership capacity (which we will dive into in the next chapter).

For Established Leaders Supporting Developing and Aspiring Leaders

As an established leader, you might have a story similar to those shared in this chapter. To support you in sharing your experiences with developing leaders in your organization, we invite you to reflect on your own journey and how you might provide a window into your experience for others. Thinking about your own journey to leadership,

- What shape has your journey taken?
- What successes and challenges can you share that might make your journey more transparent to an aspiring leader?

Thinking about sharing your experiences,

- How might you highlight specific experiences you've had as stepping stones to inspire others' pathways to leadership?
- How can you make visible an opportunity or project that could be a small, achievable step on an aspiring leader's pathway?

The path to leadership can feel hazy. Taking the time to better understand your own journey, to process your next steps or to support others, is an important aspect of achieving clarity.

For Schools or Organizations

We invite you to consider pathways your organization can provide for teachers to grow into leadership roles. You might wish to start with an informal audit:

- What's one thing that your school does well to support aspiring leaders?
- What's one thing your school can do better to solicit and support aspiring leaders?
    - For example, if your school offers a leadership program:
        - How are you inviting potential leaders into this conversation?
        - How are you including diverse voices in these communities?
        - How are you opening conversations to other school leaders in the region to provide varied perspectives?

Based on your informal audit, what next steps might you take to create a more visible pathway for aspiring leaders within your organization?

- How, where, and when are these opportunities visible to educators within your community?
- What processes or structures might appeal most to "non-traditional" leaders?
- How are you ensuring equitable access to these pathways?

As one of our Women Who Lead noted, "the pathway to being a teacher seemed really clear," but moving from teaching to leadership was like venturing into the unknown. By helping create a clearer organizational pathway, you are supporting aspiring leaders on their journey.

For individuals, it's crucial to first recognize your own potential so you can value and articulate your skills. In the next chapter, we'll explore how you can become your own best advocate.

References

Catalyst. (2020a, August 19). *Women in the workforce: Canada (quick take)* [Research report]. www.catalyst.org/knowledge/women-workforce-united-states

Catalyst. (2020b, October 14). *Women in the workforce: United States (quick take)* [Research report]. www.catalyst.org/research/women-in-the-workforce-united-states/

Cofino, K. (2021a, March 30). Exploring the unique challenges women face in pursuing a leadership position. *TIEOnline*. www.tieonline.com/article/2914/exploring-the-unique-challenges-women-face-in-pursuing-a-leadership-position

Cofino, K. (2021b, June 22). Addressing the elephant in the room: The old boys' club in international school leadership. *TIEOnline*. www.tieonline.com/article/2967/addressing-the-elephant-in-the-room-the-old-boys-club-in-international-school-leadership

Cofino, K. (2021c, September 15). Facing impostor syndrome: It Happens to Successful Leaders Too! *TIEOnline*. www.tieonline.com/article/3027/facing-impostor-syndrome-it-happens-to-successful-leaders-too-

Diversity Collaborative. (2021). *Determining the diversity baseline in international schools* [Report]. www.iss.edu/wp-content/uploads/DC-Baseline-Analysis-2021.pdf

Duevel, L., Nashman-Smith, M., & Stern, E. (2015). Moving from 'woman-less history' to women stepping up into school leadership roles. *International Schools Journal, XXXV*(1), 34–45. www.proquest.com/docview/1781327696?pq-origsite=gscholar&fromopenview=true

Eagly, A. (2020, September 8). Once more: The rise of female leaders: How gender and ethnicity affect the electability and success of women as political leaders. *American Psychological Association*. www.apa.org/research/action/female-leaders

Gipson, A., Pfaff, D., Mendelsohn, D., Catencacci, L., & Burke, W. (2017). Women and leadership: Selection, development, leadership style, and performance. *The Journal of Applied Behavioral Science, 53*(1), 32–65. https://doi.org/10.1177/0021886316687247

Grant Thornton. (2016). *Women in business: Turning promise into practice* [Report]. www.grantthornton.global/globalassets/wib_value_of_diversity.pdf

Klenke, K. (2018). *Women in leadership: Contextual dynamics and boundaries* (2nd ed.). Emerald Publishing.

Koşar, D., Altunay, E., & Yalçinkaya, M. (2014). The difficulties of female primary school administrators in the administration process and solution suggestions. *Educational Sciences: Theory & Practice, 14*(3), 905–919. https://files.eric.ed.gov/fulltext/EJ1034093.pdf

Neyra, A. (2021). What the data tells us about diversity in international school teaching staff and leadership. *CIS Perspectives*. www.cois.org/about-cis/perspectives-blog/blog-post/~board/perspectives-blog/post/what-the-data-tells-us-about-diversity-in-international-school-teaching-staff-and-leadership

Robinson, K., Shakeshaft, C., Grogan, M., & Newcomb, W. (2017). Necessary but not sufficient: The continuing inequality between men and women in educational leadership, findings from the American Association of School Administrators mid-decade survey. *Frontiers in Education, 2*(12), 1–12. www.frontiersin.org/articles/10.3389/feduc.2017.00012/full

World Economic Forum. (2021). *Global gender gap report 2021* [Insight Report, March 2021]. https://www3.weforum.org/docs/WEF_GGGR_2021.pdf

2 Recognizing Your Potential to Lead

Women will often shy away from stepping forward. We have to remember that our voices are important and valuable for others to hear. We all have to find a way to be seen and heard. The world needs more female leaders.
—Madeleine Heide

Setting the Stage

In the previous chapter, we revealed that there is no one journey to leadership, and we outlined some of the diverse pathways women have taken. This chapter will dig into the internal realizations that every successful leader, regardless of their trajectory, needs to make at some point.

Regardless of their intentions or dispositions, the Women Who Lead all had moments when they recognized their own leadership. Some had clear "aha moments," while others remembered an ongoing series of experiences over years. Many recognized their capacity not through assuming what Bridget McNamer calls "big 'L' Leadership" but through "little 'L' leadership." After taking smaller steps that came naturally, they began to see themselves as others saw them. The thread, leading from outside recognition, to ownership, to responsibility, runs through many of the WWL interviews and will be explored in detail later in this chapter.

As Madeleine Heide said during her interview, "The world needs female leaders." It can be hard to recognize that your voice has value and that you deserve to be seen and heard wherever you are on your journey. As you read the stories in this chapter, we invite you to ask yourself: *How can I share my voice?*

Reflections in the Research

In their book, *Through the Labyrinth: The Truth About How Women Become Leaders*, Eagly and Carli (2007) propose that leadership involves "being in charge of other people in multiple ways" (p. 8). They expand on this basic definition by adding that "it consists of influencing, motivating, organizing, and coordinating the work of others . . . leadership involves bringing people together to enable them to work toward shared goals" (Eagly & Carli, 2007, pp. 8–9). This expansive vision is often confirmed in the K–12 education setting, where it is very common for leadership to be exercised through both formal and informal roles.

While there is not a globally agreed-upon definition of what it means to be a teacher leader, teachers act as leaders in their classrooms and among colleagues when they "lead learning through modeling best and innovative practice, and build the capacity of colleagues" (Breakspear et al., 2017, p. 26). Middle-level leaders in K–12 education typically develop instructional practices and provide pedagogical support for their teacher colleagues (Breakspear et al., 2017). Some middle leaders provide support to teachers within a grade-level team, a department, or a curricular program and might maintain varying degrees of teaching responsibility (Breakspear et al., 2017). Education leaders including titled positions such as principal, assistant principal, and deputy principal are often members of senior leadership teams in K–12 school settings (DeNobile, 2018; Gurr, 2019). These leaders are more typically found working at the whole-school level (Breakspear et al., 2017). Regardless of their title and job description, any educator can bear leadership responsibilities.

When considering leadership potential, employers look for "qualities that signal future leadership effectiveness" (Player et al., 2019, p. 2). Research indicates that men are often elevated to leadership roles based on recognition of their leadership potential (Gaskell, 2021; Player et al., 2019; Williams, 2021). Conversely, women are deemed qualified to lead based on their past performance (Gaskell, 2021; Williams, 2021). Women must continue to prove their leadership competency over and over again (Gaskell, 2021; Williams, 2021). Being perceived as exhibiting the traditionally recognized style of leadership potential might advantage men over women because of the implicit association equating leadership with agentic traits (Player et al., 2019).

A frequently referenced statistic, attributed to internal data from Hewlett Packard and referenced in numerous articles and best-selling books, claims that men tend to apply for jobs despite only meeting 60% of the requirements (Mohr, 2014). This reference also claims that women tend to only apply for jobs when they feel they meet 100% of the requirements, which might indicate that women wait to be experts or for others to recognize their achievements. Research conducted by Exley and Kessler (2021) highlights a gender gap in self-promotion, where women present their achievements and potential less favorably than equally performing men. Women are less likely than men to self-promote, meaning they are less likely to acknowledge or recognize their own potential to lead (Exley & Kessler, 2021).

Too often, women unknowingly perpetuate the gender disparity in senior education leadership roles by avoiding them due to implicit leadership theories: the preconceived notions around leadership characteristics and who possesses them (Chen & Moons, 2015; Hoyt & Murphy, 2016). Gender-based leadership stereotypes remain firmly held across the globe (Eagly, 2020). Over time, lack of representation among senior leadership roles in international education can lead some women to feel discouraged and disengaged from pursuing their leadership ambitions (Chen & Moons, 2015; Hoyt & Murphy, 2016). Without adequate female representation among international school leaders, women can find it difficult to envision their potential and might be unable to imagine themselves taking on such roles.

Navigating the Path

In the WWL interviews, self-recognition of leadership potential often occurred in three key phases:

1. recognition from others
2. owning leadership
3. standing out and making it happen

We'll explore how these three phases interact to support your development of self-as-leader in the following sections.

Recognition from Others

As explored in Chapter 1, several of the women highlighted that they didn't initially see themselves as leaders and that it was only when others began to recognize the leadership within them that they developed the confidence to do so.

For Jasmeen Philen, it all began with giving helpful advice. She describes herself as having "an innate gift to inspire," and she took great pleasure in trying to be a positive influence for others. When more and more people started to seek advice from her, she began to realize she had the capacity to lead.

Others frequently called on Catriona Moran to lead committees, leading her to reflect that "other people realized that I had the capacity to be a leader before I did." It wasn't until she was earning her PhD that she realized she held the power to "lead an organization with ethics and morals and the ability to make change." Sometimes realizing what others see in you, as in Catriona's case, can seem clear only in retrospect.

Similarly, Madeleine Heide realized that "other people saw something in me because I did not back away from expressing myself, I wanted to be heard." She didn't start by looking to lead, but now realizes that "by being willing to get involved, that brought leadership opportunities to me." This drew her into consistently demonstrating little L leadership, which was a natural stepping stone to taking on more responsibility.

In all of these women's stories, noticing that others recognized their potential to lead helped them embrace the identity of leader, both internally and externally.

Owning Your Leadership

Many of the Women Who Lead described gaining new understanding of themselves as leaders when their experiences began to coalesce into patterns that, in turn, built confidence to seize new opportunities in more formal roles. Interestingly, this step still often involved the kind of external push described in the previous section; it seems to be very rare for women to make these realizations without some kind of outside encouragement.

Dr. Nneka Johnson first saw herself as a potential leader when people kept asking her for instructions while coordinating an in-school professional development event. Throughout her journey, she's realized that "in my leadership style, I don't mind getting dirty. I would never ask someone to do something I wouldn't do myself." Being looked up to by others, in this case, meshed with a risk-taker's recognition of her own capabilities.

Back when she was department chair, Tara Waudby had a very similar experience. She remembers sitting in the middle leadership team, thinking "my ideas are something new." She realized that not only did she have ideas, she knew how to put them into action. It was many small moments like these that gave her the confidence to apply for her first formal leadership position.

In her first school, perhaps because she had a PhD, was a visible minority, and was among one of the youngest educators, Dr. Mary Ashun found that the principal would call upon her and ask for her feedback. "That let me know that I had a certain pulpit," she says. "I didn't see it as leadership, I just thought they were asking me because I was the only Black person. I never put it all together as leadership until my second school, when I was put on committees. That's when I saw it as leadership." As in previous examples, the lead-up to her realization only became clear in retrospect.

Although Madeleine Heide didn't intend to be a school administrator, she remembers reading a job description for a principal position in the staff room and realizing that she was qualified, after which her husband encouraged her to apply. Again, this encouragement demonstrates the interwoven reinforcement of internal and external motivation that can often finally result in trying something new.

In these moments, WWL interviewees describe the internal mindset shift of finally seeing how their leadership work translated to Leadership. Being able to articulate these key skills (which we will explore more deeply in Chapter 3) helps solidify the confidence to apply for formal leadership positions.

Standing Out and Making It Happen

Full recognition of your leadership capacity enables you to take risks, stand out from the crowd, reach for bigger goals, and make a strong impact in your community.

After Lola Aneke returned to Nigeria after completing her degree, she aimed to make inclusive education a part of Nigerian schools but initially found little external support for her ideas. As she says, "If nobody is calling you, you can start from somewhere. I became my own office." She took to social media, put out calls on her blog, and went from house to house to build her own organization. "I knew there was a deficit, so I took it upon myself to address it. That was a sense of leadership." Feeling forced to be self-reliant, Lola found the strength to set a goal and achieve it.

Sometimes this self-perceived identity of leader, and the ability to act on it, is present almost from the beginning, as outlined in Chapter 1. When Kam Chohan was a child, she frequently disrupted class. Looking back, she feels this behavior represented early leadership: "I've always felt like if you are passionate about what you do and you can bring others with you, that's leadership: being authentic and completely committed to the cause. I always felt like a leader because I could bring people with me." Kam perceptively recognizes that some of the same skills that got her in trouble as a student allow her to lead as an adult.

When Kathleen Naglee began in a formal leadership position, she noticed her own attitude had "a cascading effect on the entire system; it is amplified by everyone in the room." Seeing this, she realized her responsibility to present a "caring, loving, positive authentic self" in front of the stakeholder community. As in Kam's example, Kathleen's awareness of her effect on others when leading, and feeling driven to make that effect positive, demonstrates her nuanced and evolving acceptance of her leadership persona.

In these stories of taking risks and making things happen, the WWL interviewees represent the value of being able to own, articulate, and advocate for your unique skills. Seeing yourself as a leader, combined with having the language to communicate those skills confidently to others, is what enables you to take the next step.

Embracing Your Leadership

Regardless of the unique journey that each woman shared, the moment of recognition of self-as-leader represents a key turning point. Being pushed to recognize your own strengths builds confidence in articulating your value as a leader. For many women, these strengths can feel hidden, or they can seem to be such a natural part of their approach to work that labeling them as leadership attributes can feel foreign or inconceivable. Gaining a

Recognizing Your Potential to Lead

better understanding of the essential skills developing leaders need might help you shift your perspective toward recognizing your own leadership capacity. In Chapter 3, we'll explore and label these skills to give you the vocabulary and tools to start owning your leadership.

Finding Her Path: Caroline Brokvam

Name: Caroline Brokvam
Role: Director
School: American School of Antananarivo
Location: Madagascar

Although she notes that she was always a confident achiever when young, organizing her friends and their play spaces or collecting money, when Caroline reflects on her leadership journey, she says it "wasn't particularly purposeful." When she was encouraged by a senior administrator to apply for a leadership position, she realized that although she lacked experience, she had the skills, ability, and confidence to do the job.

She believes this encouragement was based only on perceived potential, since she hadn't been actively seeking leadership roles aside from organizing student clubs and activities. After some time back in her native Australia, her next school was Copenhagen International School, where she was high school principal and the head of City Campus for five years.

When she decided to apply for director roles, including a few in Africa, she unexpectedly got the first job she applied for. The school was the right size, and the goals that lay ahead were well-suited to her skill set and experiences: moving to a new campus and implementing the International Baccalaureate Diploma Programme.

Caroline reminds aspiring leaders that it's not the end of your career if you need to leave a position. She says,

> If I hadn't left Manila, I would probably still be the assistant principal. If you want to move up in leadership, you can't just wait around for a position to come up that's going to suit you. You need to look around. That's just the reality.

Caroline feels lucky to have been initially tapped on the shoulder for leadership because "you can be doing everything in the world to show your

Seeing Yourself as a Leader

competence and never get tapped." She notes that women, unfortunately, often seem less confident than men in this area, worrying about "ticking all the boxes" before applying for a desired position.

Unpacking Her Journey

- Caroline acknowledges her competence, dependability and ability to organize from an early age.
- She gained practical experiences leading student clubs and activities.

 Take Action

For Developing Leaders

It can feel intimidating to try to name your leadership attributes. You might even be reading this right now feeling like you don't have any, but we're pretty sure that's not the case! Based on the experience of the WWL participants, it's likely that others can and will see leadership potential in you before you began to recognize it within yourself. This action task will provide a process for seeing yourself as others do, uncovering those strengths so you can start owning them as part of your unique skill set.

 Uncover Your Hidden Superpowers

The goal here is to identify things that might be such a natural part of your practices that you don't even know they are perceived as strengths by others. You can also use this stage to identify potential areas of growth to prioritize addressing in your professional progress.

Follow these steps to gather insight from past and present colleagues:

1. Think about colleagues who have worked with you in a professional capacity.

2. Reach out to at least five from the last few years whom you feel comfortable asking for feedback about you as a professional.
3. Ask for feedback about how you've demonstrated leadership, or any other specific capacity you're looking for (see suggested phrasing in what follows).
4. If you're really ready to grow, you can also ask them for areas they see as potentially having room for improvement.

You could send an email or create a survey that your past and present colleagues can complete. Here's a sample email template:

Hi There,

I'm reaching out to you today because I really value and respect your opinion and feedback. I have a quick request that I hope you might be able to help with.

I'm currently thinking about moving into XYZ position, and I'd like to be able to clearly articulate my leadership strengths. Having worked with me for 123 years, what do you see as my strengths? Where do you see me providing value to the organization or community? If you see any potential areas for growth, I'd love to hear those too!

No need to write anything too formal, I'm just looking for an outside perspective from a colleague I truly trust. If you can reply to this email within the week to share your thinking, I would appreciate it so much!

I know you're really busy, so if you don't have the time, I totally understand. But if you're able to share anything, it would help me tremendously. I really value and respect your opinion and your time.

Thank you so much!

Make Time for Reflection

Once you have this data back, think back to a time when you handled a situation but perhaps didn't recognize it as leadership. Now that you have a broader idea of what leadership can look like, reframe your own perspective to complete the following sentence stems:

- I am a leader because . . .
- I've demonstrated leadership when . . .
- One leadership trait I'm working to develop is . . .

If you want to keep this thinking at the forefront of your mind, write your responses on sticky notes and stick them somewhere visible. Or you might prefer to keep responses in your journal, here in this book, or in a document with notes from other chapters. Regardless of where you keep documentation, start thinking about, and consciously naming, your unique qualities as leadership skills to build your sense of self-as-leader.

Scenarios

To help you name and value your specific leadership skills, we invite you to consider the following scenarios. You might wish to reflect independently or talk through responses with a mentor or trusted colleague. As you think through each scenario, focus on identifying, naming, and owning your specific leadership skills:

- You step up to lead a PLC, and a colleague confronts you: "Why are you doing this? You're just a classroom teacher; are you getting paid to do this?" You're taking an action to step up to lead, whether it's consciously perceived as leadership or not, and you get challenged. How do you respond?
- Your school is looking for volunteers: Because the school lacks a service learning coordinator, the PYP coordinator is looking for someone to support a specific project, the PYP exhibition. In the past, you felt like you didn't fit the expectations of this role. Imagine taking action and volunteering for this position. How would it feel? What would you say?

For Established Leaders

From our conversations with the Women Who Lead, we know that women can struggle to own their leadership skills, often because they aren't seen as stereotypical leadership traits (an idea explored further in Chapter 3). We invite you to consider how you can make "non-traditional" leadership traits more visible in your organization. How can you call attention to these?

You might wish to start with something as simple as sending a note to an aspiring leader stating "I saw you as a leader when . . ." Once you have a structure that works, how can this become something that all leaders in the organization practice? How can it become a part of your regular routine?

For Schools or Organizations

Research indicates that women need help recognizing their potential, revealing an opportunity for established school leaders to highlight talent from within. As an organization, how are you equipping current leaders to mentor or support developing leaders?

Take a moment to reflect on your existing structures:

- Do school leaders have experience or training in recognizing talent (if not, is training provided)?
- Where in your existing evaluation process are there opportunities to highlight educators' leadership capacity?
- Do your middle and senior leaders have a shared vision of the skills a successful leader within your organization should demonstrate?
- What habits or practices does your leadership team have to intentionally recognize leadership skills among the educators within each individual's sphere of influence?

We are inviting you to revise existing evaluation structures to standardize the practice of intentionally calling out leadership traits educators might be demonstrating without even realizing it. You might find the traits discussed in the next chapter helpful as you design this process.

References

Breakspear, S., Peterson, A., Alfadala, A., & Khair, M. (2017). *Developing agile leaders of learning: School leadership policy for dynamic times.* World Innovation Summit for Education. https://alistairsmithlearning.com/wp-content/uploads/2016/02/Agile-Learning-in-Schools.pdf

Chen, J., & Moons, W. (2015). They won't listen to me: Anticipated power and women's disinterest in male-dominated domains. *Group Processes & Intergroup Relations, 18*(1), 116–128. https://doi.org/10.1177/1368430214550340

DeNobile, J. (2018). Towards a theoretical model of middle leadership in schools. *School Leadership & Management, 38*(4), 395–416. https://doi.org/10.1080/13632434.2017.1411902

Eagly, A. (2020). *Once more: The rise of female leaders: How gender and ethnicity affect the electability and success of women as political leaders*. American Psychological Association. https://www.apa.org/research/action/female-leaders

Eagly, A., & Carli, L. (2007). *Through the labyrinth: The truth about how women become leaders*. Harvard Business School Press.

Exley, C., & Kessler, J. (2021). *The gender gap in self-promotion* [Working paper]. www.nber.org/system/files/working_papers/w26345/w26345.pdf

Gaskell, A. (2021). Women's value is undervalued at work [Blog post]. *Forbes*. www.forbes.com/sites/adigaskell/2021/10/14/womens-potential-is-undervalued-at-work/?sh=3ab3444a865b

Gurr, D. (2019). School middle leaders in Australia, Chile and Singapore. *School Leadership and Management, 39*(3–4), 278–296. https://doi.org/10.1080/13632434.2018.1512485

Hoyt, C., & Murphy, S. (2016). Managing to clear the air: Stereotype threat, women, and leadership. *The Leadership Quarterly, 27*(3), 387–399. https://doi.org/10.1016/j.leaqua.2015.11.002

Mohr, T. (2014, April 25). Why women don't apply for jobs unless they're 100% qualified. *Harvard Business Review*. https://hbr.org/2014/08/why-women-dont-apply-for-jobs-unless-theyre-100-qualified

Player, A., Randsley de Moura, G., Leite, A., Abrams, D., & Tresh, F. (2019). Overlooked leadership potential: The preference for leadership potential in job candidates who are men vs. women. *Frontiers in Psychology, 10*(755), 1–14. https://doi.org/10.3389/fpsyg.2019.00755

Williams, J. (2021). *Bias interrupted: Creating inclusion for real and for good*. Harvard Business Review Press.

Uncovering Essential Skills for Female Leaders

I don't believe in wishing and hoping, I believe in being prepared. No one is going to give you anything. You have to make sure you're prepared for opportunities when they come.

—Sanée Bell

 Setting the Stage

When we think of leadership skills, we often think of stereotypes like commanding a room, giving orders, or making big decisions. However, recent global crises and technological developments have taught us that leadership can look very different from these norms—and for most people, this change is welcome. The skills in this chapter highlight 10 frequently mentioned themes from the WWL interviews that might represent a well-rounded, and likely non-traditional, leader of today.

 Reflections in the Research

The responsibilities of school leaders have shifted significantly in the early decades of the 21st century. The school leader's job was once focused exclusively on "administrative duties related to the smooth daily operations of the school building" (Marzano & Carbaugh, 2018, p. 5). More recently, we see a more pointed emphasis on instructional leadership (Marzano & Carbaugh, 2018). It is vital for education leaders to understand the dynamic interplay of operational leadership with instructional leadership and the interconnected responsibilities (Marzano & Carbaugh, 2018; National Policy Board for Educational Administration, 2015).

Leadership roles in today's K–12 education require a broad yet complex skill set such as that laid down by *The Professional Standards for Educational Leaders*, which highlight the "evolving understandings of and expectations for the profession's work" (National Policy Board for Educational Administration, 2015, p. 7). Underpinning these standards is the understanding that the ultimate purpose of education leaders is to "promote the academic success and well-being of each student" (National Policy Board for Educational Administration, 2015, p. 13). These standards paint an image of an education leader who is multifaceted. Standards focus on leaders being mission-driven, principled, focused on equity, systems thinkers, inclusive/caring, capacity builders, community builders, relationship builders, operational managers, and rooted in continuous improvement (National Policy Board for Educational Administration, 2015).

Marzano and Carbaugh (2018) extend the standards by grouping them into six domains in order to reveal the interconnectedness of instructional and operational leadership:

- Domain 1. Data-driven focus on school improvement
- Domain 2. Instruction of a guaranteed and viable curriculum
- Domain 3. Continuous development of teachers and staff
- Domain 4. Community of care and collaboration
- Domain 5. Core values
- Domain 6. Resource management

The title of each domain provides insight into what skills a leader should focus on developing and demonstrating. The standards and accompanying focus statements within each domain are an excellent resource for aspiring and practicing education leaders to self-assess current skills and areas for growth.

Many essential leadership skills identified in formal professional standards also emerged from the insights of the WWL participants. Table 3.1 draws the connections between the practical experiences and advice of the Woman Who Lead participants and the theoretical underpinnings of formal professional standards.

Table 3.1 Aligning Theory with Practice. Rooting practical experiences in theoretical knowledge can help leaders to better understand how their day-to-day actions are connected to fulfilling a broader understanding of being a successful education leader.

Essential leadership skills identified by women leaders	Essential leadership skills identified in formal professional standards	
WWL interviews (2020)	Marzano and Carbaugh (2018)	National Policy Board for Educational Administration (2015)
Agility	Domain 1: Data-Driven Focus on School Improvement Domain 6: Resource Management	Standard 1: Mission, Vision, and Core Values Standard 10: School Improvement
Authenticity	Domain 5: Core Values	Standard 2: Ethics and Professional Norms
Connection	Domain 4: Community of Care and Collaboration	Standard 5: Community of Care and Support for Students Standard 8: Meaningful Engagement of Families and Community
Emotional intelligence	Domain 3: Continuous Development of Teachers and Staff Domain 5: Core Values	Standard 6: Professional Capacity of School Personnel Standard 7: Professional Community for Teachers and Staff
Financial literacy	Domain 6: Resource Management	Standard 9: Operations Management
Inclusion	Domain 4: Community of Care and Collaboration	Standard 1: Mission, Vision, and Core Values Standard 3: Equity and Cultural Responsiveness Standard 5: Community of Care and Support for Students Standard 7: Professional Community for Teachers and Staff Standard 8: Meaningful Engagement of Families and Community

(Continued)

Table 3.1 (Continued)

Essential leadership skills identified by women leaders	Essential leadership skills identified in formal professional standards	
Inspiration	Domain 5: Core Values	Standard 4: Curriculum, Instruction, and Assessment
Integrity	Domain 5: Core Values	Standard 2: Ethics and Professional Norms
Leadership at any level	Domain 1: Data-Driven Focus on School Improvement	Standard 1: Mission, Vision, and Core Values Standard 4: Curriculum, Instruction, and Assessment Standard 6: Professional Capacity of School Personnel Standard 7: Professional Community for Teachers and Staff
Vision	Domain 1: Data-Driven Focus on School Improvement Domain 2: Instruction of a Guaranteed and Viable Curriculum	Standard 1: Mission, Vision, and Core Values Standard 4: Curriculum, Instruction, and Assessment Standard 10: School Improvement

Leveraging Your Leadership

As you explore the 10 competencies presented in this section, we invite you to reflect on where you might already be exhibiting them, as well as on opportunities you might have to build them within your current role. Even very successful leaders have gaps among these skills, and you should not feel pressure to master every single one. However, familiarity with them all might lead to increased awareness of when you are applying them. Note that without realizing it, many women might already possess several of these skills because they've had to operate from a position of marginalization or exclusion, which tends to spur the development of potential leadership traits including agility, higher EQ, and awareness of when to be inclusive of others.

1. Agility

The WWL interviews often highlighted the need for agility. Dr. Nneka Johnson references needing "to be able to think on the spot, be OK with change and work through that. Life is always going to be changing, so that is a skill that will serve us well in the future."

Carla Marschall also notes the need for cognitive flexibility and being able to adapt messaging, communication, and thinking styles based on the needs of the people you're with in the moment. Caroline Brokvam highlights non-binary thinking and being able to see multiple perspectives, and making them a part of the operating procedures of your organization.

One leader encourages "allowing ourselves to fail, to have a second chance, so that when you fall down, you have the courage to pick yourself up, dust yourself off and keep going." In this sense, agility overlaps with the essential attributes of risk-taking and resilience.

2. Authenticity

Many women mentioned developing and conveying a strong sense of self. Sawsan Jaber speaks about the importance of women sharing their voices fearlessly: "We've been muffled for such a long time. We have to get to a place where we have enough camaraderie and sisterhood with each other and our male colleagues that we need to be able to share fearlessly." This can involve trusting your instincts and not doubting or self-censoring.

In this vein, Liz Kleinrock points out that

> It's important to be unapologetic and take up space. You get so many messages your whole life that are the opposite of what you should be doing. We're seeing a lot of redefinition of what it means to be a woman, there's a lot more space for women to carve out that path for themselves. To choose the language they want and mirror who they are authentically.

As Liz and others emphasize, it can be important to realize what external and internalized messages might need to be ignored in order to confidently share who you are and what you believe in.

3. Connection

Developing skills around connection and collaboration, which can be extended to include systems thinking, influencing others, and networking, is essential for all leaders, particularly women. These skills are often referred to as interpersonal or relational skills.

Chanel Johnson notes that "a key skill for aspiring female leaders is the ability to connect with people different from you: looks, culture, economic background, and overall different mindset. It can't be the same people who think like you, look like you, feel like you." She stresses that it's crucial to "connect with people because we can't get there on our own. We all think differently, and we all have different experiences. It's our diverse experiences that help us grow and learn."

Nathalie Henderson points out that "women tend to shy away from using political skill. They don't want to be considered manipulative or selfish." She clarifies that political skill describes how you leverage or maximize relationships to meet organizational, team, or professional goals. She says that "situating what you think you need for your students is a political skill. You have to employ political skill—you can't spend all your time getting context in order to be able to act." Whether or not you call these skills "political," knowing how to connect with others, and to forge and keep relationships, can be invaluable.

4. Emotional Intelligence

Care and kindness are increasingly key in our demanding world. Jennifer Tickle says that "as leaders, we have to care, and we have to show that we care. We can be kind while still leading, and we need to be kind to ourselves as well. Care and kindness need to be de-gendered, and seen as essential components of successful leadership." Maintaining a kind approach as a leader while also making tough decisions requires great sensitivity to the variables at play.

Carlene Hamley refers to the necessary qualities of "grit and grace," saying that as a female leader, you often have to dig a little deeper because the situation requires it. She notes that women leaders have to be "brave enough to have that grit and stamina to keep going because you believe in yourself, your project, your passion." The complexity of emotional intelligence means that leaders need to care for themselves and others; build trust by being vulnerable; and then balance this with firmness, bravery, and courage.

5. Financial Literacy

Grace McCallum notes, "an unfortunate reality in the leadership community is that it is still assumed men are more financially literate than women. Being comfortable talking about money, and speaking to the state of the economy and economic trends, is very important for aspiring leaders." Along those lines, data literacy and developing an entrepreneurial mindset become more valuable the higher you go in leadership (see Chapter 11 for a discussion of the business mindset sought in prospective heads of school).

6. Inclusion

Fay Leong notes that "women are not used to taking voice; we allow ourselves to be drowned out. I am regularly asking myself: What opportunities have I crafted to ensure that everyone is required to take voice? If we don't give them the opportunity to take voice, how will they know if they have a voice? You allow people to stand up and find a voice they didn't know they had." Inclusion here means creating an environment where leadership is encouraging people to share and getting others to listen.

Similarly, Michele Mattoon refers to the concept of "facilitative leadership, which focuses on strategies to encourage people to work together for a common goal," while Lola Aneke discusses collective growth as opposed to personal growth, stressing that "it's about all of us or nothing. Let's stand as one, even in the same field. The sky is wide enough for all of us to fly." This kind of inclusion is essential to overcoming some of the issues of competitiveness and anxiety discussed in Chapter 9.

7. Inspiration

The ability to inspire others is a more "traditional" leadership skill but one that remains crucial. Many of the interviewees described behaviors such as leading by example and demonstrating passion as being key. Kathleen Naglee talks about the importance of people feeling "the charisma of your vision" and "wanting to be around that excitement and passion." If you can build into your passion, find the research to back it up, and connect with others around your passion, she explains, you'll build that ability to inspire.

Katie Koenig connects inspirational leadership to presence in the moment: "Presence with people, in listening so that they see you, and they know that you care. In the future we are going to be doing more crisis management, more complex change, more problem solving. It's easy to come up with bad solutions because you're not actually listening to people." Being an effective listener is a key component to being an inspirational leader.

Sheena Nabholz similarly stresses the importance of communication, which "differentiates between a good leader and an excellent leader. It's not leadership if no one is following you. How do you communicate a message, inspire and influence people?" These examples emphasize how complex the act of being inspirational can be, involving an interplay of behaviors, emotions, and actions.

8. Integrity

Caroline Brokvam highlights the importance of an awareness of your own vulnerabilities and biases. She points out that "unless you put processes, practices and procedures in place to make sure you can't act on your own biases, it makes no difference in organizations." Honesty about these areas might be the first step to addressing them with integrity.

Madeleine Heide describes part of acting with integrity as being open to other perspectives, including differences in areas such as ethnicity, language, and culture, so we can communicate across boundaries. In this sense, integrity means having the awareness and intercultural competence to approach everyone, and every situation, in an equitable way.

9. Leadership at Any Level

Deb Welch says women need to break free from stereotypes to see themselves as leaders: "We don't have to make ourselves in the mold of someone we think is a good leader. There are many different forms of leadership." To do this, women need to have a keen self-awareness of their strengths and be able to recognize when and where they are leading—even if not in a formal role at the time.

Katrina Charles recommends that aspiring leaders "utilize the current skill set you have to be a leader within that current position. There's leadership at every level, so bring the best you can to that particular position. Don't look at tasks as if they're too menial for you, every little bit you do helps contribute to the greater good. You need to be able to see the glass as half full." Try to notice and appreciate when you employ any of this list's leadership traits from within your current responsibilities.

10. Vision

Finally, Kathleen Naglee points out that "having a vision for education, as understood by you, is the most important skill for women pursuing a leadership career. You must have examples, understanding, and stories built up throughout your career that you can convey in a way that people want to listen to. This is the only skill that matters." Leaders need radical imagination, she adds, to think creatively and envision the future. It's this vision that helps build community, connection, and clarity.

Reflect and Set Your Next Goals

We know from Chapter 2 that naming specific leadership attributes is a key step in seeing yourself as a leader. Identifying skills that might not be perceived as traditional could help you see ways you are already demonstrating leadership. Recognizing your strengths helps build confidence and provides guidance as you determine opportunities to grow. We'll provide space to do that in the *Take Action* section in this chapter.

Finding Her Path: Deb Welch

Name:	Deb Welch
Role:	Chief Executive Officer
Organization:	Academy of International School Heads (AISH)
Location:	International

When Deb Welch looks back on her journey into leadership, she says she "didn't think about it but just did it." Even as a child, she always jumped in to lead. In elementary school, she was an officer for her class, and at university, she became a teacher and kept volunteering to take charge. Soon, she started to teach professional development courses for the district and joined the Board of Cooperative Educational Services. Over time, she became very involved with school boards and multiple school districts, which led to consulting work.

These experiences opened the door for leadership in international schools, first at the International School Bangkok, in Thailand, as director of curriculum for nine years and then as deputy head of school. Her next full-time international position was as head of school at the American School of Doha for five years. After her headship, she moved on to the CEO role for AISH and then to a role with the recruiting agency Carney Sandoe and Associates. Throughout her career, there were many times when she doubted her capacity to lead or wondered if she was the right leader for the context.

Deb says,

> There's never a smooth trajectory to head of school; that's what enables us to learn along the way. Everything is relationships. Growing into the position is made up of small incremental steps of putting ourselves out there, taking risks, getting rejected, coming back, reflecting, following your purpose.

For her, it's been a gradual, methodical progress: two steps forward, one step back.

Deb realized she had the capacity to be head of school when, as deputy head of school, she co-facilitated a retreat for heads of school. During this two-day retreat, every other participant was a head of school and a man, and it was then that she thought to herself, "I can do this!" She recognized there were many things to learn, but in terms of understanding the school as a system, considering capacities, empowering people, and technical skills, she knew she could be a successful head of school.

Unpacking Her Journey

- Deb reveals that she has been ready to take the lead and get things done all of her life.
- She took initiative to volunteer and take on leadership roles.
- She followed her interests and became involved with school boards that led to consultation opportunities.

Take Action

For Developing Leaders

Now that you have a better picture of the skills the WWL participants believe are necessary to be successful in a modern leadership role, we invite you to take a personalized leadership inventory. Using the skills highlighted in this chapter, reflect on your current leadership skills and experience, using the space in this book to document your thinking, a separate document where you keep reflections from your reading, or a journal.

Consider the following prompts:

- Which skills are you already demonstrating?
- Which skills might you focus on next?
- Which skills will require research or mentorship?

You might wish to use the following chart to document your thinking (Table 3.2):

If you'd like to be inspired further by the WWL, you might wish to download our free leadership inventory, which features more interview quotes and space for reflection.

Scenario

Now use this scenario to reflect more deeply about one or two specific skills where you have room to grow. Imagine yourself in the near future,

Table 3.2 Skill Reflection Prompts. Reflection prompts help to track skill development.

Skills I'm demonstrating	Skills to focus on next	Skills that require research or mentoring

telling the story of how you identified a specific leadership skill and made it into a strength. Conceptualizing your pathway to creating a new strength will help you think through potential avenues for your own growth and see the value in taking the time to develop this new skill:

- How did you identify the skill that needed to be developed?
- What did you do to strengthen that skill?
- How is it impacting your career "now"?

If you can imagine these steps forward, from identifying, to strengthening, to successfully using a skill, map them out and use these ideas as an action plan or template for developing this (or any other) specific skill. You might also want to consider visualizing yourself in the role: Imagine yourself already in your goal position. What are you doing, how are you speaking, what do you look like? Repeatedly seeing yourself being successful in action can help build your confidence and help you work through any potential challenges you might face.

For Established Leaders

Similar in nature to the action we offered in Chapter 2, we invite you to make time in your schedule to help aspiring leaders identify skills they are demonstrating or building. If you are already aware of an aspiring leader in your community, reach out for a conversation about how they are consistently demonstrating specific skills in their work or make it a practice to highlight certain skills for them when you notice they demonstrate them.

During these interactions, you might also want to point out a specific skill that you intentionally developed during your pathway to leadership and how you took an area of growth into an area of strength. You could also point things out to aspiring leaders in behind-the-scenes moments; for example, take them aside after a meeting to highlight how and why you used different skills.

These opportunities to see what leadership skills look like in practice, how they were developed, and how they support personal and organizational goals will help aspiring leaders take abstract concepts and make them real and context-specific.

For Schools or Organizations

Building upon the action we offered in Chapter 2, we invite you to consider whether or not your organization has articulated standards for leaders, and if so, how. You might wish to create (or adapt)

- specific standards for leaders
- a list of skills needed for leaders (perhaps building on Chapter 2)
- expectations for current leaders to mentor and encourage aspiring leaders

We invite you to consider this as the next step in building systemic structures to ensure that aspiring leaders have a clearer pathway to leadership.

References

Marzano, J., & Carbaugh, B. (2018). *2018 update: The Marzano focused school leader evaluation model* [White paper]. www.marzanocenter.com/wp-content/uploads/sites/4/2020/01/MC07-02-Focused-School-Leader-Evaluation-Model.pdf

National Policy Board for Educational Administration. (2015). *Professional standards for educational leaders 2015*. www.npbea.org/wp-content/uploads/2017/06/Professional-Standards-for-Educational-Leaders_2015.pdf

# Facing Impostor Syndrome
It Happens to Successful Leaders Too!

When I hit a wall, I just turn in a different direction. When you knock on the door, and it doesn't open, look for a window. When the window doesn't open, look for the cat door.

—Firoozeh Dumas

 ## Setting the Stage

Impostor syndrome, or the feeling that your successes are undeserved or illegitimate, is one of the most serious obstacles faced by female leaders—and one of the least visible. As noted in the *Reflections in the Research* in Chapter 2, despite all evidence to the contrary, many women feel they haven't "earned" the right to apply for leadership positions or that if they don't "tick all the boxes" on an application they shouldn't apply.

Even when women are successful, accomplished, and demonstrating leadership in a variety of capacities, they often shy away from calling themselves leaders. In fact, several of the women interviewed for WWL felt reluctant to participate because they did not perceive themselves as leaders—even though they had been identified by others as inspiring. If you feel like you're not ready for leadership as you're reading this book, you're not alone.

 ## Reflections in the Research

Impostor phenomenon was first defined by Pauline Rose Clance and Suzanne Imes in 1978 "to designate an internal experience of intellectual phonies, which appears to be particularly prevalent and intense among a select sample of high achieving women" (p. 1). Impostor syndrome, as it has come to be known, leaves many women at times doubting their abilities and feeling like a fraud despite varying accomplishments and accolades (Clance & Imes, 1978; Tulshyan & Burey, 2021). Many women who deal with impostor syndrome await the moment when someone discovers and reveals their lack of ability and intellect. This feeling is usually unfounded.

Many women wonder about the root causes of their impostor syndrome. Some sources indicate that impostor syndrome stems from feelings of "discomfort, second-guessing, and mild anxiety" (Tulshyan & Burey, 2021, para. 9) or "lack of self-confidence, depression, and frustration related to inability to meet self-imposed standards of achievement" (Clance & Imes, 1978, p. 2).

Tulshyan and Burey (2021) suggest that common feelings of inadequacy felt by women in the workplace have been falsely equated to a psychological disorder, somehow unique to women. (Since *impostor* implies an individual who seeks "fraudulent gain," while *syndrome* suggests some sort of disease, the term does seem a rather anxiety-inducing choice of words to describe understandable feelings of uncertainty.) Perhaps to better understand impostor syndrome, we might begin to unpack "the places where women work" (Tulshyan & Burey, 2021, para. 8). Workplace culture can actually contribute to women feeling like they do not belong or even cause that feeling:

> As white men progress, their feelings of doubt usually abate as their work and intelligence are validated over time. They're able to find role models who are like them, and rarely (if ever) do others question their competence, contributions, or leadership style. Women experience the opposite.
> (Tulshyan & Burey, 2021, para. 9)

While the research of Clance and Imes (1978) included 150 successful women, "they were primarily white middle- to upper-class women between the ages of 20 and 45" (p. 2). The origins of defining impostor phenomenon do not capture the feelings of self-doubt and lack of belonging that are often felt at higher rates among women of color (Exploring Impostor Syndrome from a Black Perspective, 2023; Nance-Nash, 2020). For women of color, impostor syndrome materializes beyond just doubts in their heads and takes shape as a lack of representation, prejudicial attitudes, and general lack of support in the workplace (Exploring Impostor Syndrome from a Black Perspective, 2023; Nance-Nash, 2020). The intersection of gender and race serves to emphasize, for individuals who are already marginalized, feeling like outsiders in many modern workplaces, particularly as leaders in these spaces. Perhaps it is time to shift the rallying cry from *"Let's fix women's impostor syndrome!"* to *"Let's fix workplaces to be truly inclusive of women, their ways of leading, and their ideas!"*

Manifestations of Impostor Syndrome among Women Who Lead

Many women mentioned feeling so unsure of themselves that they sabotaged their job searches before they began. Rachel Caldwell mentioned facing feelings of self-doubt and inadequacy at various times throughout her career but in particular when looking at job descriptions. Despite being confident that she met most requirements, she often wouldn't apply. In contrast, she would see her male counterparts, who seemed to have fewer of the required skills, applying successfully.

Even taking over a temporary or internal position, which might seem less daunting, can also bring up doubts. When Fiona Reynolds, who describes impostor syndrome as "faking it, and we're not sure if we're making it," had an opportunity to be acting head of school, she became stressed to the point of physical suffering. However, when she dared to be herself, rather than try to fill the shoes of the previous head, her discomfort eased and success followed.

Biases within the current system can add to impostor syndrome, according to Charlotte Diller, who points out that if you notice that, for example, most head-of-school positions are held by men, you might feel discouraged because "like only hires like." As Charlotte points out, "even though we might be intentionally trying to have diverse representation, it still is skewed." When women are consistently confronted with certain positions almost exclusively being held by people unlike them, it can worsen doubts.

Elsa Donahue believes leaning into their competence and avoiding imposter syndrome is a unique challenge for female leaders. She relates that in spite of her usual confidence, during some recent webinars for heads of school, she had found it "difficult to get a word in, to feel comfortable participating, when it's a large group and the majority happen to be male, and perhaps more dominant, voices." Women need to know "how to find that point of equilibrium, when to lean in and when to interrupt, interacting in that sweet spot," Elsa counsels.

Hopefully, these anecdotes might remind you that if you are facing feelings of impostor syndrome, you are not alone, and this challenge is not insurmountable. The WWL participants have provided a number of strategies for working through feelings of self-doubt.

Seeing Yourself as a Leader

As described in detail in Chapter 2, many of the successful Women Who Lead never initially saw themselves as leaders, sometimes even after multiple nudges from others. The following section will address four common mental obstacles holding women back from embracing their leadership.

The WWL interviews highlight many ways that teachers, instructional coaches, and other informal leaders in schools are building essential leadership skills, often without even realizing it. These interviews might offer an opportunity to reframe your current thinking so you can see the leadership capacity you're already building. If there is no one in your school setting who is offering you the nudge into leadership, please use these stories as a nudge from us!

Internal Obstacle 1: Leadership Is for Administrators, and I'm Not an Administrator

Many women say they don't want to be leaders because they believe the only way to lead is through formal, positional power. The subtext associated with this feeling is "I don't want to be an administrator." This often manifests as lack of self-belief, as Beth Dressler points out: "Women put so much pressure on themselves that they believe they can't do it. They can't possibly be the leader they want to be." Once they step into the role, however, they recognize they have the tools they need to succeed.

Mel Bland talks about a "constant companion of self-doubt, especially if you're new to the role, but once you've had a few years, you find your feet." As Charlotte Diller highlights, "often when we talk about leadership, we're thinking about positional authority. Leadership in general is more about building capacity, and everyone can be a leader at different points in their career. Sometimes we have positional authority, sometimes we don't. Leadership is contributing to make the world a better place, as a group, and perhaps influencing others, toward a common goal." Reframing your perspective on what makes a leader, and in what ways you can lead, could help you recognize your own leadership capacity. Katrina Charles talks about "being a leader within your current position and recognizing that there is leadership at every level, wherever you are in your position. If you can see the glass half full, you'll start building your leadership capacity to take that next step."

The simple fact is that leadership isn't exclusively for administrators. You can be a leader on your team, in your department, in your building, or in your hallway. You can be a leader by taking a risk and trying something new or building on something you know your school needs and moving the project forward—all with or without an official title and whether or not you consider yourself an administrator.

Internal Obstacle 2: I've Never Worked with a Leader Who Looks, Talks, Acts, or Sounds Like Me, So It Can't Be Possible for Me

It is not uncommon to go through an entire teaching career and exclusively work for the stereotypical white, male leader, which can make it hard for those who don't meet traditional expectations to see their own potential. The stories in this section highlight women of color who participated in the WWL interviews because this challenge is multifaceted for them. Because this is a truly complex challenge, we address intersectionality further in Chapter 8.

Nadine Richards notes the persistence of a glass ceiling in education: "There's a higher proportion of women in the teaching roles, but fewer and fewer as you move up into leadership positions." Nicole Schmidt talks about "the old boys' club. When I go recruiting, it is a tight network of old white men. It's hard if you don't know how to play that game; it's hard to break in."

Because of these systemic disadvantages, Dr. Mary Ashun emphasizes the importance of "being prepared and recognizing that there may be more expected of you as a woman than there might be of men. Knowing that you are going to fight for what you need, and you have to do it intelligently." Tambi Tyler talks about the lack of role models: "If you don't see anyone that looks like you doing the role, it's a far reach to imagine yourself doing it back."

The crucial issues of the lack of role models and the "old boys' club" will be looked at in even more depth in Chapter 5 and Chapter 7, respectively.

While we know it is likely many of us have never worked for a leader who looks like us, it doesn't mean it isn't possible. Our WWL project shows that it's actually the opposite: There are leaders out there who look, sound, think, and act very differently to our traditional vision of a leader, and you could be one of them.

Internal Obstacle 3: I'm Not Ready for Leadership. I Need More Qualifications

As referenced in the *Reflections in the Research* in Chapter 2, women are less likely to apply for positions until they meet the majority of the qualifications, whereas men will apply when they meet only 60%. This mindset presents an unnecessary hurdle when making the move toward leadership because, as reported in *Harvard Business Review* (Mohr, 2014), it's not actually a lack of qualifications or confidence that holds women back—it's that lists of requirements for positions are often unrealistic.

As mentioned earlier, Rachel Caldwell describes that if she couldn't check every single box, she wouldn't apply. Similarly, when a leadership position was advertised, Bin Lee was encouraged to apply, but she "hesitated until the very last minute" because she wasn't confident that she had the necessary experience. Women often self-sabotage because they worry about requirement details. This reluctance deprives women of the experience of interviewing, conceals their interest in leadership positions from peers and supervisors, and inhibits success over the long term.

Internal Obstacle 4: Fear of Failure

The mere idea of applying for a leadership position and not getting it can be enough to hold women back. Focusing on the potential vulnerability of the public step of applying for a job, thereby visibly demonstrating leadership aspirations, and then possibly failing can become overwhelming.

Fiona Reynolds points out that women are more socialized to want to put others before themselves and keep up appearances of doing well. When trying something new, you can worry you might not be good at it, and that, she explains, can be harder for women to risk. As mentioned earlier, Fiona is candid about a time when she had the opportunity to step into the role of acting head of school and felt so anxious she became physically ill. Many women might understandably give up, or decline to risk applying for a leadership role, when faced with this level of emotional and physical stress.

Helen Varney reflects on mindset changes over her career. She says that at the start, many women "don't actually believe in ourselves, because we have this role we think we should be in. That role is determined by our journey through life. It's not until you get someone else in your life that suddenly makes you think, there is more to this than I had thought. It's all about you believing in yourself. If you cannot internalize it, you cannot externalize it."

When finding her way in her position, Elsa Donohue talks about having "moments of self-doubt navigating the differences of communication styles." When working with other leaders who were more traditional, she learned to "lean into her own unique competency, to feel confident, to be able to find that point of equilibrium in her practice, where I felt I could advocate for myself and feel competent in my unique leadership style." Unfortunately, this process of resiliently finding your own style can be cut short by fear of failure.

So yes, if you take a risk, you might fail. But if you do, you're showing that you want to be a leader and are willing to take risks and stand for something. We don't usually get the first position we apply for, but we learn what works and what doesn't and where we have room to grow. If we're always feeling comfortable, then we're never growing. However, a positive mindset and willpower alone aren't always enough to bring success. Now that we've looked at some of the most common internal obstacles faced by women seeking leadership positions, the next section will look at specific strategies to overcome them.

Strategies for Dealing with Impostor Syndrome

Grow through Action

When you're questioning whether or not you should take a risk, Kathleen Naglee says, "If you're asking the question, follow your gut instinct. If you see how you can impact the lives of students, take the opportunity and apply." You will learn through the experience of applying, even if you don't get the job.

You might need to take action yourself to make things happen. Many of the WWL participants mentioned being asked by others to apply, but, as Caroline Brokvam points out, "not everyone gets tapped on the shoulder, so you could be waiting for that nudge, waiting for that tap, and it might never come." It could be time to start putting yourself out there to show your intention to lead.

Arden Tyoschin reminds us to have "the courage to be you and be courageous." The actions you take might be inspiring for you as well as others. As Emily Sargent Beasley says, "As we engage in leadership, and more women engage in leadership, we redefine leadership. From the beginning of my career to now, that notion has changed quite dramatically." As you take steps forward in your career, you will be part of defining that new vision of leadership.

You might simply need to start articulating your interest in leadership to get things moving. School leaders can't read your mind. They don't know you're ready for leadership unless you let them know, after which they might be able to support you in choosing the best next step. And if you don't have a school leader who can support you in person, you can find a mentor inside the pages of this book or in the Women who Lead online course—or find at least one personal "champion."

Cultivate Your Champions and Find Your Community

Erin Robinson notes that "women are not too bad at finding mentors" but often struggle when recruiting a champion, a role she defines as someone "who will speak up on your behalf when you're seeking a leadership position, who will speak out about your work to other leaders, someone in a position of power who can support you in your professional growth by advocating for you and your potential."

In order to cultivate your champions, Erin recommends networking to find "someone who has a lot of power and who is well-respected and who is willing to advocate for you." In some cases, champions might recommend you for something without explicitly being asked; other times, you might have to ask if they would be willing to reach out to the head of school or other leaders on your behalf. Your champion can be anyone in the school community, even, for example, board members who might be able to reach out to other boards.

The concept of finding champions to advocate for you during a job search overlaps with the more general benefits of building networks for professional encouragement and emotional support. Rachel Caldwell emphasizes "finding the people that can support you, finding your network," and the importance of "collaborating with others and having the support and being able to talk about that. Feeling that you can share those doubts that creep in. . . . You need your tribe." A supportive community of colleagues, whether or not they are leaders, will help alleviate feelings of isolation and provide encouragement as new obstacles and opportunities arise.

Don't Take Things Too Personally

Higher-level job searches usually involve background politics that aren't a reflection on you personally, according to Jane Thompson, who knows your automatic reaction might be, "if I don't get the job, I'm terrible!" She explains that as you move into higher positions, the final decision is usually much more about the broader context and that you might need to build up your self-esteem enough to see that you were just not the right fit at that time.

Jane also emphasizes that you should be willing to listen, to accept that you don't have all the answers and that it's OK to ask for advice. She notes that "everybody needs to find their own way to leadership. You will find the right way for yourself. Trust yourself and do it. We've been seeing more and more role models handling things in new and different ways in recent years." As outlined in Chapter 1, there is plenty of space for individual paths to success.

Interviews (and Beyond): Be Prepared, Be Courageous, Be Yourself

The unique challenges of interviews for head-of-school positions will be examined in depth in Chapter 11; following are some general tips that might help with imposter syndrome.

When you do find yourself heading into an interview, preparation can be key. Katrina Charles talks about the importance of having done your research and being prepared with solutions for potential problems. As she explains, we need to recognize that we all have different advantages that we have to capitalize on and don't need to "fit the mold"; instead, she suggests, highlight unique aspects about yourself. Follow things you're passionate about, and find ways to incorporate them in the interview process.

Emily Sargent Beasley reminds women to believe they were invited to an interview for a reason: The community sees something in you. She recommends being "incredibly true to who you are and don't worry about who's sitting next to you." Integrate what you came to say into the questions that are being asked and don't distort who you are just because you're trying to compete with the person next to you.

Similarly, many of the WWL participants spoke about the importance of being authentically you in interviews—and as a leader in general. Arden Tyoschin says, "In this unpredictable world, you have to have the courage to act and to make a decision and to make sure that your actions speak louder than words. It's hard but very fulfilling." Along those lines, Catriona Moran explains, "I learned I need to be authentic, that the person I was as a leader was the same person I was in life. Everything I did reflected me as a person but also me as a leader."

Dr. Chaunté Garrett adds, "Vulnerability is one of the things I'm most proud of the leader I'm becoming right now. Nobody is ever going to get to know anything other than what you share, and if you're really going to thrive in a space, you have to bring your authentic self."

Don't Give Up

"When I hit a wall, I just turn in a different direction. When you knock on the door, look for the window. When the window doesn't open, look for the cat door." This is how Firoozeh Dumas describes her persistent approach, adding that she's always looking to evolve: "You have to keep growing. If you ever think 'I'm done, I've arrived' you're going to be sorely disappointed—the world is constantly evolving. I'm always thinking, 'what unique contribution can I make?'" As difficult as it might seem at times, finding and maintaining this kind of resilient mindset can be essential to progress on a journey to leadership.

You Are Not Alone

If you recognize your own negative self-talk in the anecdotes, you are not alone. Many of our very successful women leaders have felt this way too, and hopefully their stories and strategies might help you recognize that feelings of inadequacy are both common and conquerable. As you're going through this process, don't hesitate to connect with others to share challenges and opportunities you have encountered along your leadership pathway. For many, the support of a mentor is critical in this journey. We'll explore the power of mentorship in Chapter 5.

Finding Her Path: Madeleine Maceda Heide

Name: Madeleine Maceda Heide
Role: Superintendent
School: Asociación Escuelas Lincoln School
Location: Buenos Aires, Argentina

Madeleine Maceda Heide grew up in Manila with a Filipino father and a Canadian mother. Both parents were professional pianists, and her ethnomusicologist father's global reputation brought many international scholars to their home. From a very early age, Madeleine was exposed to a diverse, multicultural, trilingual academic environment, which had a profound impact on her, bringing respect for a global mindset very early in her life.

Madeleine earned her undergraduate degree in early childhood education, taught preschool at an international parent cooperative school in Manila, and completed graduate studies in the United States, after which she was hired as the education coordinator for Head Start in Indiana. This was a substantial position of leadership, requiring oversight of programs across six counties—a massive job—and she was just 25 years old. She realized that while she was an outsider in many ways in the United States, her knowledge and experience could positively impact many people's lives, and she felt a deep desire to represent her position of responsibility through wise choices and actions.

Madeleine continued her international career at Taipei American School (TAS) when she moved to Taiwan with her American husband. As a teacher at TAS, she again realized her impact on other people. Rather than sitting by and allowing decisions to be made, she chose to raise her hand and get involved. She believes that "other people saw something in me because I wanted to be seen." She was invited to be the team leader because she clearly cared about the school and was very vocal about decisions, and her principal recognized the value of her voice. She says, "it was wanting to get involved that made me be a leader."

Madeleine remembers a critical moment when she saw a job posting for a principal position and realized that she had the required qualities. When she showed the posting to her husband, who encouraged her to go ahead and apply, something clicked forward in her sense of self and she thought, "Why not?" She recalls that preparing this application was a very intense process of self-reflection. She advises

> it's a process people should take very seriously. It's not just about documenting all that you did, but considering how best to express who you believe yourself to be, so that others gain confidence in what you can do and will ultimately hire you.

She moved on from her first-grade teaching position to the principalship at the International School of Brussels in Belgium (ISB). She notes that at the time, it was quite unusual for a teacher to make the leap into administration. It was even more rare for a woman to get a senior position of leadership, especially a non-European woman, at such a prestigious school in Europe. As the founding principal for early childhood in 1994, Madeleine established the Early Childhood Centre at ISB, one of the first of its kind in the international school world.

After six years in Brussels, she became lower school principal at Hong Kong International School, then assistant superintendent at the American School of Bombay in India, then head at Academia Cotopaxi in Ecuador, then superintendent at Asociación Escuelas Lincoln School in Argentina. Madeleine views this wide range of leadership positions she has held in various parts of the world as having given her continuous opportunities to grow her professional skills.

When looking back on her career, Madeleine feels a sense of urgency for a world with more women in leadership roles. She says that "women will often step away rather than step forward," reflecting that there are many barriers for women to move into leadership, yet women form half the world's population. She encourages women to

> believe that your voice is important, and that it is valuable to hear diverse perspectives, and especially diverse female perspectives. We have to find ways to express what matters, engage those with ideas different from our own, and share our values and priorities to evolve to a better, more equitable world.

> **Unpacking Her Journey**
>
> - Madeleine recognized the value of her cultural and linguistic identity as valuable assets that set her apart from other women leaders.
> - She was eager to share her ideas and opinions because he was motivated to make a difference.
> - She pursued and achieved a wide variety of leadership roles around the globe that provided her with an invaluable depth of knowledge and experience.

Take Action

For Developing Leaders

As we have shown, even very successful women leaders deal with impostor syndrome. You might feel now ready to identify when and how these feelings appear for you.

In this activity, we invite you to engage with a memory of a time you let impostor syndrome take the lead and did not pursue an opportunity that appealed to you even though you had the necessary skills and experience. Using the table provided (Table 4.1) or in your own notes or in your journal, organize your thinking into three sections:

1. Start by unpacking the reasons you hesitated (it might help to review reasons listed in this chapter, but don't feel limited to them).
2. Next, identify which aspects of impostor syndrome held you back (perhaps as noted in the *Reflections in the Research* section).
3. Finally, note specific skills from your leadership inventory that provide evidence that you would have been, and are, capable of stepping into this role.

The purpose of this exercise is to help you see exactly what stopped you from stepping up and to note evidence of your skills and experience so you don't let these same patterns repeat themselves.

Table 4.1 Impostor Syndrome Table. A table to reflect on your experiences with imposter syndrome.

	Reasons you hesitated	Unpack	Leadership inventory skills
Example: Applying for a head of dept. position	Didn't have experience formally leading a team	Felt like I needed more credentials. Second guessing my competence.	Ran student council, organized several small committees. I'm often the person people come to for support on our team.

If you discover that there are blank spaces in your table, that's totally fine! This reflection is designed to give you an initial data set that will help you either make a different decision in the future or identify a specific pathway for growth.

Scenario

To help ensure that you don't allow similar feelings of impostor syndrome to interfere in the future, we invite you to explore the following scenario. You might choose to simply think through the process or to document your self-talk in your journal:

Mentally, go back in time to the example you referenced earlier. Picture yourself in the moment that you decided not to step forward. Talk to your past self with the knowledge you have now. Explain, with kindness, how well-prepared you are to take on this new challenge and how everyone deserves the opportunity to grow.

For Established Leaders

To help an aspiring leader in your organization navigate the challenges of impostor syndrome, find an opportunity to have a mentoring conversation. You might wish to approach the conversation in one of two ways:

1. Flip Roles! Allow your aspiring leader to mentor you through an impostor syndrome moment. This could involve stepping back into

your past to bring up some of those previous feelings and allowing your aspiring leader to walk you through changing your mindset or recognizing your leadership capacity.
2. Unpack! Ask your aspiring leader to share the impostor syndrome moment from the *Developing Leaders* section earlier in this chapter and walk them through sifting the data from the emotion.

Stepping into leadership can feel like an isolating and unfamiliar experience. Taking steps with the support of a mentor can have a huge impact on your growing confidence and capabilities. In the next chapter, we'll explore the power of mentorship.

For Schools or Organizations

Continuing on the work from Chapters 2 and 3, after reflecting on the leadership standards in your organization, we invite you to consider areas such as the following:

- How inclusive are those standards of diverse leadership styles?
- How does your organization recognize or delegate leadership capacities that are more stereotypically adopted by women (e.g., taking notes, organizing projects)? (You might find the *Reflections in the Research* section of Chapter 6 helpful for identifying these specific capacities.)
- Within existing leadership teams, is there equitable division of who's taking the labor of leading?

After reflecting on these elements, you might wish to return to the activity in Chapter 2 to ensure that they are represented in the standards you created or adapted.

As your organization seeks to support more diverse leaders, building structures for mentorship opportunities could be a natural next step. This is addressed in further detail in the next chapter.

References

Clance, P., & Imes, S. (1978). The impostor phenomenon in high achieving women: Dynamics and therapeutic intervention. *Psychotherapy*

Theory, Research and Practice, *15*(3), 1–8. www.paulineroseclance.com/pdf/ip_high_achieving_women.pdf

Exploring Impostor Syndrome from a Black Perspective. (2023). https://online.maryville.edu/blog/impostor-syndrome-black-perspective/

Mohr, T. (2014, April 25). Why women don't apply for jobs unless they're 100% qualified. *Harvard Business Review*. https://hbr.org/2014/08/why-women-dont-apply-for-jobs-unless-theyre-100-qualified

Nance-Nash, S. (2020, July 27). Why imposter syndrome hits women and women of colour harder. *bbc.com*. www.bbc.com/worklife/article/20200724-why-imposter-syndrome-hits-women-and-women-of-colour-harder

Tulshyan, R., & Burey, J. (2021). Stop telling women they have impostor syndrome. *Harvard Business Review*. https://hbr.org/2021/02/stop-telling-women-they-have-impostor-syndrome

# The Power of Mentorship for Women Seeking Leadership Positions

Mentorship is the secret sauce to becoming a leader and being a good leader. If we have as many women leaders mentoring us, as we do women leaders, we would be unstoppable.

—Tambi Tyler

 ## Setting the Stage

Many of the women interviewed for WWL recognized that mentorship had been extremely valuable for them. Although some women felt strongly that a mentor should share similar lived experiences, many also highlighted that they had had valuable mentorship experiences from men. There might be no "one size fits all" mentorship model, but this chapter highlights how you can begin to approach a mentor and what that relationship might look like for you.

 ## Reflections in the Research

Because women often face greater barriers than men as they pursue leadership roles, their need for guided career support is crucial (Duevel et al., 2015; Hideg & Shen, 2019). Women who work with mentors to grow as education leaders experience positive career outcomes, such as advancement into leadership roles and general overall career satisfaction (Hideg & Shen, 2019).

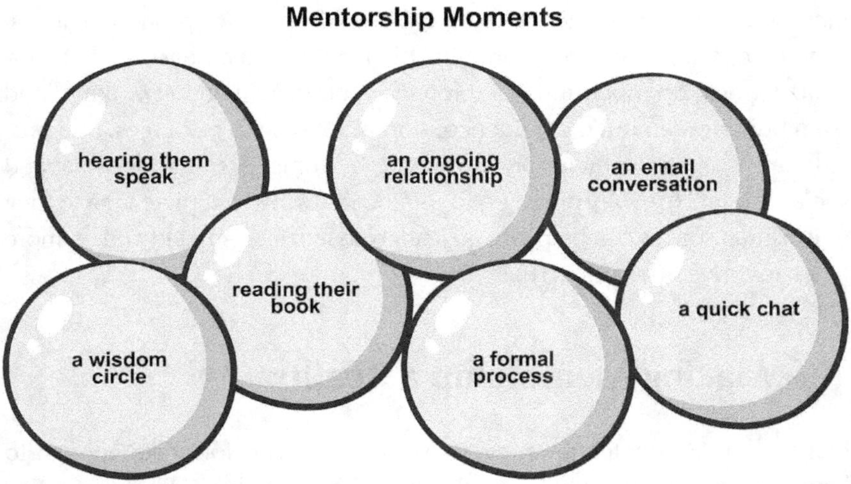

Mentorship Moments

- hearing them speak
- an ongoing relationship
- an email conversation
- reading their book
- a quick chat
- a wisdom circle
- a formal process

Figure 5.1 Mentorship Moments. Mentors provide support to developing and established women leaders in many ways, some of which are indicated in this graphic.

Mentoring and coaching opportunities are key to strengthening the leadership pipeline for women. Working with an executive coach can provide real-time feedback that can develop leadership skills and competencies, offer opportunities for critical feedback, and ease impostor syndrome. According to Klenke (2018), group coaching "can be employed to create virtual networks of executive women who support one another in their leadership development" (p. 56). Both individual coaching and group mentoring provide women leaders opportunities to "build confidence, stop isolation, tap resources, and provide a systematic vehicle for developing a women's social network and social capital" (Klenke, 2018, p. 56). Seeking mentors and coaches who look like them can provide an opportunity for women to see themselves physically represented by successful leaders and to diminish feelings associated with impostor syndrome (Exploring Impostor Syndrome from a Black Perspective, 2023; Nance-Nash, 2020).

There is a strong need for both men and women to become allies and advocates of female leaders. Finding mentoring options in a relevant experiential context can be challenging for female leaders (Duevel et al., 2015; Gipson et al., 2017). Encouragingly, a growing catalog of networking opportunities are available to female leaders in international schools, including conference sessions, multi-day workshops, asynchronous learning experiences, and weeklong summits. Klenke (2018) emphasizes that "formalizing network opportunities through group coaching, networking, and team building can build confidence, stop isolation, tap resources, and provide a systematic vehicle for developing a women's social network and social capital" (p. 56). Forming and joining networks that meet face to face or in virtual spaces can help female leaders to feel less isolated and be more likely to thrive (Klenke, 2018).

 ## Making Mentorship a Reality

During the WWL interviews, every woman who was fortunate enough to have had a mentor highlighted the experience's value. However, many women also described their struggles to find mentors who looked like them or who had undergone similar life and professional challenges. The unfortunate reality is that for those who need it most, finding a mentor is often the hardest.

What a Mentor Can Do for You

A mentor can be invaluable in helping you identify, build on, and communicate leadership skills. Caroline Brokvam notes that "if you don't have recognition by the administration where you are, then having a mentor can help you build the skills and create the opportunities" to gain the sort of initial recognition that, as discussed in Chapter 1, is often the first step in a journey to leadership.

Mentors can also be invaluable as mirrors and sounding boards. Beth Dressler says, "You have to allow yourself time and space to reflect. The more you can talk about it, the more you can reflect, and get feedback the more you can learn and grow. Mentorship formalizes the opportunity to do that." In this sense, mentors can act as coaches, bringing to light what you are unable yet to see on your own.

Mentors can transmit their experience; Chanel Johnson describes it in terms of a heavy responsibility to "prepare for the next generation, even if the next generation surpasses them. We still live in a world where in many places, there are just men in the boardroom. As women we need to help another woman get to that room so there are more diverse thinkers in there." Mentors don't actually need to be older as long as they have more experience in relevant areas.

By acting as role models, mentors can also inspire, build confidence, and provide a possible career template. Katie Wellbrook says that "mentorship is invaluable because if we can't see role models in our workplace, it's hard to aspire to those positions." This aspect of mentorship might need to be approached carefully because emulating someone else can get in the way of making the best choices for yourself.

The Importance of Having a Female Mentor

All the Women Who Lead who had had mentorship experiences described them as valuable regardless of the mentor's gender. However, several of those who were able to compare the experiences of being supported by both women and men did highlight specific advantages to working with women.

Carla Marschall notes that female mentors might more easily contextualize some of the challenges that women experience in their roles, like implicit biases that can exist in organizations; because they might not have experienced them personally, it might be more difficult for men to notice the impact of some of these issues. Similarly, Daniela Silva points out that there are key differences between men and women leaders. She referenced a study (McMaster University, 2013) in which "female leaders are more likely to consider the rights of others and take a comparative approach to decision making" because they are more engaged in listening and consensus building.

Grace McCallum also notes the importance of having a female mentor, pointing out that "it's transformational to have the support of someone with similar experience and talk frankly and transparently about what that's like. The further you go up in the ranks, the more lonely it is. It's so key for female leaders to find your leadership tribe, cultivate those relationships and value them because that's what will get you through to be successful." Although she has had amazing and supportive male leaders, Grace recognizes that it is often easier for women to establish a shared perspective.

Things sound similar on the mentor's side of things; when Rachel Hovington began mentoring aspiring women leaders, she was surprised to hear feedback like, "I feel like I can talk to you more than I can talk to anyone else." Because she had always simply tried to help anyone she thought could go to the next level in leadership, she hadn't specifically realized the power of being a woman to coach, mentor, and empower women leaders until she heard that feedback.

What Mentorship Can Look Like

If you feel isolated in your leadership journey in your current school context, you're not alone! Many aspiring women leaders feel exactly the same way. Trying to find a mentor isn't always easy, and it doesn't have to start as a one-to-one relationship.

Often when we think of a mentorship relationship, we envision a formal process with clearly outlined goals, roles, and responsibilities. However, Bridget McNamer thinks of mentoring as "a moment," describing it as "a mindset or a behavior, but not necessarily a formal relationship." In fact, mentoring can happen in varied configurations and degrees of formality and participation.

Dr. Chaunté Garrett echoes this, noting that "mentorship is not always about connection, it can be about what you value in someone you admire." You don't have to be in a real-time interpersonal relationship with a mentor; you can gain inspiration even from a distance, by reading their work or listening to them speak.

According to Katie Ham, mentorship can just be a connection you create that works in the moment. She says that "mentoring used to be scary, formal and sit-down." This more informal view of mentorship has helped her take advantage of many opportunities to learn that she might not have fully appreciated earlier in her career.

Grace McCallum's mentorship experience did not fit the stereotype, either. She grew as a leader as part of a group of women who helped each other. She says "we all went into leadership together, all new, all not knowing where we were going, and we supported each other without ego, without competitiveness." This peer mentorship helped all the woman as they advanced into leadership.

Joellen Killion had a similar experience with a group of women she refers to as a "wisdom circle," what she describes as "a circle of women colleagues that have been meeting for over 20 years together, who I deeply trust and value, who have committed to my growth as much as I committed to theirs. It feels right because it is a circle of women. For me that has been something I have valued throughout my entire career. It has always been a circle with no hierarchy. We pushed and prodded each other, we've challenged, held each other up, picked each other up. I am blessed to have that experience."

Finally, Deb Welch asks us to "view mentorship as a continuum, to not be fixed in our definition of what mentoring is." She notes that it's possible to learn from many different people, some of whom might not even realize they've provided just the right inspiration at a particular stage in your career. She advises "being open to growth and mentoring from many. It might be long term or short term. To be continually open to what others can teach you, never feeling as though you've got it all yourself." This flexible view of mentoring allows you to embrace mentoring moments when and wherever you need them, without feeling like the learning has to look or feel a certain way.

Challenges of Finding a Mentor

Tambi Tyler didn't grow up seeing a lot of African American leaders, but fortunately, "the few that I did see were great and instrumental in reaching back and getting others to replace themselves." She emphasizes that if you "don't see anyone that looks like you doing it, it's a very far reach to see yourself doing it," highlighting the challenges of finding guidance for women, and in particular for Black women, when available mentors or role models are lacking among school leadership.

Similarly, Junlah Madalinski points out that "mentorship is critical and crucial, but it is a privilege. For women of color in education leadership, it's not something that is afforded to us. Especially if we're seeking out mentors who are also women of color, especially if we're seeking out heads who are actively doing social justice work." This has led Junlah to struggle to find a mentor within the international school community.

Clarissa Sayson, describing comparable challenges, says that "it's only been in the last five years that I've been able to look to female leaders." She, like several others, notes that there were limited opportunities to connect with women leaders in the early stages in her career. Unfortunately, this is precisely when these connections would be the most valuable.

Seek Out a Mentor

If you're struggling to find a mentor, don't hesitate to ask. You don't have to limit yourself to one mentor or to your immediate school community; there are many ways to seek out mentorship. It might seem intimidating, but most leaders are not only willing but eager to mentor others. Suzanna Jemsby highlights that mentorship won't happen all on its own. She says, "We're all sitting here waiting; you need to ask." In her experience, very few people do, and they end up missing valuable opportunities to learn, share, and grow.

As you are building your leadership capacity, you might find that you need more than one mentor—and that's OK too! Similar to Deb Welch's advice in *What Mentorship Can Look Like* in this chapter, Katrina Charles mentions that "it's good to have a plethora of mentors to do with a variety of things: physical health, education career, having a family. Thinking one mentor can do everything for you is probably unlikely." It's acceptable and appropriate to reach out to a variety of people to get support that meets your needs in different facets of your life.

You might feel you don't have opportunities for mentorship within your local school community, but your mentor can be anywhere! Abeer Shinnawi notes that mentorship is even more important when you are feeling isolated, as women leaders often are. She points out that often in leadership circles, "you can be the only female, and if you're a woman of color, forget it." Even if your mentor is not within your school community, you can lean on them and channel their energy to keep you going and focused on your goals. You don't have to be in the same physical space to learn from each other.

Create Your Mentorship Moments

Regardless of the level of formality or structure you are aiming for, ultimately you are responsible for finding mentorship for yourself. While some might be fortunate enough to have the support of an experienced leader within their school community, others might have to work harder to cultivate the right relationships. We urge you to use the *Take Action* section in this chapter to begin considering the right mentorship opportunity for you. As you embark on Part 2 of this book, Facing the Realities of Leadership for Women, you might appreciate having a mentor for support.

Finding Her Path: Tambi Tyler

Name: Tambi Tyler
Role: Head of School
School: The Colorado Springs School
Location: Colorado Springs, Colorado, United States

Tambi Tyler has had a "long leadership journey," spanning 25 years. Her journey began in Des Moines, Iowa, where she acted as an associate before moving on to senior administrator roles at various schools, including Atlanta International School.

She first began to recognize she had the capacity to lead as an associate. A respected veteran teacher came to her and asked for help with a specific student. She realized that even teachers with all the "bells and whistles" might still not be able to reach kids but that she could and that this was an area where she might be able to lead.

She became department head after her third year as a teacher, and she still didn't quite feel she officially "had the mantle of leadership," but she gradually began to see how her increased responsibilities allowed her to make a greater positive impact on classroom practices. Eventually, after her fifth year of teaching (and after much urging from mentors and fellow African American women colleagues), she became a dean of students.

Tambi had several strong female mentors who pushed her to return to school to pursue a master's degree. She notes that these women were very direct in their mentorship, teaching her how to trust and believe in herself despite her struggles with impostor syndrome. She says, "they gave me the wings."

Tambi had three African American women and one African American man as mentors, which she notes was extremely rare, particularly in Iowa. She points out that young women of color are not often sought after from a teacher associate role to become the next principal or leader of an institution. Because her mentors were all African American, they convincingly demonstrated the possibility of her own leadership, although this was never discussed openly. She says "mentorship is so essential that we don't even give it credit," and she feels she was extremely lucky to have had so many mentors in her career. Tambi refers to herself as a "unicorn," noting that the research shows that there are still not many people of color in school leadership. This is especially true in independent schools, where numbers are less than 10%. She wonders "What happens now, when we retire?"

Overall, Tambi believes that mentorship is "part of making a leader a leader. Mentorship is the secret sauce to becoming a leader and being a good leader. If we have as many women leaders mentoring as we do women leaders, we would be unstoppable."

Unpacking Her Journey

- Tambi recognized that she had skills that allowed her to reach and support students in ways not all teachers could.
- She sought out and accepted guidance and mentorship from colleagues.

Take Action

For Developing Leaders

Now that we have seen that mentorship can take many forms, we invite you to consider multiple ways you can intentionally seek out mentorship right now. We've structured these opportunities into varying levels, from "safety" to "spendy," so that you can embrace multiple mentor moments on your journey.

Level: Safety

For this mentorship level, we're asking you to consider someone you can learn from who might never even need to know that you consider them a mentor. Think about an aspirational person you want to follow. Can you read their work, listen to their podcasts, take their courses, go to a workshop, or learn from them, even at a distance, in some other way?

Consider creating a custom feed of content from aspirational mentors so you can be inspired by them whenever you need support. For example, we like to use "stations" on Apple podcasts to create specific playlists around themes or Twitter lists to create a stream of content from specific authors or thought leaders.

Level: Supported

For this mentorship level, we're asking you to consider creating a community of support within your local context. Whether they are in your school, your city, or your region, who is in your work circle of colleagues who are also working toward leadership? Is there an opportunity to create your own "circle of women" whom you can grow with over time? This might include people you currently work with who lead in ways you admire, people you know from conferences or local events, or people you have previously worked with.

This community can start as something simple, like a WhatsApp group, or can build to a regular meeting in person or over Zoom. Your circle will require effort, organization, and continued commitment from everyone involved to continue to grow. Use this opportunity now to plant some seeds, but make sure to keep the connections and conversations alive over time.

Level: Stretch

For this mentorship level, we're asking you to take a risk. As mentioned in previous chapters, your current leaders won't be able to support you in your leadership goals if they don't know you have them. Take this opportunity to share your goals with your school leaders. If speaking to your head of school or superintendent feels like too big of a stretch right now, start with a middle leader or a head of department. The important part is letting others know that you will be looking for support in your journey toward leadership.

While you are having these conversations, you might also specifically want to ask one of your school leaders to mentor you in this process or consider seeking out a champion, as described earlier by Erin Robinson, within your professional network. When you reach out for mentorship, you might notice that it feels more intimidating to ask for support without knowing what you want to achieve. You can alleviate that feeling by creating a mini action plan that includes, for instance,

- What are the three things you would like to know?
- Why is this the person you want to reach out to?
- How would you like to work together/what kind of support do you need (is this an email, a conversation, a long-term relationship)?
- What would you like to accomplish or learn from this mentoring relationship?

Regardless of where you begin, or what level you are working toward, remember to be open to the mentor having insights that you might not expect. The value of having a mentor is in the learning (and the reason you're seeking mentorship is because "you don't know what you don't know").

Level: Spendy

If none of the aforementioned options feel right for you, remember that you can always pay for mentorship or coaching. This is a service that Kim offers through Eduro Learning, and there are many coaches or mentors who provide formal mentoring packages without having to navigate complicated work relationships.

Scenario

To help you think through the process of seeking out a mentor, we invite you to consider the following scenario. You might wish to share your thinking with someone in your network or simply document notes in this book, a document, or journal:

> Although you've been a teacher for many years, you've never worked with a leader who looks, talks, or acts like you. It feels like there's no path to leadership for you. It's hard to imagine how you go from being a teacher to a leader. What would your journey look like if you had a mentor? Who would this future self be, as a leader? How would this person act? How would they present themselves?

Table 5.1 Levels of Mentorship. A comparison chart of the different types of mentorship developing leaders might seek.

	Mentorship level	*Descriptor*
1	Safety	A mentor you can follow through their work without interacting personally
2	Supported	A mentor who is already within your current professional community
3	Stretch	A mentor you don't know yet who could be able to provide specific support around a focused area of growth
4	Spendy	A professional mentor or coach you can hire

Now that you've thought through the answers to these questions, is there someone who comes to mind who possesses one (or some) of these characteristics? Is there someone you have crossed paths with who you can reach out to?

For Established Leaders Supporting Developing and Aspiring Leaders

We know that mentorship is crucial in a leader's journey. As Catriona Moran says, "good organizations try to grow leaders. Not so that they'll stay with us forever, but so that they will go on and do great things at other organizations." We invite you as an established leader to take this opportunity to offer mentorship to aspiring leaders in your organization and to make this a regular part of your leadership practice. We're offering three different levels of support you can provide.

Level: Nudge

As described in each chapter in Part 1 of this book, many of the WWL participants weren't considering leadership until they received a tap on the shoulder. At this level, we are inviting you to consider developing an intentional practice of "nudging" developing leaders within your organization.

You might wish to

- note who is demonstrating leadership capacity in your organization right now
- offer a nudge or tap on the shoulder to invite them to consider leadership opportunities
- provide opportunities for more responsibility
- specifically invite them for interviews

Consider how you can invite other leaders in your organization to make these steps an intentional part of your practice to help grow great leaders.

Level: Mentorship

Although mentorship does not always need to be formal, as discussed in this chapter, we are inviting you to consider how you can create a structured mentorship program in your organization to provide a transparent process for nurturing leaders.

You might wish to

- create a simple application process using a digital form, ensuring that the process for reviewing applications is transparent and equitable
- identify specific leaders who are willing to be mentors
- clearly state or describe what mentorship entails, ideally with the input of those seeking mentoring
- invite experts/coaches in to elevate the conversation with aspiring leaders
- provide leadership professional development opportunities for middle-level leaders
- add this feature as a benefit to your compensation package, as part of your contract

Level: Champion

We invite you to use your leadership authority to be a champion for someone in your professional community or to leverage your professional network to support an aspiring leader. This could be someone who is not the right fit for leadership in your organization right now but for whom you see an appropriate next step elsewhere.

You might wish to

- offer to mentor an intern or student teacher
- offer to connect a head of department with someone from another school in a similar position

You might find there are opportunities for all of these levels of support within your organization or for just one or two right now. This action is about implementing options wherever and whenever you have the capacity to bring mentorship moments to your developing leaders.

For Schools or Organizations

We invite you to consider the organizational structures you might have in place (or not) to support opportunities for mentorship, both within and beyond your local setting. You might wish to think about issues such as the following:

- How does your school support individuals seeking mentorship?
- What kind of funding does your school offer if the mentoring provided on site is not suitable for a particular candidate?
- Is there a formal process to provide mentors?
- Do your school leaders have experience mentoring aspiring leaders (if not, is training provided)?

Ideally, the actions described here should help establish clear pathways to mentorship at the organizational level rather than putting the burden on the individual to navigate in isolation.

The unfortunate likelihood is that most schools might not currently have these types of supportive structures in place; if you are an individual aspiring leader reading this, it's important to be aware of the variety of difficulties you might face on the path ahead, obstacles that are the focus of the next several chapters of this book.

References

Duevel, L., Nashman-Smith, M., & Stern, E. (2015). Moving from 'womanless history' to women stepping up into school leadership roles. *International Schools Journal, XXXV*(1), 34–45. www.proquest.com/docview/1781327696?pq-origsite=gscholar&fromopenview=true

Exploring Impostor Syndrome from a Black Perspective. (2023). https://online.maryville.edu/blog/impostor-syndrome-black-perspective/

Gipson, A., Pfaff, D., Mendelsohn, D., Catencacci, L., & Burke, W. (2017). Women and leadership: Selection, development, leadership style, and performance. *The Journal of Applied Behavioral Science, 53*(1), 32–65. https://doi.org/10.1177/0021886316687247

Hideg, I., & Shen, W. (2019). Why still so few? A theoretical model of the role of benevolent sexism and career support in the continued underrepresentation of women in leadership positions. *Journal of Leadership & Organizational Studies, 26*(3), 287–303. http://doi.org/10.1177/1548051819849006

Klenke, K. (2018). *Women in leadership: Contextual dynamics and boundaries* (2nd ed.). Emerald Publishing.

Nance-Nash, S. (2020, July 27). Why imposter syndrome hits women and women of colour harder. *bbc.com*. www.bbc.com/worklife/article/20200724-why-imposter-syndrome-hits-women-and-women-of-colour-harder

PART II

Facing the Realities of Leadership for Women

Double Standards for Women Leaders

What women really need to do is own their voice and communication style. We need to shift the narrative on what makes a good communicator. There is a place for storytelling and more than one message in one story. We need to trust that people will figure it out instead of transforming our communication styles to be more like male leaders.

—Fiona Reynolds

Setting the Stage

Most women are keenly aware of existing double standards based on gender. The expectation that, for example, women run the household while men manage the finances might feel easy to dismiss as an outdated stereotype, but many of those traditional expectations continue to subtly but profoundly affect the recruiting process.

Almost all of the WWL participants interviewed had at least one story to share, some of them outright laughable and others infuriating. If you don't fit the traditional middle-aged cisgender white male stereotype of a leader, you might have come across many of these yourself. The WWL interviewees have not only faced these obstacles, but they described a variety of strategies for dealing with them that you can apply to your own leadership journey!

Reflections in the Research

Popular media reinforces stereotypical beliefs that women are caretakers who are better equipped to look after children and aging parents than to lead organizations. These gendered norms inform many workplaces that continue to adhere to the expectation of a nuclear family with gender-specific roles (Cullen & Perez-Truglia, 2021; Klenke, 2018; Tarbutton, 2019). Persistent social expectations can prevent women from pursuing school leadership roles because teacher roles are more connected to caretaking responsibilities (Tarbutton, 2019).

In the 21st century, words used to describe leaders often include *strong*, *direct*, *aggressive*, *powerful*, and *charismatic*. These words have positive connotations when they are associated with men. Furthermore, these words help to define a gender-centric culture of leadership that continues to be based in "male-dominated theories and research" (Klenke, 2018, p. 19). Where these gendered norms of leadership prevail, men will continue to dominate the top leadership positions. Other adjectives used to describe expectations of leaders typically include *charismatic, visionary, inspiring, upright, decisive, efficacy-oriented, integrative, dependable*, and *diplomatic* (Braun et al., 2017).

Gender bias is defined by the American Psychological Association (2023a) as "any one of a variety of stereotypical beliefs about individuals on the basis of their sex, particularly as related to the differential treatment of females and males." Research continues to confirm that women are held to a higher standard than men (Gaskell, 2021) while proving their competence in ways that men do not have to (Klenke, 2018; Williams, 2021). Gender bias takes form in a variety of ways that can decrease women's ability to do their best work, to remain engaged in a professional field, and to find satisfaction in their careers (Chen & Moons, 2015; Williams, 2021).

Among the myriad hurdles faced by women leaders is the various contexts they negotiate—family, workplace, community (Klenke, 2018). They act as leaders within various contexts that include "their families, the workplace, the church, and sports they are involved in" (Klenke, 2018, p. 17). Each context in which women lead and interact is guided by certain beliefs about their "leadership competencies and sex role stereotypes" (Klenke, 2018, p. 18).

The context within the field of international education is informed by its way of "doing" gender. The profile of the international school head has historically been heteronormative and dominated by middle-aged white men, who tend to knowingly or unwittingly appoint other men who resemble them in certain ways. This exclusivity of senior leadership roles in international schools has undoubtedly led to missed opportunities due to the absence of new ideas and diverse perspectives (more on this in Chapter 7). Additionally, leadership styles are often presented as a common binary labeled masculine or feminine, and the most prevalent stereotype of leadership might be that as leaders, women take care and men take charge.

Agentic Leadership Characteristics

Agentic characteristics, which are commonly used to describe leaders, are behaviors that are more assertive, authoritative, or confident. Agentic leaders are perceived as "being ambitious, dominant, independent, self-sufficient or aggressive, and caring more about the task than about people" (Braun et al., 2017, p. 378). Not surprisingly, a man quickly comes to mind for many individuals when they hear such descriptors.

Communal Leadership Characteristics

Conversely, communal traits are attributed to women such as "being affectionate, helpful, or gentle" (Braun et al., 2017, p. 378). It seems counterintuitive that leaders who possess nurturing characteristics would be excluded from leadership profiles. After all, how else might a group of people move forward together toward a common goal if not by the individuals' exhibiting communal traits?

When women lead with strong agentic tendencies that are more commonly associated with men, they often receive negative feedback. This is known as the backlash effect. Not surprisingly, similar-to-me hiring practices coupled with the backlash effect lead to "fewer women in leadership positions and more negative evaluations of female leaders" (Braun et al., 2017, p. 379).

Change initiatives are often framed as women's issues when it is men who more frequently hold positions of power (Grant Thornton, 2022). Since men hold a majority of leadership roles in international schools and are involved in making decisions that impact policy and strategy, their active support in breaking cycles of gender inequality is mandatory. Men in leadership roles must actively engage as allies.

Stereotypes in the Real World

Getting an insight into how these stereotypes could manifest in interactions with others could help you be more prepared to deal with them. Highlighted here are several stories that stood out during the WWL interviews.

Managing Misogyny

Both Jennifer Tickle and her husband are school administrators, so they have each sat in the candidate's chair while the other was the supportive spouse. Jennifer finds that when they're interviewing together, her own CV is often ignored. Once, when asked what she can do to support her husband, she jokingly said "I bake very good cupcakes," and the interview team wrote it down as a serious answer. When she interviews for a leadership position with her husband in the room, no one asks what he can do to support her—and we can imagine the response if he replied about his baking prowess.

Similarly, Katie Wellbrook has heard comments like, "Your earrings are too big, they're a distraction. Is that a power suit you're wearing? Is it possible to be too ambitious?" during the interview process. As she says, "women have to determine if these comments are misogynistic. Would they ask this to a man?" These kinds of comments highlight a need to shift the culture, but it might also be a clue to determine if the recruiting organization is the right fit for the individual.

The Maternal Wall Bias

Many of the Women Who Lead expressed frustration with interview questions about being a parent and feeling pressured to specifically point out that they can both parent and lead. Carla Marschall recalls an experience when she was pregnant with her first child while interviewing and faced questions about how the "emotional state" of being a parent could influence her role. She points out there "needs to be a high level of trust within the organization that a person can play both roles of parent and leader." In the end, these interview questions led her to pull her application because she could tell there was not a culture fit between her and that particular school.

Similarly, Michelle Khuns shares a story about coaching aspiring school leaders and noting that women often get comments about how to be a successful principal while also being a parent, but men rarely do. She wonders, "How do we respond to that question? What are our words? That's what we need to figure out as female leaders." Positively addressing these frequent questions about family can clearly be a constant, draining challenge for women.

Additional Challenges of Motherhood

Jennifer Tickle notes that a lot of the women she saw in leadership positions weren't mothers, so she found it hard to envision being both until she happened to be working in a school with four women with leadership ambitions who all had children around the same age. She says "it was really powerful to see that there were others with the same challenges. The more we can share our stories, the better." Unfortunately, it's often hard to find these kinds of role models or exemplars.

Michelle Khuns notes that "people sometimes think that leadership and family life are not compatible." She points out that "you can make it compatible, because everything you're doing that makes yourself whole is going to help you in your leadership position." You don't have to choose, she adds, saying, "you can be an effective school leader and be an effective family member or friend. You don't have to give up all of that to be an impactful leader." It might be important to consider discouraging advice in this area with detachment and to seek out and focus on perspectives that align with your own values.

Rashida Nachef noted that being a parent in a busy leadership position might be even more challenging in the Middle East, where often "men don't give as much support." Despite the pressure she felt to stay home once she got pregnant, she never gave up her career, appeasing her family by saying, "if, at any time, you see that I'm not taking good care of my daughter, you have the full right to tell me to stay home." Although it was not easy to raise three children while leading, she credits her success to being able to manage time well, setting aside time for her children as well as time for herself: "If you give the attention you need to give to your children, without compromising, you can keep your career and success in the workplace, and at the same time give your family the attention they deserve, and they will appreciate that."

Many of the WWL interviewees described finding similar ways to support their families without compromising.

Michelle Remington recalls adjustments she needed to make as an established administrator who was simultaneously nursing an infant, recognizing that, "It's hard for women in leadership . . . there are definitely sacrifices that are unique to women; traveling across the world when you're trying to breastfeed a baby isn't easy." While admitting that it might not be for everyone, she concludes, "I'm a better parent because I work," a positive perspective shared across several interviews.

These stories make clear that women leaders face definite obstacles both in the demands of leadership roles and in the area of family life. It's worth noting that in some school and host-country cultures, no amount of positive thinking by individuals might shift those barriers. On the other hand, some seemingly impossible dilemmas might just be illusory stereotypes. This is why it's important to share these interviewees' stories about their experiences as parents—they reflect all of the frustrations and paradoxes of being a woman in leadership but might also provide some reassurance around potential paths to success.

Managing the Mental Load of Motherhood

Carla Marschall elaborates on the double standards around motherhood and parenting that women face, noting that while it is rarely a concern if a male leader has children, judgments abound for pregnant women or those with younger children. As she explains, "The motherhood piece is probably something that many female leaders experience. Although I need to take care of my children at the end of the day, it doesn't mean that I switch off when I get home. In reality a person can play both roles of parent and leader."

Carla also notes that in society, not only are women generally the primary caregivers but even when both parents are involved, the cognitive load to organize and do all the planning often still falls on the women: "Just because the father is present, doesn't mean that he's the one doing the thinking. In most cases, the mother is doing exactly the same job at home, carrying the cognitive load for the family. Generally the same expectation doesn't exist for men, and fathers have more freedom to choose their hours."

Grace McCallum also reflected on this challenge, highlighting that "the mental load of being a woman and a parent, it's invisible but it's big. All these little tiny nitpicky things on our minds that are unseen but important." The extra energy required to work against these unbalanced expectations can be a significant stress on women pursuing leadership roles.

Stereotypes and Cultural Expectations

Women leaders are frequently labeled as bossy or aggressive, but unfortunately, being the opposite can also work against them. Catriona Moran has often been told that she is "too nice" for a stereotypical leader. She shared a revealing story about being the lead administrator for the design of a construction project: "One meeting, there were twenty people in the room (nineteen males, I was eight months pregnant). Anytime a decision needed to be made, the others looked to my male colleague—even though I was making the decisions." As she points out, there is a perception that "nice" women aren't capable of being decisive leaders.

International school educators might find themselves facing varying levels of stereotypical expectations due to influence from the surrounding culture. Caroline Brokvam has observed that she gets "challenged in a way that wouldn't happen to a man" more frequently in her current region of the world, Africa, than in her previous, Europe, but she finds it hard to pinpoint why. She has found that gender-associated stereotypes sometimes seem cultural but also sometimes particular to specific parents or teachers: "I feel like you get challenged and people assume that you will back down because you're a woman."

Unfortunately, this behavior is not exclusive to individual parents or teachers; it often finds its way into executive board conversations as well. Jane Thompson shares that she has often found herself in executive board meetings with businessmen where her ideas are completely dismissed, only to be rephrased by a man and received with appreciation. Jane recommends that "we should call it out and laugh at it: the old boys' club in international schools. They're lovely people, but it does feel like a group. It does make you feel excluded and makes you draw back." This "elephant in the room" at international schools will be addressed in the following chapter.

Strategies to Manage These Challenges

Given that these double standards continue to exist on a societal level, we recognize that we can't expect the burden to fall on individual women to change the system. Many of the WWL interviewees whose stories we share were able to make progress in the face of great structural and cultural challenges. However, the reality is that such progress might simply not be possible for many women, no matter their individual approach or effort, due to wider systemic issues. It is with this caveat that we share the following strategies for confronting work–life balance stereotypes.

Be Bold: Stand Out, Speak Out, Stay Positive

Grace McCallum recommends that aspiring female leaders "be bold." Defying cultural expectations to be direct enough to say "I want this" can be a game changer. As Grace says, "the answer is always no, unless you ask." She notes that it can be hard to boldly advocate for what you believe in when getting started, so sometimes you have to "fake it till you make it."

Now that she is more confident in her boldness, Grace talks about being clear in her communication and standing up for her beliefs. As a leader, she is transparent about who she is, what she believes in, and what she stands for. This might mean that not every potential future position is a match, and, she explains, that's OK. The last thing you want to do is accept a leadership position in an institution with an incompatible philosophy.

Often, when women do not feel confident in their leadership skills, they will pull back from expressing themselves. In addition, impostor syndrome can cause women to remain silent and not share their thinking, which makes them easy to overlook. Madeleine Heide recommends that aspiring and growing leaders "find a way to be seen and heard because the world needs female leaders." Confident expression isn't always easy, but the fact is that remaining quiet will likely not lead to change.

Recollecting earlier experiences with double standards and microaggressions, Jane Thompson recognizes that at the time, she was oblivious to the negativity, which therefore didn't get under her skin. Now, although she acknowledges the importance of recognizing those behaviors and being aware of them, she cautions, "don't waste time being angry about it; it's not going to help you." She notes that there is a lot more sensitivity to the issue among male colleagues than in the past, and "they do want to help. Over time, the atmosphere is changing and becoming much more supportive and respectful."

Be a Role Model at School and at Home

Many interviewees pointed out the importance of being a role model, including for aspiring female leaders who want to have families, for their own children, and for school community members. By being a parent and being a leader, these women demonstrate that leading while having a family is possible.

Grace McCallum discussed the importance of "taking on leadership as a young woman" and emphasized that "we all have the responsibility to be sure that we're making this experience normalized." She initially felt some pressure to keep family and work separate, but she knew that that was never going to work for her, saying "it was really important for me to set the tone of 'This is who I am, this is what I bring to the table, this is what it's going to look like. If that doesn't work, I'm out.'" At one point in her career, she had to bring her newborn to meetings and nurse her at the table. She says "if you want to be involved, and your baby is young, you can do both if you want to. You're going to have to rip off the band-aid and make it normal to everyone." For her, being a role model as a female leader means not hiding the fact that she's a parent.

Rashida Nachef highlights that because she worked while raising her children, she taught them to be self-reliant and how to appreciate work. She says her "girls can't imagine themselves getting married and being simply a housewife," and they never missed any of the attention or affection their cousins had. She is proud to have provided a role model of a successful working mother to her daughters.

Nicole Schmidt addresses the challenge of being a leader in a small international school, where "you're always the principal, even at a birthday party or game." She uses those opportunities to say "I'm here as a mom, I need to be a mom today" to help other parents recognize the varying roles she has within the community.

Melanie Vrba shared that she was considering accepting a leadership role when her elementary-school-age daughter said, "Mom, but principals are boys," and she realized that every other principal at the school had been a male. She decided to take the role then and there because she wanted her daughter to see that families can function in different ways.

Jennifer Tickle appreciates that international schools have helped with these issues, because they're family-oriented environments, and she's worked to foster that within schools that didn't have those structures set up. She says, "It's really important as a school leadership that we set up structures so that people can manage working while having children. We've learned that it's OK and we are human and sometimes kids will come in and be more of a pressing priority." Leaders like Jennifer show that it's possible to be role models to one's children and families while also working on structural changes to make possibilities more visible for the whole community.

Defining Your Path

These realities are not going to change overnight. It's likely that many scenarios similar to those shared here will arise in your journey to leadership, but they don't have to stop you! Recognizing how you might face these kinds of challenges, and having specific strategies and tools to manage them, is a critical step in taking your leadership to the next level. Throughout Part 2 of this book, we'll be exploring different challenges and providing opportunities for you to determine how you want to manage them.

Finding Her Path: Jennifer Tickle

Name: Jennifer Tickle
Role: Secondary Principal
School: Dresden International School
Location: Dresden, Germany

Jennifer Tickle says her journey to leadership has been "planned, but not planned." She says she's made leadership steps along the way and it "felt like a very natural progression." At each point in her career, she's chosen to take on what felt like the next logical role. When she felt she was hitting a ceiling, she tried to find the next route upward.

Even though it's been a natural progression, she notes that she was sometimes frustrated along the journey because, for example, gender differences in parental leave policy meant she had to take five months of leave because her partner only got two days, so that in a professional sense "having two children really slowed me down," but in retrospect, she recognizes that it was a chance to reflect and refine her craft. She describes the journey as interesting and as having always felt "right" along the way.

Jennifer notes that her experience as a theater director prepared her well for leadership; she's used to organizing people to build an ensemble. She says "leadership is an immersive experience; you want to move people through it, so when they come out of it they feel empowered." She emphasizes that she loves learning, which has always felt very positive to her.

As a leader, Jennifer recognizes the challenges that women leaders face when trying to strike a balance among roles that can include parent, partner, and school leader. She "really wants to empower women to shift that balance, and empower men as well, because they're just as trapped as women in these situations."

Unpacking Her Journey

- Jennifer always looked for the next opportunity that would take her to the next level of leadership or a new experience.
- She used the time when she was more focused on raising her children to reflect and refine her craft as a leader.
- She recognized that the skills she had developed as a theater director transferred well into leadership.

Take Action

For Developing Leaders

Knowing that you will likely be confronted with stereotypical expectations of leadership styles based on gender, we invite you to take this opportunity to be prepared.

This activity is designed to help you see how your specific leadership style is uniquely you. We've provided a Venn diagram (Figure 6.1) for you to map both your agentic and communal traits as described in the *Reflections in the Research* section of this chapter.

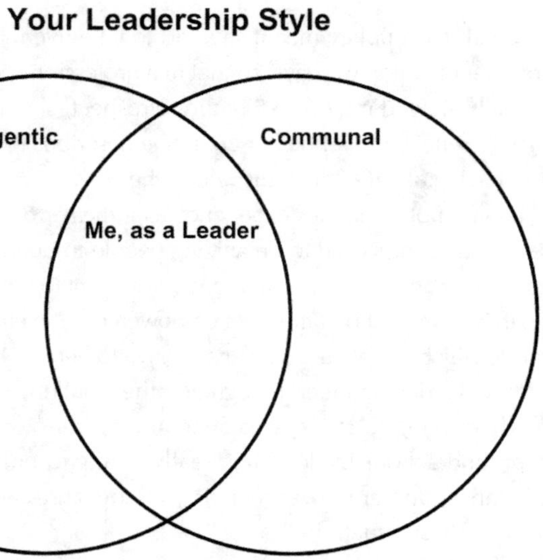

Your Leadership Style

Figure 6.1 Agentic and Communal Traits. Using a Venn diagram can be helpful for categorizing agentic and communal leadership characteristics in order to identify what might be your personal leadership style.

Scenario

To help you handle an uncomfortable or even insulting interview question, we invite you to think through some of the specific examples shared in this chapter and imagine how you might respond in the moment. If you're not sure which story to focus on, we recommend the following scenario. You might wish to role-play a similar conversation with a colleague or document your thinking here in the book, in a document, or in your journal:

Imagine you're in the same situation as Jennifer Tickle in the interview process, and you're asked what you bring to support your partner in leadership work. What concrete statement could you make that would emphasize your skills and abilities as a professional?

For Established Leaders

In order to help you create and maintain equitable hiring practices, we invite you to use this as an opportunity to reflect on your own perceptions of what makes a great leader.

Table 6.1 Leadership Skills T-Chart. It is important to categorize leadership skills in order to examine beliefs and attitudes.

My leadership skills	
Agentic	Communal

This activity has three parts:

1. Define leadership skills.

Write down skills, behaviors, attitudes you associate with a "good leader."

2. Organize skills.

Organize the skills or traits that you identified in step 1 into the T-Chart (Table 6.1).

3. Reflect.

Review your T-Chart. Do you notice that your perception of a good leader leans too heavily to one side or the other? If so, this could be a good opportunity to reflect on your hidden biases. You might also wish to bring this conversation to your leadership team to help uncover any other potential beliefs that could be unknowingly shaping your hiring practices. You might also wish to develop structures within your hiring practices to remove these biases.

For Schools or Organizations

We invite you to reflect on the distribution of leadership in your organization. When you see leadership teams in action, consider scenarios such as the following:

- Who takes on certain types of tasks? Do the women take on planning the pancake breakfast while men take on "Sports Day"?

- Who do you see consistently taking notes or planning and organizing meetings?
- Who do you see consistently leading visioning or meetings focused on school direction and goals?
- Who is leading in the elementary school vs the secondary school? In the academic leadership positions vs coordinator or curriculum positions?

Reflections for men to consider in their pursuit of active allyship include the following:

- How are men in leadership roles actively leveraging their power to support women who are interested in leading or who are already in leadership roles?
- How have men sought guidance from women about how they need to be supported?

As you consider the reality of the breakdown of tasks on various leadership teams in your organization, you might also want to envision

- How can these roles be more evenly distributed?
- What structures can be put in place to ensure that the responsibilities of note-taking vs facilitating are equally shared among leaders?
- Where and when can you create opportunities for this type of distribution to be visible to all stakeholders?

Unfortunately, the distribution of these roles is often entrenched in the underlying culture of schools and their leadership, an area we address further in the next chapter.

References

American Psychological Association. (2023a). Gender bias. *APA Dictionary of Psychology*. https://dictionary.apa.org/gender-bias

Braun, S., Stegman, S., Hernandez Bark, A., Junker, N., & van Dick, R. (2017). Think manager—think male, think follower—think female: Gender bias in implicit followership theories. *Journal of Applied Social Psychology, 47*(7), 377–388. https://doi.org/10.1111/jasp.12445

Chen, J., & Moons, W. (2015). They won't listen to me: Anticipated power and women's disinterest in male-dominated domains. *Group Processes & Intergroup Relations*, *18*(1), 116–128. https://doi.org/10.1177/1368430214550340

Cullen, Z., & Perez-Truglia, R. (2021). *The old boys' club: Schmoozing and the gender gap*. [Working paper] (Conditionally accepted at the American Economic Review). www.hbs.edu/ris/Publication%20Files/BODY%20--%20Cullen%20and%20Perez-Truglia%20--%20Old%20Boys%20Club_e9d852d9-3277-461c-b7eb-27d46b896318.pdf

Gaskell, A. (2021). Women's value is undervalued at work [Blog post]. *Forbes*. www.forbes.com/sites/adigaskell/2021/10/14/womens-potential-is-undervalued-at-work/?sh=3ab3444a865b

Grant Thornton. (2022). The role of male allies in progressing towards gender parity. *Grant Thornton International Ltd*. www.grantthornton.global/en/insights/articles/the-role-of-male-allies-in-progressing-towards-gender-parity/

Klenke, K. (2018). *Women in leadership: Contextual dynamics and boundaries* (2nd ed.). Emerald Publishing.

Tarbutton, T. (2019). The leadership gap in education. *Multicultural Education*, *27*(1), 19–21. https://files.eric.ed.gov/fulltext/EJ1250147.pdf

Williams, J. (2021). *Bias interrupted: Creating inclusion for real and for good*. Harvard Business Review Press.

 # The Old Boys' Club in School Leadership
The Elephant in the Room

Leadership in international schools really is an old boys' club. There's a bubble around access and the engagement and conversations that happen in those social circles. And they are not particularly welcoming unless you're in that clique. If you don't know how to play that game, it's hard to break in.

—Nicole Schmidt

Setting the Stage

It's not hard to notice in the head-of-school announcements every year that the top leadership positions at international schools often seem to be passed around within the same small circle of (mostly) white men. As the following stories will show, most female leaders have had very similar experiences in this area. Fortunately, many of the interviewees have also discovered constructive approaches to moving forward in spite of feeling excluded from this network of influential connections, sharing in this chapter some strategies that might help women break into this club.

Reflections in the Research

One factor that causes women to lag behind men in reaching senior leadership roles is the "old boys' club" (Cullen & Perez-Truglia, 2021; Elting, 2018; Gray & Barbara, 2013), a network that operates much like high-school cliques, defining who is "in" and who is "out." As cliques do, the old boys' club controls access to the spaces they inhabit (Elting, 2018). This informal network often thrives within "traditionally male spaces like country clubs, golf courses, sports events . . . places where women are generally not likely to be invited" (Elting, 2018, para. 7). The old boys' club provides men with insider access to promotions since they can access and network with other men in more senior and powerful positions in spaces that are less accessible to women (Cullen & Perez-Truglia, 2021). Members of these informal networks "promote from within and provide networking and professional mentoring opportunities that are simply not available to anyone who isn't a part of them" (Elting, 2018, para. 2). They further exclude women by condoning high levels of toxicity and a reliance on some level of "sexist humor and objectification" (Elting, 2018, para. 2). The exclusivity created by the old boys' club can lead to a self-perpetuating cycle where men in leadership "promote a disproportionate share of male employees, who continue promoting other men" (Cullen & Perez-Truglia, 2021, p. 2).

It is not uncommon for women to be excluded from male-dominated social situations and networks that include golf courses, soccer pitches, and happy-hour events after work. According to Gray and Barbara (2013), "81% of women say that they feel excluded from relationship-building at work, and many also feel excluded from after-work hours socializing" (Cullen & Perez-Truglia, 2021, p. 2). These are important opportunities for men to gain favor and engage in self-promotion while learning more about each others' efforts, achievements, and experiences, as well as insider information that could lead to promotions. Yet 92% of men believe that they are not excluding women (Gray & Barbara, 2013). This data point indicates that there is a significant blind spot.

Recommendations for developing more inclusionary practices are numerous. International schools can incorporate best practices that support the advancement of women (Klenke, 2018), provide career support for women (Hideg & Shen, 2019), and host workshops for men and women to understand gender-specific needs (Duevel et al., 2015). Women can create open alternatives to the old boys' club with their own girls' club (Elting, 2018), organize conferences and workshops for aspiring female leaders (Duevel et al., 2015), and leverage online social networks for career purposes (Klenke, 2018).

The Reality: Navigating the Old Boys' Club

Within the small community of international schools, it's very common to walk into cocktail events during leadership recruiting fairs and see almost exclusively older white men. When she walked into one such event, Nicole Schmid couldn't help but think "this is really an old boys' club": "There's a bubble around access and the engagement, and conversations that happen in those social circles are not particularly welcoming unless you're in that clique. If you don't know how to play that game, it's hard to break in. They all knew each other, they'd all been recycled through schools, and they all get jobs."

As Junlah Madalinski points out, getting a foot in the door for a leadership position is often overly reliant on who you know. It's very common to hear that "you need a network" or "you need to put yourself out there," but if you don't yet have that social currency as a newer leader, self-advocating can be much more difficult. Junlah also notes that because the international school community is so homogenous, it's even harder for women of color to make the supportive social connections that will help them leverage a network.

Similarly, Grace McCallum recalls an experience at a school heads meeting earlier in her career. Men in the room patronizingly assumed she was a teacher, then kindergarten head, then finally realized she was head of the elementary school. As Grace notes, when these experiences happen to female leaders, "it can shake your confidence a bit." Grace emphasizes that she tries to use these opportunities to be bold and stand up for what she believes is right so she can set an example for the female leaders who follow in her footsteps.

Even when our Women Who Lead reach the top levels of international school leadership, like Suzanna Jemsby, they still have to deal with this tight network of men making assumptions about the roles of the women in the room. Suzanna shares a story of participating in her first heads-of-school meeting. When she walked into the meeting, it was all men, all quite tall, slapping each other on the back, calling each other things like "coach." When they saw her, they assumed she was there to take notes, which of course she was not.

Several Women Who Lead in technology director positions mentioned how rare it is to see anyone but a middle-aged white man in the position.

Daniela Silva believes that it's a real challenge to be a woman tech director; she couldn't recall seeing another woman in the final run with her for any of those positions. Similarly, Anita Chen recalls that at her first tech director meeting in Asia, there were about 40 white men, and she was the only Asian woman. The stereotype of what a tech director looks like ends up excluding women even when they have extensive experience and an innovative perspective.

Carla Marschall notes that "in international education, there's definitely a gender, race, and age preference in who is leading international schools." Katrina Charles notes the same dynamics: "For a lot of places in the international circuit, a lot of the time, a certain look is required and a certain standard is what is being paid for. What that means is that it's a lot more masculine-heavy and -led. Because within those societies, there is a belief that only men can lead effectively. Women are rarely seen as leaders." In her experience, Katrina has often been the only woman on the senior leadership team or the only woman or minority on a leadership team. The traditional expectation of what a leader "looks like" makes networking even more difficult for non-traditional women.

Navigating the Challenge of Networking

Almost every chapter of this book includes strategies for moving forward on your path to leadership, including detailed lists of crucial strategies around topics like finding a mentor (Chapter 5) and being aware of double standards around gender (Chapter 6). In addition to those, the following brief additional examples came up in discussions of ways to positively address the challenges of networking in the realm of the old boys' club.

Know Your Worth

Kam Chohan emphasizes that she shouldn't be expected to "assimilate to the white male leadership that came before me. My background is an advantage." She points out that women of color as leaders are underrepresented and argues that we shouldn't expect women of color to change themselves to be just like those who came before. We should expect them to be who they are because they bring a wealth of experience. She feels that there's no better role model for other women than being able to see people like themselves in those positions, making a difference.

Similarly, Carlene Hamley shares that female leaders have amazing skills but don't always know it. As she describes it, "learning the skill of knowing who you are and what you enjoy doing, knowing your values and where you sit with certain issues, is a huge skill for aspiring female leaders." Since it's not likely you will be able to change the entire system overnight, one of the most positive strategies for dealing with the old boys' network might be to know yourself and to be confident in your strengths.

Stay Active and Involved

Catriona Moran reminds aspiring women leaders that it's not enough just to have the certifications, it's also crucial to demonstrate commitment to leadership by, for example, being involved in committees and taking every opportunity to interview. She points out that "every time we interview or put ourselves forward, we have to reflect on our beliefs, the underpinnings of our pedagogical approach, and ourselves."

According to Catriona, when you persist in interviewing for leadership positions, even if it doesn't initially succeed, you're letting your head of school know that you aspire to be a leader. Then, when a role arises to lead, they might ask you—even if you're not a part of the boys' club. "Ultimately," as she explains it, by being persistent you will have "put yourself on their radar."

Include Men in the Conversation

Finally, Clarissa Sayson highlights that it's important for men to be a part of this conversation, as they are often currently the ones in a position to mentor or sponsor women in their schools, to encourage them to pursue leadership, and to find out if there are any aspiring leaders in their midst. While it's unfortunate that this is the status quo, as Clarissa explains, male administrators or decision makers often currently have more power to move the conversation forward, so it might be valuable to inform them of your perspective and enlist their help.

Making Your Move

Although breaking into the old boys' club of senior leadership networking will likely continue to be a challenge, recognizing that others have come before you and intentionally worked to break down these barriers can provide not only inspiration but also a strategic pathway forward. Taking action right now to be better prepared for unspoken obstacles will allow you to make decisions with awareness and intentionality. As more and more women make progress, whether individually or together, we can help wedge the door open wider for all those who come behind us.

Finding Her Path: Nicole Schmidt

Name: Nicole Schmidt
Role: High School Principal
School: American International School of Johannesburg
Location: Johannesburg, South Africa

Nicole Schmidt describes her journey to leadership as unplanned, saying that it "happened by accident." She began her teaching career at The Linden School in Toronto, a women-centered school based on feminist pedagogy—the only time she has ever had a woman as her boss.

Her first step into a leadership role was as the pastoral care coordinator at Windhoek International School in Namibia, which she says she "fell into" and had "no idea" she was getting into leadership. Her next role was at NIST International School in Bangkok, Thailand, as the professional development coordinator. At the time, she didn't realize she had leadership skills or qualities, but when she looks back, she can see that people recognized her work ethic, energy, and growth mindset.

During the lead-up to her first formal leadership role at NIST, she was a passionate IB Middle Years Programme practitioner, but she wasn't focusing on leadership for her professional learning. Nicole's first principal role was in Angola, and after she earned that position, her confidence in her leadership skills skyrocketed. Looking back, she wishes she had been more intentional in her path earlier in her career.

In her first year as a formal leader, she recognized that she was going to make a difference. She had a moment of realization that what she would do in this role was going to have a massive impact on kids—her main focus as a leader. She says she had "the stamina, was resolute, had ideas, and a network of people who I could call and ask for support, and a head of school who let me do what I needed to do." It was at this point that she was "all in."

Reflecting on her journey, Nicole notes that "no one sat me down to have that conversation" about becoming a leader. In fact, she only had her first mentor when she was already in a leadership role. Now she is very intentional about the conversations she has with young women. She tries to point out that they have a lot to contribute, can have a strong voice, and should not let anyone silence them.

Unpacking Her Journey

- Nicole possessed skills and competencies that translated naturally to leadership: a strong work ethic, lots of energy, and a growth mindset.
- She leveraged her network to seek support and guidance when needed.
- She maintained a focus on doing what was right for kids.

 ## Take Action

At some point you will begin the formal process of seeking a leadership position. To be prepared for the potential challenges presented in this chapter, we invite you to proactively strengthen your professional network now. Building connections before you need to lean on them will help create more meaningful and lasting relationships.

For Developing Leaders

Wherever you are in the recruitment process, develop a research process that will help you identify the school culture as well as the potential support networks you can activate for each specific school.

Here are several steps you can follow to get started:

- Do initial research about the schools you're interested in, and start to identify any connections you might have to the leadership team in those schools.

- Work your networking muscles—even if these are further connections via LinkedIn or another social media platform—and specifically reach out to people you know who have connections to this leadership team.
- Seek out a champion to speak on your behalf in the recruitment process. Who do you know that could introduce you to a couple of people who might be connected with this leadership team?

If you are realizing that you need to broaden your network, you might wish to create a visual map (using pen and paper or a digital tool) to actually track and graph the connections you have built over the years. Sometimes just documenting connections helps you see relationships you might not have been aware of previously.

Scenario

To help prepare you for the recruiting process, we invite you to consider the following scenario. You might wish to role play this conversation with a trusted colleague or friend or simply document your thinking here in this book, in a separate document, or in your journal:

> You're recruiting at a leadership event, at the cocktail hour, and it's almost exclusively older white cis male recruiters. Someone approaches you and makes an assumption that you're an elementary teacher or someone's wife. How do you respond?

For Established Leaders

As an established leader, you are in a position to support equitable hiring practices both informal and formal. We invite you to take this opportunity to reflect on recent experiences and consider how you might "be the change" within school leadership to continue forward momentum of this movement.

- During social events, particularly when there are only a few women present, how do you make them feel included and welcome?
- During private conversations among recruiters and school leaders, how can you highlight the ways that leaders can be more inclusive of women candidates?
- With recruitment organizations, how can you highlight the ways that aspiring female candidates need to be supported throughout the process?

Identify ways to create networks that support developing (and established) women leaders in your school/organization:

- Create support networks that provide women with mentorship, sponsorship, and opportunity equivalent to their male counterparts.
- Form a brunch group or movie night that socializes on a regular basis to allow coworkers to connect, find opportunities to network, and share relevant opportunities.

For Schools or Organizations

We invite you to consider social events for leaders within your organization.

- What events are planned for leaders? Who is being excluded if it is
  - a golf outing,
  - an after-hours dinner, or
  - at a bar where alcohol is served?
- How much time do certain leaders have to socialize outside of school? Which educators are excluded from these activities because they're not asked or they have other commitments?
- What decisions are being made at social events, in particular those that are ongoing and regular, where certain leaders or staff member voices are excluded?

If you uncover that the outside-of-school opportunities to socialize for leaders are focused on events that provide additional barriers for women, how can you be more intentional about being inclusive?

This could be a community-specific challenge that is difficult to address through policies, and it could be dependent on host-country culture or activities available in your location, but perhaps some first steps might be to

- encourage a women's leadership club that provides women with their own professional opportunities to develop from within
- survey the staff to see which kind of social engagements they would like to participate in
- consider how and when decisions are discussed and made to ensure that those conversations are happening when there is equitable access to participate

Social interactions are just one barrier women can face on their pathway to leadership. These become more layered and multidimensional when we begin to explore intersectionality in the next chapter.

References

Cullen, Z., & Perez-Truglia, R. (2021). *The old boys' club: Schmoozing and the gender gap* [Working paper] (Conditionally accepted at the American Economic Review). www.hbs.edu/ris/Publication%20Files/BODY%20--%20Cullen%20and%20Perez-Truglia%20--%20Old%20Boys%20Club_e9d852d9-3277-461c-b7eb-27d46b896318.pdf

Duevel, L., Nashman-Smith, M., & Stern, E. (2015). Moving from 'womanless history' to women stepping up into school leadership roles. *International Schools Journal, XXXV*(1), 34–45. www.proquest.com/docview/1781327696?pq-origsite=gscholar&fromopenview=true

Elting, L. (2018). How to navigate a boys' club culture [Blog post]. *Forbes*. www.forbes.com/sites/lizelting/2018/07/27/how-to-navigate-a-boys-club-culture/?sh=37a0eb394025

Gray, J., & Barbara, A. (2013). *Work with me: Eight blind spots between men and women in business*. Palgrave Macmillan.

Hideg, I., & Shen, W. (2019). Why still so few? A theoretical model of the role of benevolent sexism and career support in the continued underrepresentation of women in leadership positions. *Journal of Leadership & Organizational Studies, 26*(3), 287–303. http://doi.org/10.1177/1548051819849006

Klenke, K. (2018). *Women in leadership: Contextual dynamics and boundaries* (2nd ed.). Emerald Publishing.

# Exploring Intersectionality for Women in Leadership Positions

> *In terms of unique challenges facing women pursuing a leadership path, for me as a hijabi, there's an extra layer. There's always preconceived notions of what I will be like. I know automatically that they don't get what they thought they were going to get when they see me.*
> —Abeer Shinnawi

 ## Setting the Stage

Along with all of the well-known stereotypes about gender and leadership, the WWL interviews highlighted additional layers of expectations and bias facing women of color pursuing a leadership path. The intersection of all these can multiply the challenges that women face in their leadership journey. Better understanding those challenges as you embark on your leadership career, or as you recruit and hire women, is an essential first step to challenging and overcoming them.

While anyone might find themselves facing microaggressions in the work environment, women in leadership (and women of color even more so) often encounter particularly elevated levels of these negative interactions since in their positions, they so visibly combine the lightning-rod issues of gender and power dynamics.

This chapter will provide a closer look at the following intersectional challenges:

- microaggressions
- unconscious bias

- linguistic expectations
- cultural backgrounds
- physical size and height
- skin color

As you read, you might find one or several of these challenges resonating with you. Please note that they could bring up past experiences and trauma. Please read with care and caution.

Reflections in the Research

Words matter. The words we use influence our perceptions of people and events. Knowing the right words and expressions can help women to accurately convey personal experiences in the workplace. Using a common lexicon can help leaders to name experiences in order to identify, confront, and root out biased behaviors all too commonly experienced by marginalized groups (Table 8.1).

Table 8.1 Types of Biases. Identifying some ways bias appears can help women leaders name, confront, and root out behaviors that discriminate and impede their ability to access leadership roles.

Implicit bias	unconscious preferences that individuals have based on identity traits such as gender, race, or sexual orientation
Intersectionality	"the complex, cumulative way in which the effects of multiple forms of discrimination (such as racism, sexism, and classism) combine, overlap, or intersect, especially in the experiences of marginalized individuals or groups to produce and sustain complex inequities" (American Psychological Association, 2023)
Maternal wall bias	bias against mothers and motherhood
Microaggressions	"commonly occurring, brief, verbal or nonverbal, behavioral, and environmental indignities that communicate derogatory attitudes or notions toward a different 'other'" (American Psychological Association, 2023)

(*Continued*)

Table 8.1 (Continued)

Prove-it-again bias	the expectation that disadvantaged groups must continuously prove themselves in ways that advantaged groups do not
Tightrope bias	the narrow range of behavior seen as acceptable for people from non-dominant and stigmatized groups compared with the leeway afforded to those from dominant groups
Tug-of-war bias	when members of a marginalized group compete against each other in an unhealthy way for scarce career opportunities

Intersectionality is a term that emerged to address "the particular manner in which Black women are subordinated" (Crenshaw, 1989, p. 140). In a 2017 interview, Kimberlé Crenshaw spoke of intersectionality as "a lens through which you can see where power comes and collides, where it interlocks and intersects" (*News From Columbia Law*, 2017, para. 4). Crenshaw acknowledges that race, gender, class, or LGBTQ+ problems rarely exist in isolation but that people often possess multiple combinations of these marginalizing aspects (*News From Columbia Law*, 2017). There are a number of nuanced ways in which women might experience intersectional bias in the workplace.

Implicit bias refers to the unconscious preferences that individuals have based on identity traits such as gender, race, or sexual orientation (Fiarman, 2016). Implicit bias can inform hiring tendencies within professions, such as within international schools, where leadership hiring has favored white men (Charles et al., 2021). As women begin their ascent into leadership roles in international schools, they can experience multifaceted challenges based on the intersectionality of identity characteristics that are often connected to implicit biases.

Maternal wall bias is a bias against mothers (Williams, 2021). Women who become mothers are often confronted with assumptions that they are somehow less competent and less committed to their careers (Williams, 2021).

Prove-it-again bias refers to the all-too-familiar expectation that disadvantaged groups must continuously prove themselves in ways that advantaged groups do not (Gaskell, 2021; Williams, 2021). While white men are often judged on their potential, members of less privileged groups are more typically judged on performance, over and over again (Benson et al., 2022; Williams, 2021). This is a bias experienced all too often by women in leadership and becomes a double-bind for women of color.

Tightrope bias acknowledges that political savvy is necessary for members of some groups to succeed (Williams, 2021). White male leaders are often praised when they display such valued leadership characteristics as authoritativeness and ambition. However, women walk a metaphorical tightrope when displaying the same traits, since they can be perceived as "abrasive if they are authoritative and unqualified if they aren't" (Williams, 2021, p. 6). Female leaders must regularly be guarded about what they say and do; otherwise they risk diminishing the validity of their own opinions and arguments.

Tug-of-war bias captures the negative impact of conflict within a group that is the target of bias (Williams, 2021). This bias can lead members within a marginalized group to not support each other or stand up for one another when they experience discriminatory behaviors.

Microaggressions are biases that emerge as comments or actions that subtly express a prejudiced attitude toward a member of a marginalized group (such as a racial minority) (Merriam-Webster, n.d.). The effects of gendered and racial microaggressions can have negative health implications that include increased psychological distress (Burton et al., 2020). When women find themselves on the receiving end of a stressful situation, they make an assessment to either engage or withdraw from the situation (Burton et al., 2020). As a result, women of color often develop a variety of coping strategies, including using their voices as power, using support networks, and self-protective disengagement (Burton et al., 2020).

Layers upon Layers

Until now, this book has primarily focused on the experiences of women pursuing a leadership pathway in general. However, once we begin to look more deeply at the intersectional challenges of women of color, or women who belong to other groups or subgroups, even more nuanced and specific challenges become visible.

Microaggressions

Once they take on the mantle of leadership, women, and women of color in particular, no longer have the safety of "staying in their classroom." Being in the more public eye of a leadership position leaves them more exposed to these daily attacks unless there is action taken to improve the school culture. While the stories shared next might not all fit the precise definition of microaggression, that is how they were presented in the interview process.

Junlah Madalinski describes this clearly:

> What happens when women of color are in leadership positions is it makes them more visible. Instead of having yourself within your classroom, you have more of a larger audience, and microaggressions tend to play themselves out in that way.

Renée Green highlights the many intersectional challenges she is constantly trying to grapple with and assess to determine what's going to be the priority in each moment. She says she's constantly negotiating different parts of her life:

> I'm American by passport, Jamaican by values, I'm a woman, I'm Black, and I wear my hair natural. These are all things that may seem like minor details, but the entire package, in the spaces that I've worked in, I haven't always had a seat or even been welcomed.

Throughout her career, she has needed to explicitly think about how to read the room and how to comport herself in each space. She highlights that "there are different challenges revolving around being able to code switch and times when I have to defend my pedigree." These constant additional layers to contend with on a daily basis add additional barriers to leadership for women of color.

Chanel Johnson shares her experience of staying true to her authentic self and being told she doesn't "look the part" of a leader:

> I'm not the type of woman that likes to wear suits and high heels. I'm not a well-spoken and poised model of a woman. I'm my authentic self, and sometimes being your authentic self, even when you clean it up, gets you overlooked.

She is intentional about being both respectful to others and true to herself. As a leader, she recognizes how conscious of her appearance she needs to be and how her choices have impacted her journey.

Linguistic Expectations

Elsa Donahue realized early on that not only her gender but her accented English got in the way of her being offered head-of-school positions. She points out that at "schools that were defined as being American schools, I didn't potentially fit. Though that was never explained to me, I could figure it out." Elsa discovered that an unspoken requirement of speaking English with only an "acceptable" accent, particularly for women, might impede their progress or even tip the balance one way or the other during hiring.

Marta Medved also feels that she has been categorized as "different" in terms of not appearance but language profile. She describes experiencing this inequality when attending professional learning and being "surrounded by a group of 20 native speakers [of English] and the only second language speaker [of English]." She notes further that in these situations, it can take longer to process content when it is delivered in your second language.

Cultural Expectations

Along with accents, these conversations surfaced common prejudicial assumptions about people from specific cultural backgrounds. From Asian and Muslim women tending to be perceived as "meek" to Black/African American women being perceived as "angry," these cultural and gendered biases can be unspoken obstacles during the interview process—and often continue as ongoing challenges even once the position is secured.

As Abeer Shinnawi points out, "for me as a hijabi, there's an extra layer. There are always preconceived notions about what I will be like. I know automatically that they don't get what they thought they were going to get when they see me." Being the only young Muslim woman in her school community, she always felt she had to prove herself. Even among peers and colleagues, she always had to push against the perception of being a meek "wilting flower" because of her status as a covered Muslim woman. Fighting against stereotypes that involve visible signs of cultural and/or religious affiliation like the hijab can seem like a never-ending battle for many women.

Physical Size

Many women also spoke about realizing that their physical stature had been an unspoken obstacle to securing a leadership position. A unique set of intersectional challenges is created when combining physical size, cultural heritage, linguistic profile, and other qualities that influence bias. As Madeleine Heide highlights,

> I am very short. I don't have the profile of being a leader. I'm a woman. I come from early childhood. I'm not a white woman. I'm biracial. My heritage is Filipino and I claim my Filipino-ness. These are all points against me in terms of stepping up to the top leadership position. In my experience, people have stereotyped notions about what leadership looks like. I can see them wondering when they look at me, "Can you lead?" Here I am!

Clarissa Sayson also shares experiences influenced by the biases held by others. She describes herself as "short, Asian, with a youthful appearance." More times than she can count, she has heard comments like, "You look too young to be in a position of leadership." She is aware that she does not fit the stereotype of what others expect to see in a leader, and she has to manage these kinds of comments on a regular basis. Regardless, she sees herself as "a powerhouse."

Skin Color

Jasmeen Philleen talks about the weight of responsibility she feels not only representing herself as a Black woman but also representing a long line of African American people. She is forced to carefully navigate the world knowing that when she is new to an international school, parents can be initially reluctant to have her as their child's teacher, simply because of the color of her skin. While these stereotypes exist at all levels of education, it remains exceptional to see many faces like Jasmeen's in leadership positions in international schools. As a leader, she recognizes that she is unique, and this, as she mentions, "makes me strive even harder to prove myself, to prove that I am worthy."

Similarly, Tambi Tyler highlights that she had "three strikes [against her] coming out of the gate as a leader. I'm young. I'm black. I'm a woman." She highlights that she had to see herself leading and deal with the criticism

Layers Upon Layers

Skin Color	Facing stereotypes & assumptions based on skin color
Physical Size & Height	Navigating assumptions based on youthful appearance or physical size
Language & Accent	Expectation to speak with the desired English-language accent
Code Switching	Needing to read the room to identify how best to comport yourself, given the audience
Visibility	No longer "safe" in your own classroom, more visible for critique
Sexism	Assumptions & different treatment, based on gender

Figure 8.1 Layers upon layers. Inside (and outside) the leadership space, women of color experience the impact of intersectionality to a greater extent than white women. Like a brick wall, each characteristic represents a layer, building upon each other to form a significant barrier that can stand in the way of ascent into leadership roles.

knowing that even when she's doing a great job, she knew she would be unlikely to hear about it. She's "seen a lot of women shy away from the role because they don't have enough support around them."

Dr. Chaunté Garrett shares that she has served in spaces where her "degree was valued more than her intellect"; where she was treated as a figurehead and the men ran the show; where her male boss was told that he needed to "control me and keep me in check"; where others have clearly tested her to see what she was going to do. In these experiences, she says intersectionality can make it "hard to tell which thing you're facing: racism or sexism."

Finding Solutions

Each of these women has or has had to battle some combination of stereotypical assumptions that confront(ed) them every day. Since they are often the only person who looks like them in their school community, they are usually on their own to process and persevere. Although there is not one simple solution to any of these issues, several women spoke about ways the challenges can be confronted and, potentially, surmounted.

Own Your Voice

Fiona Reynolds mentions the importance of women owning their own voice and communication style. By emulating traditional expectations of leadership styles (that often are about being direct), we might be missing opportunities to benefit from individual or cultural styles of communication. As women, "we need to shift the narrative on what makes a good communicator. Trust that people will figure it out instead of transforming your style to a stereotype."

Embrace Your Unique Strengths

Anita Chen notes that in her first meeting of technology directors in Asia, there were about 40 white men and she was the only Asian woman. At that time, being surrounded by men was intimidating for her. She shares that she "felt a little bit small in that moment. I didn't know how to find my voice and speak out." Later, during a job interview for a leadership role, she was told that the school was particularly interested in working with her *because* she was Asian and a woman. She recognizes that "in that moment, something that I thought was a weakness became a strength."

Find the Right Fit

Sawsan Jaber talks about the importance of making yourself marketable without compromising what is important to you as a professional or person. She shares that her focus is on finding the right fit for her values and beliefs: "If they're not proud to have a person of color, who is a proud Muslim, who wants to work for the betterment of all kids, I'd rather not work for that district." In a leadership position, this match of values is even more crucial.

Embrace Your Leadership Opportunities

Not all women feel ready to make the leap into leadership, but the majority of the participants in the WWL interviews highlighted the importance of taking the risk. Jasmeen Philen points out the need for people from diverse backgrounds in positions of leadership "because when you're in leadership, you have the 'ear' of the highest-level leaders." As she says, "when you root for the underdog, everyone wins." When international school leaders begin to more accurately reflect the world around them, and the diverse communities they serve, the voices of the "underdogs" will become more clear, acknowledged, and represented in all aspects of learning.

Katrina Charles notes that the notion of women in leadership needs to be normalized to model for the next generation what leadership can look like:

> If we want to see more women in leadership, those who are in it have to keep digging and make it easier for our sisters to follow us. It's about solidarity. More voices with different experiences, backgrounds, and perspectives working for the same cause.

Sheena Nabholz says that in her experience,

> you don't know if you don't get a position if it's because of your gender, or your color, or you just weren't a good fit. As women we have to take the locus of control back into ourselves and go for the jobs we want, and learn from the experiences of the jobs when we don't get the job we want. When we convince ourselves that that's what's holding us back we don't take risks the way we might."

Develop School Structures

One of the first steps organizations can take to begin to challenge unconscious bias and daily microaggressions is to develop processes to systematically check bias before any action can be taken.

The reality is, we all have biases, and even though we can do training and practice self-reflection and personal improvement, we can't recognize unconscious bias because it is, by definition, unconscious. As Caroline Brokvam states, "Unless you put process and practices and procedures in place to make sure you can't act on your own biases, it makes no difference in organizations."

An example of the types of procedures schools can put in place, shared by Caroline, is accepting and reviewing blind CVs when hiring. When school leadership comes to recognize that hiring practices do not reflect the diversity, equity, and inclusion practices they aspire to, even the small and practical step of removing photos, names, and pronouns from applications can help work toward more equitable hiring processes.

In *From Resistance to Sustainability and Leadership Cultivating Diverse Leaders in International Schools* (Shaklee et al., 2019), the authors note that "critical factors that influence successful international schools on issues of diversity, equity and inclusion appear to be intentionality and developing a comprehensive, long-term, strategic commitment" (p. 6).

On the Forefront of Change

This is not a problem for women to tackle on their own; we know that building systemic change takes time. Increasing your awareness of both the stereotypes and expectations faced by women as they seek leadership roles, and developing strategies to deal with these challenges, could help you feel more confident in taking the next steps toward your dream job. The WWL interview participants shared that recognizing that many women face these challenges has helped them own their leadership. This feeling of solidarity has empowered the WWL to stop holding themselves back from pursuing leadership positions.

Finding Her Path: Junlah Madalinski

Name: Junlah Madalinski
Role: Assistant Head of Primary
School: Nanjing International School
Location: China

At the time of her interview, Junlah had already spent 15 years in education, having worked around the globe in countries such as Ethiopia, Japan, Cambodia, and China. She was assistant head of primary at Nanjing International School in China and was preparing to transition to Schutz American School in Alexandria, Egypt, assuming the role of elementary and middle school principal.

When reflecting on her leadership journey, Junlah noted the importance of taking on the role of International Baccalaureate Primary Years Programme (PYP) coordinator at the International Community School in

Addis Ababa, Ethiopia, where she was able to apply facets of instructional leadership in moving the school's PYP from the candidacy phase to full authorization, a position she feels gave her the experience to pivot into her next role as assistant head of primary at Nanjing International School.

Junlah defines her leadership through what she refers to as her "three conceptual cornerstones" that honor the collective experiences that have shaped her throughout her life. She calls one cornerstone relational heritage. Growing up as a Laotian American, she observed family matriarchs making decisions for the community and nurturing the collective family. Junlah attributes the cornerstone of responsiveness to her childhood experiences in Chicago, where she developed an innate ability to pay attention to her surroundings in order to be ready to advocate for herself and her community at any given moment. With design thinking rounding out her leadership persona, Junlah says, "one of the major skills you will have to cultivate as an education leader is to be able to utilize design thinking in a way that helps bring ideas or notions to the table that were not on the peripheral. It means coming up with 'right now' solutions because we are in an exceptionally fluid and dynamic situation, where we need to address the 'right now.' The skills around that, including flexibility, adaptability, design thinking, and having a solution-based stance."

Rather than pinpointing a moment when she recognized for herself that she was a leader, Junlah honors that collective experiences have shaped her over time and will continue to do so into the future.

Unpacking Her Journey

- Junlah possesses a depth of knowledge and experience due to a wide variety of international school experiences as both a teacher and a leader.
- Junlah's cultural identity has informed her personal conceptual cornerstones that have helped her to bring forth her authentic leader self.

Take Action

We know that with every additional intersectionality, the path to leadership becomes more challenging. We are inviting you to create an environment for yourself in which you are reminded that it is possible to achieve your leadership ambitions.

For Developing Leaders

Create your space: In your office or in another visible space, curate examples of leaders who look, talk, and sound like you. This could be a bookshelf with specific books, a vision board of images, inspirational quotes, or anything that will help remind you that there are women who look, talk, and act like you who are also successful leaders.

Prepare your language: There will be times when you might be caught off guard by the behavior of others; prepare yourself for these moments by developing and practicing specific language that might help you address the issue in the moment. Craft a response to a typical microaggression/stereotypical comment you have received (or in response to one of the stories shared in this chapter). You might wish to rehearse with a safe colleague or friend so you feel confident in what you might say should a similar situation arise.

Scenarios

To help you prepare for a potential conversation addressing intersectional challenges, we invite you to reflect on one of the scenarios that follows. You might choose to document your thinking here in this book, in a separate document, or in your journal.

Scenario 1: During an Interview

> You're in an interview, and the person interviewing you asks a question that crosses one of your personal boundaries, similar to anecdotes you might have already read in this book, for example commenting on your choice of earrings in the interview, asking about when you plan to have children, asking if you bake for your husband, asking who will take care of your children if you're working full time in this job, or saying you seem "too nice" to handle this job. How would you respond? Once you have thought through your response, you might wish to practice with a safe colleague or friend.

Scenario 2: At School

Your school is doing a curriculum review. You know that the resources are primarily white male authors, and you see a potential to be more inclusive. How will you start this conversation? Once you have thought through your response, you might wish to practice with a safe colleague or friend.

For Established Leaders

With a focus on the intersectional challenges faced by women of color, we invite you to unpack your own biases about leadership, for instance considering

- What does society tell us about leaders?
- What are my perceptions of men's roles vs women's roles?
- What are my perceptions about women of color vs white women?
- What are my perceptions about tall people vs short people?
- What are my perceptions about people who speak with accents?

As you're thinking about these different facets of intersectionality and your own hidden biases, you might also consider if you use the phrase "our parent community expects" to cover the reality of any of those biases.

As you reflect on your own perceptions, you might also wish to consider the ways that you are potentially demonstrating hidden biases. You might choose to do this through an audit of the leadership/inspirational resources you share with or present to staff (Figure 8.2). As you are reviewing your most frequently used resources, consider this an opportunity to include and share works from a diverse group of leaders.

While you are uncovering any potential hidden biases with your leadership team, this might also be an appropriate time to work with your human resources department to develop a process for using blind CVs in the recruitment process. You might also consider reflecting on the questions that you typically ask during an interview through the lenses from this chapter.

Facing the Realities of Leadership for Women

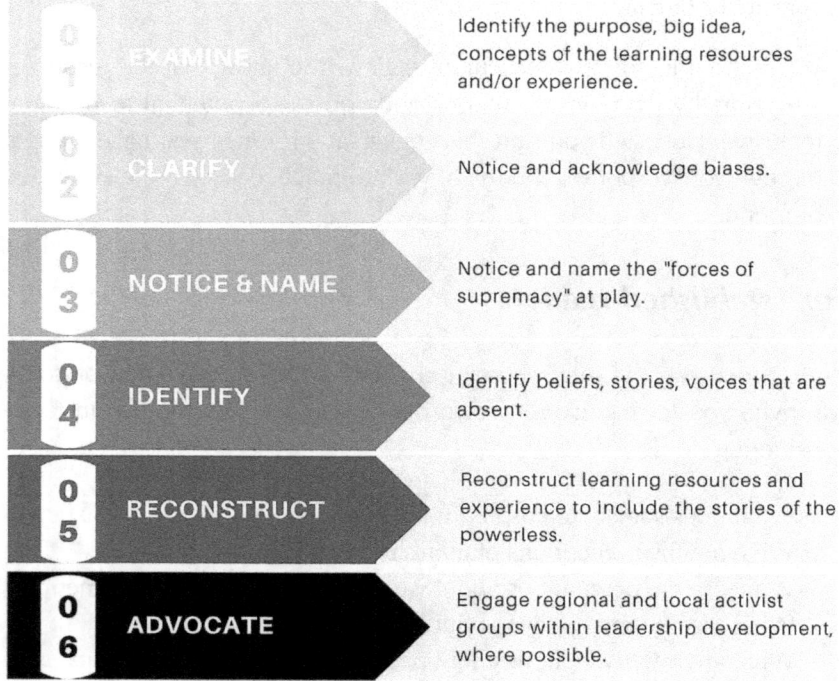

Figure 8.2 Equity Audit. Conducting an audit of leadership and professional learning resources for diversity, equity, and inclusion can provide opportunities for international school leaders to consider how their own biases influence how they lead others. We must inquire into power dynamics to understand what gets shared, as in what is allowed to be shared and who holds the power to decide and approve.

For Schools or Organizations

We invite you to consider the organizational bias you might be presenting to your community (and beyond) without even thinking about it. For example,

- When you visit your school's "About our Leadership Team" page, what do you notice?
- When there are pictures of school leaders (or teams of leaders), who do you see?

If you uncover a visual message that demonstrates exclusionary practices (unintended or unintended),

- Where might there be opportunities to discuss the message that these pages are sending?
- What type of workshops or opportunities are you offering to staff to recognize their own intersectionalities?
- How are you as a school advocating for diversity with your parent community?

Visible representation of diverse leaders can also help in the perceived availability of opportunities for women seeking leadership positions, an additional challenge we address in the next chapter.

References

American Psychological Association. (2023). *Inclusive language guidelines*. https://www.apa.org/about/apa/equity-diversity-inclusion/language-guidelines

Benson, A., Li, D., & Shue, K. (2022). *"Potential" and the gender promotion gap* [Working paper]. https://danielle-li.github.io/assets/docs/PotentialAndTheGenderPromotionGap.pdf

Burton, L. J., Cyr, D., & Weiner, J. M. (2020). "Unbroken, but bent": Gendered racism in school leadership. *Frontiers in Education, 5*(52), 1–13. https://doi.org/10.3389/feduc.2020.00052

Charles, A., Chandler, J., Neitzel, K., & Welch, D. (2021, August 11). *Promoting a gender-inclusive hiring process* [Blog post]. www.ecis.org/gender-inclusive-hiring/

Crenshaw, K. (1989). Demarginalizing the intersection of race and sex: A black feminist critique of antidiscrimination doctrine, feminist theory and antiracist politics. *University of Chicago Legal Forum, 1989*(1), 139–167. https://chicagounbound.uchicago.edu/cgi/viewcontent.cgi?article=1052&context=uclf

Fiarman, S. (2016). Unconscious bias: When good intentions aren't enough. *Educational Leadership, 74*(3), 10–15.

Gaskell, A. (2021). Women's value is undervalued at work [Blog post]. *Forbes*. www.forbes.com/sites/adigaskell/2021/10/14/womens-potential-is-undervalued-at-work/?sh=3ab3444a865b

Merriam-Webster. (n.d.). Critical. *Merriam-Webster.com*. www.merriam-webster.com/dictionary/well-being

News From Columbia Law. (2017). *Kimberlé Crenshaw on intersectionality, more than two decades later.* www.law.columbia.edu/news/archive/kimberle-crenshaw-intersectionality-more-two-decades-later

Shaklee, B., Daly, K., Duffy, L., & Watts, D. (2019). From resistance to sustainability leadership: Cultivating diverse leaders in international schools. *Results of the 2019 Diversity Collaborative Survey (DCS).* https://www.iss.edu/wp-content/uploads/DC_Report_Survey2019Results.pdf

Williams, J. (2021). *Bias interrupted: Creating inclusion for real and for good.* Harvard Business Review Press.

Clarifying the Lack of Opportunity for Women in Leadership

As female leaders, we need to focus on both personal and collective growth. I desire to see more of a horizontal growth, not just personal growth, but others growing along with me. It's about all of us, or nothing. Let's stand as one, even in the same field. The sky is wide enough for all of us to fly.

—Lola Aneke

 Setting the Stage

Women face an especially complex challenge around lack of leadership opportunities, both perceived and real. As mentioned repeatedly throughout this book, there are far fewer women in positions of leadership in education than there are men, although the majority of educators are women. This leads to several frustrating and compounding scenarios.

In some cases, there is the perception that there are only a finite number of jobs available for women and that therefore they must compete among themselves for them. In many cases, there is truly an inequitable hiring process that disadvantages women, either through unconscious bias, intentional discrimination, or societal stereotypes. In all cases, this means women must work harder and appear more competent than their white cisgender male counterparts to earn a leadership position. In this chapter, we'll explore the experiences of our WWL interviewees in these frustrating areas—and then we'll look forward, exploring approaches to overcoming these problems and building a culture of women supporting women.

Reflections in the Research

Women in leadership roles often face contradictory messages from, and judgments by, other women. Women in leadership expect positive support from other women as they take up the 'women in management' mantle, but they can end up being negatively evaluated for displaying agentic, stereotypically masculine, behaviors (Mavin et al., 2014). Hostility of women toward their female counterparts in senior leadership roles is too frequently noted as a challenge to women's progress (Mavin et al., 2014).

We are all too often met with negative images of workplace relationships among women. In reality, women's relationships with each other, inside of and outside of the workplace, are far more profound and nuanced, if under-explored in academic research (Carr & Kelan, 2016). As such, we expect that when individual women ascend into senior leadership roles, they "will become the mentors and role models so desperately needed for younger employees of their group" (Morley, 2018, p. 120). However, it is not uncommon for some women to 'pull up the ladder' behind them. Women are often met with indirect aggression from other women, creating a greater obstacle to their ascension than "overt bias from the opposite gender" (Morley, 2018, p. 120). Some women in senior leadership roles act in ways that abandon and leave other women behind (Carr & Kelan, 2016). Carr and Kelan (2016) refer to this as 'queen bee syndrome,' describing a perceived need to ward off any threat of competition from her female counterparts.

Another barrier to women's pursuit of senior-level leadership positions in K–12 education is career positioning (Tarbutton, 2019). A common ascension pathway for women is teacher, elementary principal, central office director, and then superintendent. In contrast, a common career path for men tends to be teacher, high school principal, and then superintendent (Robinson et al., 2017). The pathway to a head-of-school or superintendent role is closely connected to the role of high school principal (Superville, 2017; Tarbutton, 2019). According to the National Center for Education Statistics (NCES, 2013), almost 70% of high school principals are men. An additional stepping stone on the path to high school principal is "closely aligned to that of the athletic director" (Tarbutton, 2019, p. 20). Statistics indicate that men are three times as likely as women to be athletic directors (Maranto et al., 2018).

How might we "do gender well and differently"? Mavin et al. (2014) suggest multiplicity: an approach inviting women (or men) to leverage both agentic and communal behaviors that could lead to new approaches to leadership over time. Similarly, Chin and Trimble (2015) highlight an evolving leadership landscape inclusive of styles exhibited by women and racial and ethnic minorities that contribute to androgynous leadership styles that "emphasize both task and people skills" (p. 110).

A Culture of Competition

Perceived Scarcity of Opportunities

Many WWL interviewees spoke of a competitive and tense zero-sum atmosphere around female leadership positions, driven by the pervasive sense of scarcity.

Liz Kleinrock highlights that women pursuing leadership have nearly everything going against them, from "men who unconsciously or consciously chose to lock you out of opportunities, to women who are fed all these messages how we need to be in competition with each other all the time." When women are surrounded by other women who believe that only one woman can be successful, they try to drag each other down instead of supporting each other. Liz also talks about the prevalence of "toxic femininity," where women amplify traits like demureness and subservience, which only exacerbates societal expectations of who could and should be a leader.

Lack of Visible Role Models

As described in previous chapters, the lack of female mentors and role models in leadership is particularly noticeable in the international school environment, where leadership teams tend to be very male-dominated. Katrina Charles highlights that it's difficult to find women, particularly strong women, within leadership. Throughout her career, she has often been "the only woman on the senior leadership team, or the only women within an ethnic minority, or the only leader within an ethnic minority on a leadership team."

Just becoming a successful leader isn't enough. As Katrina continues, "if it's deemed you are a leader, the words used to describe your work are not necessarily positive. You put forward a point, you're seen as aggressive. Your voice raises too much, you're emotional. Not the same words that would be used for a gentleman." Rachell Caldwell echoes the same sentiment, as did many others in the WWL interviews: "When you're a female leader, there does seem to be this indication that you're not a 'strong leader,' you're a 'bossy leader.'"

Disproportionate Representation in Leadership Positions

Ultimately, pursuing a leadership pathway in an environment where, as Nadine Richards notes, "the glass ceiling still exists" is an ongoing challenge. As she points out, "it's been an historical factor, and things just don't change overnight."

Madeleine Heide highlights that although we might see more women in lower leadership positions, the gap widens when you begin applying for a head-of-school position, and "women have to work harder to successfully secure a position at the very top level of our schools." Madeleine recalls that she was interviewed for 15 different positions and was rejected. Because women are not commonly found in head-of-school positions, she could feel others "wondering, as they are looking at you, 'Can you lead?'"

Tara Waudby remembers being asked by a prospective school's board about her thoughts on possibly being part of an "all-female" leadership team. Her response was, "There are plenty of all-male teams; I hope this isn't a reason why I wouldn't be hired. If we need male support, we would just reach out." This perception that an all-female team would be less successful than an all-male team is pervasive likely in part because of how rarely we see all-female leadership teams.

This combination of the lack of visibility of strong, successful women leaders, the societal expectations of leaders, and the all-too-prevalent belief that there are limited positions for women, can cause women to feel as though they're competing with each other, exacerbating feelings of isolation and hindering inter-woman cooperation. Career success depends on access to "good advice, feedback, and those in leadership who can open doors for you" (Lee, 2014, para. 7).

Approaches toward Solutions

Pull Up People Behind You

In almost every interview, there was a story, or a piece of advice, about reaching back and supporting the women who are rising up behind you. If you have the capacity to be a mentor for others, several women recommended that you go out of your way to do so. Grace McCallum notes that "the highest call to leadership is when you're pulling up the people behind you." As women in leadership, we all have the responsibility to be sure that we're normalizing female leadership.

Tambi Tyler says, "All women should be reaching back for other women across the depth and breadth of the organization. Be better mentors." Catriona Moran recognizes how difficult it can be to approach a head of school for mentorship, so she actively works to find those who could benefit from mentorship because others did the same for her. She feels it is part of her role as head of school because she believes "our organizations need to grow great leaders."

Women Supporting Women

Informal sources of support have been reported by women to be particularly effective and influential (Hideg & Shen, 2019). Nina Shoman Danji emphasizes that all women should "support other women, even if you never got that support." One of the most important skills that we should have as women leaders is to make sure that we are very collaborative, not only within our department but also across campus. Her experiences have shown her that although many women who seek support from other women might not get it, "that doesn't mean we shouldn't give it." We need to remain educated about the experiences of other women so we can support them in their journey, even if it doesn't mirror our own.

The ultimate takeaway from these conversations is that all of us can do more to support women and that everyone should try to lift up our aspiring women leaders. As Clarissa Sayson shares, "The world and our workplaces need to be more open and empathetic to women." Each day, we can make small differences to build to these changes, one step at a time.

Developing a Circle of Support

Many of our Women Who Lead spoke about having a supportive circle of women to grow with. In particular, Joellen Killion shares the story of a circle of women colleagues whom she has been meeting with for over 20 years, "who I deeply trust and value, who have committed to my growth as much as I committed to theirs." She notes that it has always been a circle with no hierarchy because they didn't distinguish themselves from one another. Inside this circle, "we pushed and prodded each other, we challenged each other, held each other up, picked each other up. Every woman needs to be held up by her sisters."

Using Your Voice

With or without the support of other women, it's critical for all women to use their voice. Dr Chaunté Garrett, superintendent of a K–12 charter campus in North Carolina, USA, highlights the importance of speaking up on your own behalf. She notes that she was raised in a space where it was not acceptable for anyone to "project inequities, inequalities, and disrespect" upon others, where you correct people where they stand: "When you are a leader, you have to be really clear about how you're showing up in a space. If you can't manage those spaces, they're going to become more and more miserable if you're walking away feeling disrespected, hurt and unsafe. That's what gets created when we don't say how certain things have made us feel. Everyone has a voice and everyone has value." Every woman needs to use her voice.

Be a Model for the Next Generation

Several women mentioned challenging the idea that women leaders need to be more stereotypically masculine, moving toward modeling leadership that isn't constrained by older ideas of gender roles. As Katrina Charles mentions, "Sometimes I notice now, women who are trying to go into leadership, they think they have to be 'like men.' We have to look like the people we're trying to be when in actuality we can lead with our femininity

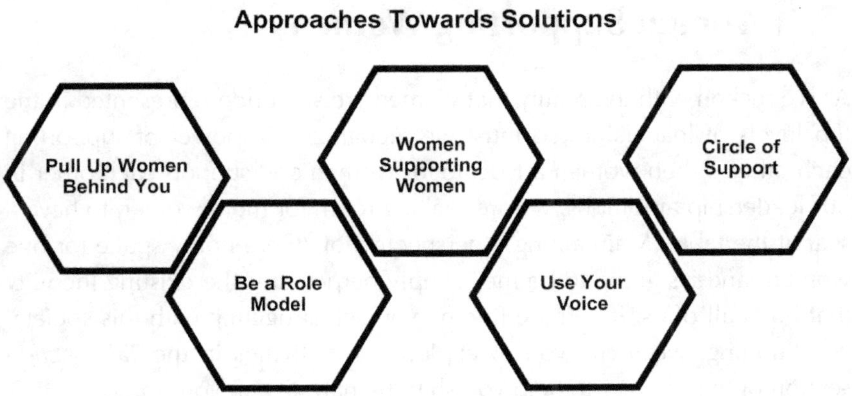

Approaches Towards Solutions

- Pull Up Women Behind You
- Be a Role Model
- Women Supporting Women
- Use Your Voice
- Circle of Support

Figure 9.1 Approaches Toward Solutions. There are many ways that women in leadership roles can help to support aspiring and developing women leaders as they begin on their pathways to leadership.

and still be effective leaders. At the end of the day, why should I have to downplay my femininity to prove my worth?"

Similarly, Katie Wellbrook remembers, "When I got into leadership, there were two types of female leader: mother hen or bulldog (one of the guys) and I didn't identify with either of those things. Being a young female leader, I had to carve my own path and determine what my leadership looks like. It's very important for young women to see different versions of female leaders." This leads to one of the important areas where women can support others—providing a model for the next generation.

This important sense of responsibility to model leadership for other women and future leaders to look up to was mentioned by many of the Women Who Lead. As Chaunté Garrett explains, "Somebody has to come behind me. There has to be another Black woman that comes behind me. I'm not there to be the only one, I'm there to clear the pathway for someone else." In the words of Katrina Charles, "It's about solidarity, more voices, with different experiences, backgrounds and perspectives working for the same cause. Women in leadership needs to be normalized. This is a next generation we need to model for." After all, female leadership is not a pie that will run out, and, as Abeer Shinnawi says, "We need to fix each other's crowns instead of tearing each other down."

Women Supporting Women

As we reckon with the reality that women are still underrepresented in the top levels of leadership, so must we recognize the power of supporting each other. When women advocate for women and support each other in our leadership ambitions, we are making room for more women to have a seat at the table. Maintaining a perspective of "there's only space for one woman, and it's going to be me" simply perpetuates the existing inequity that hurts all of us. If you are finding yourself struggling with this societal conditioning, we invite you to explore the activities in the *Take Action* section of this chapter to help you shift the narrative in your mind.

As we move forward into Part 3: Strategies and Skills for Success, we'll start exploring structures that support women in being successful as leaders.

Finding Her Path: Dr. Chaunté Garrett

Name:	Dr. Chaunté Garrett
Role:	Superintendent
School:	a K–12 charter campus
Location:	North Carolina, United States

Dr. Chaunté Garrett feels like she had a long journey to leadership. Even as a young child, she realized the types of changes and impacts she wanted to make in the world. Throughout her career she has focused on being prepared and making sure that she "checked all the boxes." Looking back, she says that as she began to hit roadblocks on her path to leadership she discovered "that checking all the boxes didn't create the guarantee."

When she started intentionally pursuing leadership, she realized that each barrier on her path sent her to the place she was meant to be. Although the positions she was offered along her journey might not have been what she was seeking at the time, each step "became a blessing to land where I was sent." Her path to school leadership has included stopovers as a teacher, an instructional coach, a school administrator, and a district administrator.

When she looks back on her journey, she can't help but smile. She says "there was a lot of learning." Everything about her journey helped her become who she loves being today. She underscores the importance of how you show up in your space and appreciating all the gifts along the way.

In the classroom, she developed great relationships with her students. Her ability to connect and serve other people's needs is a leadership skill. As an instructional coach, she was moving from space to space all around the district, creating outcomes all over the district, not just in her own classroom. This speaks to her own skills and capabilities as well as the ability to develop and build capacity in others. She refers to this moment as a surprise and remembers a feeling of "this is really happening! I'm doing this!" In this role, she was able to see how she was able to serve a need and to be a problem solver. She developed the skill of being able to walk into very established spaces and ask, "What are the challenges?" and then develop systems and processes to provide solutions to some of those challenges.

When she thinks about her experience as an instructional coach, she notes that it was a defining role in terms of who she wanted to be the rest of her career. She found it to be one of the most valuable spaces that prepared her for every other space she has worked in.

Thinking about her path to school leadership, she says, "I've never labeled myself as a leader, I say I'm the lead servant here. I'm in a space to serve."

Unpacking Her Journey

- Chaunté sees herself as a servant leader who is eager to help and support others.
- She is a problem solver who is able to work through challenges and fill gaps by developing systems and process.
- Her positive outlook has allowed her to find the opportunity in every teaching and leading experience she has had.

Take Action

For Developing Leaders

After uncovering some of the perceptions women have about multiple women in leadership positions, we invite you to consider this as an opportunity to reflect on the story you tell yourself and the media you consume that could contribute to that narrative.

You might wish to reflect on what you see

- in your social media feeds
- on the shows or movies you watch
- within your community
- within your friend group

Consider how women are portrayed in these environments and what messages you are hearing on a regular basis. Where did you see normalizing of women acting in ways that "abandon and leave other women behind"?

As you think of these examples that you may encounter on a regular basis, break down the stereotypes or tropes that you see and consider how these may be influencing your own thinking. How might you shift the narrative that comes through your chosen media?

Scenario

As you reflect on the different viewpoints that women can have about other women aspiring to leadership, consider the following scenario. You might wish to document your thinking here in this book, in a separate document, or in your journal. After documenting your thinking, you might also consider reflecting on this scenario with a trusted colleague or mentor.

You've looked up to a female leader in your organization for a while. When a position opens up that you're considering applying for, you reach out to her for support. You let her know that you're planning to apply and her response is (directly or indirectly): "There's only room for one woman in this leadership team, and I'm going for that position, so you're unlikely to be successful."

- What might you say in response?
- How do you ensure that this response doesn't 'get in your head'?
- How might you avoid accidentally repeating this pattern with someone who looks up to you?

Reflecting on this scenario, does this bring up personal experiences for you?

- Have you experienced feelings of indirect aggression from another woman?
- Have you ever treated another woman like that?
- What precipitated the encounter?
- How might you react or act differently in a similar situation?

For Established Leaders

Reflecting on the stories shared in this chapter, consider this an opportunity to reflect on your perspectives and habits when hiring and creating teams within your current leadership structure. You might wish to discuss the following scenario as a leadership team.

When hiring for a final position on a leadership team, a woman on the hiring committee makes the comment, "We should go with the man, because you know what it'll be like with an all-female team?" What could you say to break this stereotype?

For Schools or Organizations

Within your organization, we invite you to consider what pathways your leaders are taking, including the steps different leaders need to take to arrive at their goal position, and therefore what pathway you are paving for them (intentionally or unintentionally).

To help uncover this journey, you might wish to review your company's organizational chart:

- What do you see?
- Where do you see women being successful vs men?
- What are the expectations from your school community about who holds which positions?

Once you have made your observations, consider the following:

- What is the pathway that men vs women take in order to earn a senior leadership position?
- On average, how many career transitions precede a woman becoming head of school versus a man?
    - for example, men stepping from head of social studies to athletic director to head of school but women taking many more steps: from head of department to instructional coach to Middle Years Programme coordinator to vice principal to curriculum director to principal to head of school
- What message is this sending?
- How can you provide a more equitable pathway for all aspiring leaders?

Within Part 2 of this book, we have hoped to identify the specific challenges women can face on their pathways to leadership while also providing actions that individuals and organizations can take to overcome these barriers. While you as an individual might not have the power to change your organization, we hope the actions provided in this section offer a productive starting point for conversation within your community. In Part 3, we look at skills and strategies that can help aspiring and established leaders be successful in their roles.

References

Carr, M., & Kelan, E. (2016, September 6–8). Femininities at work: How women support other women in the workplace [Conference proceedings]. *British Academy of Management (BAM2016) Conference: Thriving in Turbulent Times*, Newcastle. https://dspace.lib.cranfield.ac.uk/bitstream/handle/1826/14416/Femininities_at_work_How_women_support_other_women_in_the_work_place-2016.pdf?sequence=1&isAllowed=y

Chin, J., & Trimble, J. (2015). *Diversity and leadership*. SAGE.

Hideg, I., & Shen, W. (2019). Why still so few? A theoretical model of the role of benevolent sexism and career support in the continued underrepresentation of women in leadership positions. *Journal of Leadership & Organizational Studies, 26*(3), 287–303. http://doi.org/10.1177/1548051819849006

Lee, A. (2014). How to break up the old boys' club in your office [Blog post]. *Quartz*. https://qz.com/196273/how-to-break-up-the-old-boys-club-in-your-office

Maranto, R., Carroll, K., Cheng, A., & Teodoro, M. (2018). Boys will be superintendents: School leadership as a gendered profession. *Kappan, 100*(2), 12–16. https://doi.org/10.1177/0031721718803563

Mavin, S., Williams, J., & Grandy, G. (2014). Negative intra-gender relations between women: Friendship, competition, and female misogyny. In S. Kumra, R. Simpson, & R. Burke (Eds.), *The Oxford handbook of gender in organizations* (pp. 223–248). Oxford Press.

Morley, C. (2018). Women vs. women: Gender tokenism, indirect aggression and the consequences for career advancement. In S. Adams (Ed.), *Time for solutions! Overcoming gender-related career barriers* (pp. 119–138). Routledge.

National Center for Education Statistics. (2013). *Characteristics of public and private elementary and secondary school principals in the United States*. https://nces.ed.gov/pubs2013/2013312.pdf

Robinson, K., Shakeshaft, C., Grogan, M., & Newcomb, W. (2017). Necessary but not sufficient: The continuing inequality between men and women in educational leadership, findings from the American Association of School Administrators mid-decade survey. *Frontiers in Education*, *2*(12), 1–12. www.frontiersin.org/articles/10.3389/feduc.2017.00012/full

Superville, D. (2017). Few women run the nation's school districts. Why? *The Education Digest*, *82*(6), 14–19.

Tarbutton, T. (2019). The leadership gap in education. *Multicultural Education*, *27*(1), 19–21. https://files.eric.ed.gov/fulltext/EJ1250147.pdf

PART III

Strategies and Skills for Success

10 Seeing the Big Picture

> Leaders need to be able to find leverage points to maximize growth. If you have only a big-picture approach, it's difficult to take action on anything. If you only have details and no big picture, you're on the hamster wheel; you can't move forward. Being able to see systems and toggle between micro and macro level thinking are essential skills.
> —Carla Marschall

As leaders, not only do we have our own goals and ambitions, but we are responsible for moving our institutions forward. We have goals that range from school-wide, to divisional, to small group and individual, and we need to make progress on all of them, each year. Ideally, all of those goals are grounded in the vision and mission of the school, but that doesn't always make it easy to prioritize or manage wide-ranging responsibilities.

The WWL interviewees were each asked how they deal with the many demands of their roles and what effective strategies they have developed. Their insights offer ways in which busy leaders can manage the needs of a school or division from a big-picture perspective, allowing leaders to toggle between urgency and importance while considering the impact of the effort required.

To capture the interviewees' approach, we combined the "Eisenhower Principle" (based on a speech where the former president said "I have two kinds of problems, the urgent and the important. The urgent are not important, and the important are never urgent," which was later visualized by Stephen Covey as quadrants of a matrix) with another well-known scale called the Impact/Effort Matrix (Eisenhower, 1954; Covey, 2020; Andersen et al., 2010). See Figure 10.1.

DOI: 10.4324/9781003426110-13

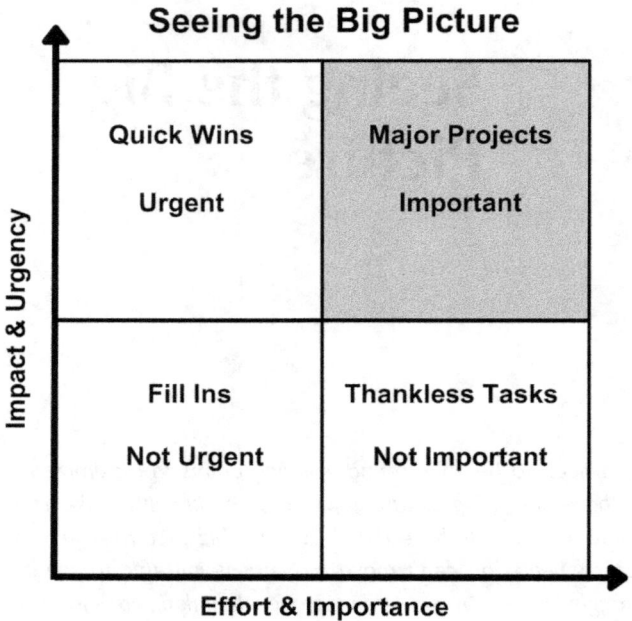

Figure 10.1 Seeing the Big Picture. Women leaders find value in using a decision-making matrix that balances Impact & Urgency against Effort & Importance to navigate conflicting demands (adapted from Stephen Covey's visualization of the Eisenhower Principle and the Impact/Effort Matrix by Andersen, Fagerhaug, & Beltz).

Reflections in the Research

As human beings, we can easily find ourselves overwhelmed by the complexity that confronts us on a daily basis, and international school educators are certainly not immune. From state and local mandates to accreditation visits to tumultuous political climates, educators often lack the time, resources, and emotional energy necessary to implement all of the possible policies, procedures, and practices. In order to resist "initiative fatigue," it is vital for education leaders to find their focus (Reeves, 2011). The primary object of a school leader's focus is to promote the success and development of each student. An essential function performed by school leaders is removing distractions and barriers so that educators can focus their efforts on student learning (Marzano & Carbaugh, 2018).

The International Successful School Principal Project reveals practices of highly successful principals that lead to improving curriculum, pedagogy, and assessment. Since it is impossible for one person to be an all-around expert, successful leaders ensure improvements "most often by working with other school leaders to influence teacher practice" (Gurr, 2015, p. 138). Evidence suggests that making the most of each person's knowledge, skills, and abilities by distributing leadership across all levels in a school sets the scene for high-quality teaching directly impacting student outcomes (Gurr, 2015; Leithwood et al., 2020; Simpson, 2021). When leadership extends throughout a school, it has a greater influence on improving instructional practices and student learning. Some research indicates that teachers feel more committed to a school where leadership responsibilities are shared based on experience and expertise (Leithwood et al., 2020).

When school leaders set clear and consistent goals, they are able to guide the organization and its members in a collective direction. How school leaders assemble, lead, and collaborate with teams is a key factor in aligning the day-to-day actions of a school community with its mission and vision. Research indicates that diverse leadership teams in schools perform more effectively and work smarter than groups composed of similar individuals (Charles et al., 2021; Rock & Grant, 2016). According to Rock and Grant (2016), "diverse teams are more likely to constantly reexamine facts and remain objective. They may also encourage greater scrutiny of each member's actions, keeping their joint cognitive resources sharp and vigilant" (para. 7). Sharing leadership among a diverse team can lead to better decisions as varied perspectives are considered, and diverse leadership teams are often able to better serve their learning communities.

Building Your Team

Caroline Brokvam reminds us of the importance of working as a team. She points out that 30 years of research indicates that team decision making is better than individual decision making and that diverse teams experience greater success than homogeneous teams. As a leader, she says, you might be making some decisions on your own but a lot fewer than you might think, so having processes in place with the people you work with will help you make better decisions.

Likewise, Charlotte Diller thinks about leadership as a shared responsibility and points out the importance of creating goals together as a team: "They become the hooks to hang on all the other things you do. That helps give the bigger focus. Are we all working towards the same purpose and goal?" She notes that you don't need too many goals, perhaps three to five, and stresses the importance of making sure that these goals are simple enough that you can keep referring to them. If your goals are simple enough, you can intersperse them into everything you're doing.

Although she recognizes the importance of a principal's visibility in terms of symbolic leadership, Jennifer Tickle says that "it can't be the culture of Jen, it has to be the culture of the team." Having shared goals means the strategic plan can be "owned" by everyone. Then, even as priorities change over the course of a busy school year, when you come back to the strategic plan, you can remind yourself of the big picture. Having that big-picture view helps you stay positive because you can look at what you've been doing and see how you've contributed to the overall plan of improvement. That can be a daily reminder that you are making progress, even if you get caught up in the business of the day to day.

Focus on the Future

Elsa Donahue says that "leadership is not about the now, it's about what's coming down the road." Knowing that, and recognizing what she refers to as her own self-diagnosed ADD, she realizes that her leadership "can not be about the things that are urgent, it also has to be about the things that are aspirational and inspirational." She consistently pays attention to the days and weeks ahead so she doesn't get "stuck in the now" (Table 10.1). She builds time into her schedule to think about what's coming down the road.

Madeleine Heide also recognizes that urgent tasks "tend to get immediate play," but she knows that she has to find time to plan ahead for what's coming (Table 10.1). Like many of us, she finds it frustrating to put out the daily fires because she knows that those fires are there because of things that didn't get dealt with in the past. But, she points out, "the truth is that you have to put out those fires, and then you can plant the seeds and work on the roots." It can be hard to get the ball rolling, but the more purposeful planning time you can build into your day, the more time you'll have for it in the future.

Table 10.1 School Year Overview. Women leaders can sketch out a month-by-month view of key events that occur throughout the school year in order to focus on what lies ahead.

August	September	October
• New Staff Induction • All Staff Inservice • New Student Open House • Student Registration	• First Day of School • Back-to-School Open House • MAP Testing	• Parent-Teacher Conferences • Re-Accreditation Visit • Q1 Report Cards
November	**December**	**January**
• Regional Leadership Conference	• First Day of School	• First Semester Exams • End of First Semester • Q2 Report Cards
February	**March**	**April**
• Regional Leadership Conference	• IBDP Mock Exams • Q3 Report Cards	• Spring Break
May	**June**	**July**
• IB World Exams	• High School Graduation Ceremony • Final Report Cards	• Leadership Retreat

Define Your Priorities

Catriona Moran believes that it's important to be familiar with current theories on prioritization and leadership, but it's even more important to understand what works best for you. She prefers collecting data, asking questions, and engaging in conversations when she's prioritizing. Then, she takes the time to share the "why" behind her prioritization with her team. This is important because "how we define the priority may change, but the rationale and the thinking behind it remain constant." When teams have a great sense of understanding the "why" behind the priorities involved when they are making decisions, Catriona points out, then they can explain which priority they were addressing and why.

Katie Ham finds that being authentic and true to herself as a leader helps keep those defined priorities in her focus. Because she has such a strong belief in the school mission and vision, those priorities become part of her narrative and discourse. After articulating them at the beginning of the year, she consistently comes back to them as "the big rocks she's pushing." Having those clearly articulated priorities helps; when people ask why they're *not* focusing on something, she points back to the established priorities.

Once those priorities are set, Lola Aneke works with her team to split them into quarters (or even shorter time frames), so that whatever comes in between, "unless it's aligning with what we planned to, unless it's life or death, we ignore it." If something comes up that doesn't align, she uses the priorities to determine how important it is to the goals before adding something new. Lola also points out the importance of having lots of opportunities for review and recalibration as they go through the year to make sure daily tasks are in alignment with their goals.

As teachers, we're very familiar with the concept of backward design for unit planning. Nadine Richards believes it's the same with leadership. She starts with understanding what the vision is, what she's trying to accomplish. She asks herself, "Where am I trying to go? What do I want to see accomplished in five to ten years whether I'm here or not?"

Nadine reminds leaders that in the process of team-based design thinking, we can get stuck in the ideation phase so long that nothing is implemented. She points out the importance of action steps after ideation and outlining who will be responsible. What clouds progress and process, according to her, is when it's not clear what the next steps are to move a team from an ideation phase into implementation. It's essential to know who is in charge of decision making.

Once Sheena Nabholz has a strategic direction set, she just stays the course. After that, she says, "there's no more need for wayfinding." As a former head of school, she notes that staying the course and thinking several steps ahead are important skills. Referring to the Eisenhower Matrix, she describes this approach as necessary "so you don't get lost in the noise, or caught up in the 'urgent and unimportant' quadrant," expending constant activity that's unproductive in the long run.

Articulate Your Challenges

Arden Tyoschin points out the importance of having precise and shared language to ensure that everyone is talking about the same thing. By articulating any challenge you face and assigning it a name, you now have the ability to refer to something directly rather than talking around the topic: "Being intentional with language is so important when you're building and co-creating a culture." Having precise terminology and shared vocabulary are essential when communicating among a leadership team or with community members, as it will also reduce misunderstanding and tension while keeping focus on the impact of the most important projects.

Put Relationships First

Nicole Schmid reminds us of the importance of getting out of the office. She says, "When the relationships I'm building are working, everything else falls into place." She explains that so much happens when she's out in the community that she needs a game plan for every day. She looks at her calendar the night before and determines exactly who she needs to talk to and when she'll be out of her office so she can prioritize her time around their time: "I set my priorities around relationships. There's a sacred time in the day when you have the ability to interact with other human beings that is essential."

Once you're in the position of leadership, Kathleen Naglee cautions that "the work that you need to get done can rarely get done at school. The distraction is the job." It gets easy to focus on the quick things instead of the important things, so she has learned she needs to write down which are the real things to focus on and not be so focused on being perfect with the little things. She has to handle the big things, and "the big things are people."

Process, Reflect, Then Act

Tambi Tyler knows she needs processing time to make decisions, so she asks as many questions about her priorities as she can. Once she gets to a place where it's time to act, she's had time to think it through so that the decision has bubbled to the top.

Tara Waudby knows that teachers and leaders often like solving problems, and it's easy to go into "fixer mode." When teachers come to her with a feeling of urgency, she focuses on being responsive, not reactive. She is a "huge believer in not creating a sense of urgency." She listens, stays calm, and works to de-escalate urgency so she can give each party time to download their thoughts.

Strategies and Skills for Success

To enable herself to do this, she prioritizes entering the day calmly by getting out her thoughts before leaving home. She also created a short decision-making matrix and helps her colleagues practice asking questions so they don't feel like they have to make decisions right then. She notes the importance of ontological coaching, paying attention to the language of how we speak: "Just because I've listened doesn't mean I agree." We need to be explicit about not making assumptions after a conversation, as well as be clear about making explicit requests and stating what's needed.

Finding Your Personal Process

This chapter has shared some prioritizing tips and approaches that came up during the WWL interviews, but keep in mind that every school context is different; some of these processes will work in your context, and some might not. Gathering these and other similar examples for inspiration, and testing out different methods, can help you recognize what might work in your setting, but ultimately, you will find yourself creating a process that works for your school community.

Finding Her Path: Clarissa Sayson

Name: Clarissa Sayson
Role: Elementary School Principal
School: International School of Beijing (ISB)
Location: Beijing, China

Clarissa Sayson started her career in South Korea as the head of an English as a second language department. From there, she moved to the Philippines, where she stayed for 13 years.

Even early on in her career, she knew she wanted to have a greater impact on students. While she was in the Philippines, she thought that working with teachers on professional growth would be the way to make a bigger impact, so she told her head of school at the time that she aspired to leadership.

Ultimately, she took on the role of elementary school principal and helped grow her small school to medium sized. In this role, she learned a lot through being "able to wear many hats." She moved to the role of middle school assistant principal, where she was able to learn about middle-level education in a larger school. In her heart of hearts, she knew that she wanted to return to elementary education, which led her to ISB.

Thinking back over her leadership career, the first moment that Clarissa remembers realizing she was a leader was not necessarily a positive one. She moved from being a teacher in a small school to becoming the principal of that same school. During one of the first weeks of the school year, a teacher who was her friend said to her, "Things are going to be different [between us] now." She realized that just by having a leadership title, her personal relationships and social networks would be impacted.

She realized she had the capacity to lead when she moved into the middle school assistant principal position at a larger school. Tasked with a major school restructuring project, she found herself working with many different community members and juggling many different priorities but having a vision for what was going to happen.

She has learned over her years as a woman in school leadership to let go of the lack of confidence that she has in her ability and capacity to be a leader. She now recognizes that she can lead, that people will listen to ideas if they know 'the Why,' and that the work will be really fantastic. Moving through many positions has helped her gain the skills and experiences that have shaped her perspective as a leader.

Unpacking Her Journey

- Clarissa expanded her knowledge as a school leader by leading in a division outside of her experiences at the elementary level.
- She knew where her leadership heart needed to be and followed that desire to her preferred leadership space in the elementary school.

Take Action

After considering the shift in perspective necessary to be successful in a leadership role, we invite you to "try on" some leadership thinking to see how it feels.

Strategies and Skills for Success

For Developing Leaders

Start by experimenting with shifting your perspective from the micro to the macro view (Figure 10.2). Review your school's strategic plan and identify an objective that is meaningful for you. Start thinking about the systems and structures that need to change or adapt to make this goal a reality. Identify all the parts of the whole that need to come together to achieve this goal. As a thought experiment, take one of those goals and backward plan it, as if you were the school leader during this process.

Consider the following questions:

- What does the timeline look like?
- Who needs to be involved in the decision making, and the actions?
- How will you communicate the stages of this process?
- When will you provide time to make progress?
- Where are there opportunities for accountability in the process?

There's no need to share this with anyone (unless you come up with a brilliant idea!). The purpose is to go through the practice of looking at the big picture and breaking it down into tangible steps.

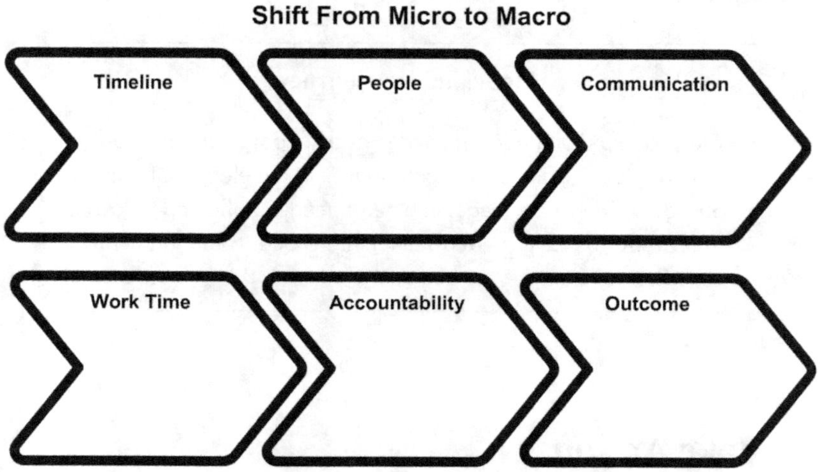

Shift From Micro to Macro

> Timeline > People > Communication
> Work Time > Accountability > Outcome

Figure 10.2 Shift From Micro to Macro. While the small details are important, it is important for leaders to be able to zoom out to envision and understand the big picture.

Scenarios

To put you in a leadership mindset, we invite you to think through either one (or both) of the following scenarios. You might want to document your thinking here in this book, in a separate document, or in your journal. After reflecting, you might want to review and discuss your ideas with a trusted colleague or mentor:

- Your school is beginning the self-study process. There are 10 standards you're collecting evidence for, and the school needs one chair to lead each committee. You have volunteered to lead a committee. What's your plan for leading this deeper dive into one of the accreditation standards (for example, school culture, finance, governance, tech integration)? How will you have a successful outcome leading a group of people from across the school?
- Your school has just been through an accreditation visit. One of the recommendations is to more broadly support English language learners in your school. As the head of department for your subject area, how might you address this recommendation within your team?

For Established Leaders

Consider offering the opportunity for aspiring leaders in your organization to explore or learn more about how the school operates from a systemic, big-picture view.

To provide you with some guidance for this conversation, you might want to try an Affinity Mapping protocol from Critical Friends Group. A simplified description is: On post-it notes, write different parts of the organization, put them all up on a board, and move them together to talk about how different parts interact, impact, affect, or repel each other.

See the book website for more details.

For Schools or Organizations

We know from the *Reflections in the Research* section of this chapter that diverse leadership teams perform more effectively and work smarter than groups composed of like individuals.

We invite you to take this as an opportunity to reflect on the ways that you can embrace different ways of thinking and working to form diverse teams, for instance,

- Do you know the strengths that your different team members bring to the table?
- How do you identify the strengths? Have you used an organizational tool like Strengthsfinder, Compass Points, or a leadership inventory?
- How do you ensure that you're diversifying those strengths?
- How does your organization leverage those diverse strengths?

After you consider the make-up of your current leadership teams, you might find that specific skills or strengths are overwhelmingly represented (or underrepresented). If so, consider the following:

- How can your organization prioritize creating diverse teams?
- In alignment with the actions in Part 2, when you identified leadership standards and shared vision of leadership skills for your organization, where and how can you ensure that diverse strengths are represented in your standards and expectations for leaders?

In this chapter, we talked about seeing the big picture as an individual school leader and the importance of being able to make the shift from micro to macro perspectives. In the next chapter, we'll focus on one specific real-world challenge that pushed many of our Women Who Lead to confront the scope and expectations of the biggest-picture lens within a school organization: the interview process to become a head of school.

References

Andersen, B., Fagerhaug, T., & Beltz, M. (2010). *Root cause analysis: Simplified tools and techniques: A step-by-step guide.* Quality Press.

Charles, A., Chandler, J., Neitzel, K., & Welch, D. (2021, August 11). *Promoting a gender-inclusive hiring process* [Blog post]. www.ecis.org/gender-inclusive-hiring/

Covey, S. (2020). *The 7 habits of highly effective people.* Simon & Schuster.

Eisenhower, D. D. (1954). *Address at the Second Assembly of the World Council of Churches, Evanston, Illinois*. www.presidency.ucsb.edu/documents/address-the-second-assembly-the-world-council-churches-evanston-illinois

Gurr, D. (2015). A model of successful school leadership from the International Successful School Principalship Project. *Societies, 5*, 136–150. https://doi.org/10.3390/soc5010136

Leithwood, K., Harris, A., & Hopkins, D. (2020). Seven strong claims about successful leadership revisited. *School Leadership & Management, 40*(1), 5–22. https://doi.org/10.1080/13632434.2019.1596077

Marzano, J., & Carbaugh, B. (2018). *2018 update: The Marzano focused school leader evaluation model* [White paper]. www.marzanocenter.com/wp-content/uploads/sites/4/2020/01/MC07-02-Focused-School-Leader-Evaluation-Model.pdf

Reeves, D. (2011). *Finding your leadership focus*. Teachers College Press.

Rock, D., & Grant, H. (2016, November 4). Why diverse teams are smarter. *Harvard Business Review*. https://hbr.org/2016/11/why-diverse-teams-are-smarter

Simpson, J. (2021). Fostering teacher leadership in K–12 schools: A review of the literature. *Performance Improvement Quarterly, 34*(3), 229–246. https://doi.org/10.1002/piq.21374

Lessons Learned from Head-of-School Interviews

You often think to yourself, "should I apply for this job or not?" If you're asking the question, follow your gut instinct. If you see how you can impact the lives of students, take the opportunity and apply.
—Kathleen Naglee

As we move up the "ladder of leadership" in international schools, the interview process changes, becoming increasingly demanding. This chapter highlights 10 key lessons about head-of-school interviews that emerged from the WWL interviews. Although we recognize that there are different professional pinnacles for each educator, interviews at this level are the most distinct from other administrative positions. We chose to shine a light on head-of-school interviews because they demonstrate the biggest shift in thinking from one interview "level" to the next and often highlight different aspects of leadership that might not be seen in other administrative positions. These interviews most clearly expose the expectations that can be placed on women at the higher levels of leadership. Even if you're not planning on applying for head of school positions, or anything similar, in the near future, the following insights are likely to be helpful to you before you even begin thinking about the process.

Reflections in the Research

Workplace diversity, and especially diversity among leaders within an organization, has been positively connected to increased success rates across many sectors (Hunt et al., 2015; Rock & Grant, 2016). Diverse workplaces help team members to keep their biases in check and increase innovative thinking (Rock & Grant, 2016). When considering these factors, the significance of a hiring process that engages the right educators and leaders in any school cannot be understated.

In international schools, search agencies are often key players in recruiting for senior leadership roles and for headships. Such agencies frequently serve as gatekeepers to leadership roles, determining which candidates are put forth to school-based hiring committees. Since 2020, when strong calls for greater diversity, equity, and inclusion (DEI) erupted in the international educator community, these agencies have developed DEI statements and continue to align their actions and practices with these statements.

This shift, even if somewhat forced, to embrace and implement DEI practices helps to break up the old boys' club and to address implicit bias in leadership recruiting and hiring practices. These agencies have committed to promoting diverse groups of highly qualified candidates (Charles et al., 2021; Magagna, 2020). Search agencies are more transparent about the practices they incorporate to ensure equitable access to leadership roles (Charles et al., 2021). In some cases, these agencies also support and grow diverse talent and provide coaching and mentoring support (Charles et al., 2021).

The first step into an interview for any leadership role often reveals a process that is different from interviewing for a teaching role. Leadership searches typically involve a multi-stage interview process whether the role is for middle leadership (e.g., head of department, coordinator), for senior leadership (e.g., principal), or for head of school. The search/interview process at each level of leadership brings with it additional layers of interview teams, constituents, and performance tasks (Table 11.1).

Welch (2022) suggests two action steps for candidates to consider when preparing for the content of a head-of-school interview. First ask yourself, "What are the school's projected needs?" (para. 4). To answer this question, a candidate will review the description of the position being pursued. This description is often prepared by a recruiting agent who has spent significant time speaking with a wide variety of school constituents to understand the wants and needs of the community (Welch, 2022). First, home in on specific details of desired qualities and qualifications to understand the priorities of the role. Second, reflect on your own "leadership accomplishments that match the school's projected needs" (Welch, 2022). Specifically, familiarize yourself with "behavior questions" that seek to

Strategies and Skills for Success

Table 11.1 Interview Process Progression from Teacher to Head of School. This table might not reflect every step in an interview process, but it captures the various interviews with school community members and related tasks as the pursuit of leadership roles becomes more complex and demanding.

	Teacher	*Middle leader*	*Senior leader*	*Head of School*
Number of interviews	1–2	2–3	2–4	Exhaustive across multiple constituent groups
On-campus interview	Rare	Rare	Common	Almost Always
Possible members of interview teams	• Principal or • Head of School	• Teachers • Middle Leaders • Senior Leaders • Head of School	• Recruiting Agent • Teachers • Middle Leaders • Senior Leaders • Head of School • Students • Parents	• Recruiting Agent • Teachers • Middle Leaders • Senior Leaders • Head of School • Students • Parents • Board Members
Possible performance tasks (asynchronous or synchronous)	• Submission of video/live teaching example	• Pre-recorded self-introduction video • Writing prompt exercise • Leadership philosophy	• SWOT analysis based on strategic plan • Data analysis	• Data analysis
Possible performance tasks (on-site)	• Demo lesson	• Lead professional learning experience	• Lead staff meeting or professional learning experience	• Board presentation • Presentation of action plan

uncover your philosophy and approaches to various issues that a head of school might confront (Thompson, 2022; Welch, 2022).

Ten Lessons Learned from Head-of-School Interviews

1. Connect with Varied Stakeholders

When you are interviewing for a head-of-school position, you're going to be speaking with all community stakeholders. Rachel Caldwell notes that you need to demonstrate that "you really deeply care and that you can connect equally well with students, staff, and parents. People need to feel that you're genuine in your desire to connect."

In order to make those genuine connections, Elsa Donahue focuses on communicating an authentic, consistent, crisp, and clear message about who she is and what she can offer the school community. She warns that "a trap that one may fall into is to think you might want to target your audience and say what you think that audience group is looking for." Instead, she recommends staying true to who you are and focusing on sharing a consistent message across all meetings.

2. Prepare for Board Members (and Other Non-Educators)

Something completely new for most educators not currently in a leadership position is being interviewed by non-educators. When you are interviewed for a head-of-school position by the school's board, they're very often men from the business world who are thinking about things differently. Madeleine Heide recommends preparing for questions from the board's perspective: "They will ask you about managing change, future of education, and how you would handle all the components of a school."

Similarly, Deb Welch explains that "they are typically people with different backgrounds than you: They can be host nationals, corporate executives, parents, or embassy employees. In a for-profit school, you'll be interviewing with the CEO and senior leadership of the company." Being aware of some of the major differences between your own perspective and that of these stakeholders from outside of the world of education, and anticipating the kinds of questions they might have for you can be key.

3. Focus on the Big Picture

According to Tambi Tyler, a successful head-of-school interview is all about common language and systemic thinking. In our day-to-day work, she explains, we often speak in the language of immediate tasks, but the head-of-school role is not really about "tasks"; it's about "leadership as a whole and concept, in theory and conceptual knowledge.

Demonstrating that you understand systemic challenges and roles is essential in the interviewing process." You want to show that you will be capable of persuasively working with and guiding others to move the whole school forward.

4. Be Aware That Interviews Will Be Intense

Whether it's a head-of-school interview or a principal interview, it's intense. In a head-of-school context, you are hired by the school's board. Deb Welch notes that, "if you have made it to the finals and are brought to campus, you have an exhausting two days of being in front of every group imaginable, from faculty (maybe even in front of the other finalists), to parents, students; as well as dinners and evening events. It's exhausting. The last interview typically is the interview with the board, and they are looking at data that's come in from the past few days, frequently in the form of a survey where they're getting perception ratings from people about you. By that point, you're exhausted."

Jasmeen Philen shares her experience of being flown to a campus with five other candidates to have five interviews over the course of two days, including the principal and assistant principal, the leadership team from all divisions, the head of school, a 12-teacher panel, and the curriculum coordinator plus class visits and observations. In the evening, there were social events with everyone who conducted the interview and the other four interviewees. She sums it up by saying, "It's a more complicated process. You're vying for very few positions, so the process becomes a little more challenging." If you're facing this kind of intense interview gauntlet, keep a careful eye on your own levels of fatigue, stress, or jet lag and make an extra effort to refocus and center yourself during any downtime available.

5. Own Your Leadership

During the interview process, you need to present yourself as a leader even if you don't have experience in every aspect of the role. Madeleine Heide has noticed that women often confess to not being an expert in one or more areas but warns that "you're dead in the water if you do that." She advises aspiring heads of school to "present yourself as an executive leader who has an incredible skill set." To do this, she counsels, "You have to begin to shape your language around what they're looking for and how you can be that person. Prepare, think about it, and write it down. Do what you need to do to be prepared. You want to look like you're prepared."

Along those lines, instead of stating what you haven't done, or what you don't know, Bridget McNamer recommends sharing your point of view. Rather than saying "I haven't done this before," she suggests explaining what you think about the issue: "Don't call attention to what you haven't done. Instead, say 'This is what I think about XYZ, this is how I would imagine starting the process.'" The important thing is to find strategies that allow you to project overall confidence and competence when answering any question.

6. Show Understanding Beyond "Just" Education

As educators, we are passionate about education, but head-of-school interviews are about more than just education; they're about being the director of an organization. Kathleen Naglee reiterates that, as mentioned in some of the earlier items in this list, a head-of-school interview is completely different from any other interview that you would have in education: "You have to understand that you're applying as a CEO. You're hired by boards, and they are often business people. You have to look like, have the language of, and have the confidence of a CEO. For most women, the biggest barrier is to believe you can run the show." You might need, she continues, to make sure you've taken courses in finance because you have to be prepared to manage a large budget.

Jane Thompson echoes, "You're being interviewed by the board, and they are responsible for the financial sustainability of the school and for making sure the school is as brilliantly led as an organization as possible. The education side is just a piece of that. For most of them, it's not the most interesting piece."

Sheena Nabholz also emphasizes that aspiring heads of school need to recognize that the role is often really about finance, communication, and management. When heads of school struggle, Sheena explains, it's often because they haven't had this level of management experience, particularly focusing on finance and facilities.

7. Do Your Research on the Board

When Caroline Brokvam took her first head-of-school role, she wasn't prepared for how much of the job was working with the board. As mentioned in earlier items on this list, the fact that they're not educators means that the conversations can be very different, and board members will often have very diverse opinions and expectations. You need to be prepared for those close relationships once you get the job, so Caroline recommends gathering as much information on the board as possible before you interview.

8. Know What You Want Them to Know

During the interview process, make sure you're clear on the story you're sharing. Madeleine Heide recommends that you decide on at least five things you want to make sure they know about you and find a way to share those five things no matter what their question is. Madeleine emphasizes,

> When you leave the room, you want them to have those five things about you in their head. Find a way to weave that in, no matter what they ask you. You have to know yourself very well and what you want them to know about you.

Fay Leong recommends that you start by identifying specific achievements and skill sets that you can bring to your next position. You need to "name it in your head and articulate for yourself exactly how you specifically contributed. When you're in a team and you're contributing, what part can you own?" Not only can this help you tell your leadership story, but this change in perspective can help you step up and do more, enabling you to be even more prepared for the next step in your leadership journey.

As Nathalie Henderson notes, a district-level position interview is "not so much about theory, more about 'tell me about a time.'" She explains that every leadership role she has interviewed for has included questions like "tell me a time where you have done XYZ." The higher up you go, the more you might be expected to speak to the impact and the results of the actions you took: "The questions that you are asked can be a chance to reflect on how you overcame past dilemmas, expose a bit of vulnerability, or show how you exhibited grace and empathy during difficult situations." To prepare for the interview, plan out your story with these goals in mind.

9. Start with the Headline

Bridget McNamer points out that when it comes to leadership roles, "Women tend to do inductive answering; they'll get to the answer by going through the story. What would serve them better is deductive, starting with a headline. Talk about a time when you faced a challenge, start with the headline. Keep the headline in mind and then draw the details in later, if asked." This might differ from your usual style, but you don't want interviewers to think your anecdotes are unfocused, or for a point to get ignored because you didn't underline it clearly enough.

10. Level Up Your Skills

Catriona Moran highlights that "it's not enough to get certification. You have to get the certification, but you also have to have demonstrated that you have contributed to the organization which you're in." She recommends that you take every possible opportunity to interview because "every time we interview or put ourselves forward—when we have to reflect on our beliefs, the underpinnings of our pedagogical approach, and ourselves—helps us become stronger in our beliefs." As mentioned in Chapter 7, Catriona believes that applying to interviews even when the position is not a perfect fit can have multiple benefits, including showing your head of school that you have aspirations and are willing to step up and take risks.

The Ladder of Leadership

You will find that each step upwards adds new elements to the interview process. Being aware of the expectations at each level will help you identify areas where you need to grow and intentionally prepare for. Taking the time to develop skills and competencies that will be needed at the next level will help you move up the ladder with confidence.

Finding Her Path: Kathleen Naglee

Name: Kathleen Naglee
Role: Head of School
School: International School Helsinki
Location: Helsinki, Finland

Early in her career, Kathleen Naglee recognized that one of her strengths is being a problem solver. She says when she was teaching, she was never satisfied when students weren't learning to the depth that she intended. When she was teaching world history, she realized that there was a problem with the course content and resources. She identified a potential solution, implemented it, and solved the problem herself. She says,

> when you're working with leadership in a school, you need to position your solution in terms of solving a problem that the school is working on, instead of offering a strange new program. Learn how to phrase your initiatives in the format of, "here is the problem and this is the solution."

In the second part of her career, when Kathleen had moved into senior leadership, she noticed her work again focused on problem solving. At the time, she was IB Diploma Programme coordinator and upper school principal at an international school in Estonia. The school was heading toward bankruptcy, and Kathleen offered to step in as the director for a year, paid at a teacher's salary, to see if she could turn things around. She notes that it is not uncommon for women to be promoted to high positions of authority and responsibility during times of crisis or when an organization is failing, a phenomenon known as the "glass cliff." Kathleen points out that cases like this might theoretically be great for building leadership skills but can be precarious and even dangerous for your career because "you're trying to figure things out in crisis mode."

Even as an upper school principal, Kathleen didn't see her influence. It was only when she became head of school that she began to see herself as a leader. She points out that it took her so long to see because "early in your career, you're often speaking to your own credibility, so you're trying to prove why you should be there." Through that process, she realized that she needed to stop talking about why she should be in a given leadership role. She needed to shift the focus from "me" to "we" to bring her staff into focus.

Kathleen recognized that as a leader, the language she uses can have a cascading effect on the entire system. She also noticed that the energy she brings into a room is amplified by everyone there.

Once she recognized her leadership, she realized that her mood had an impact on the entire system. She had to focus on being present for others and could no longer share her worries with colleagues because those worries would be passed on and felt by others. She had to focus on presenting her caring, loving, positive authentic self in front of all members of the learning community. She notes that it can feel strange to have such influence, that it's at times terrifying to have the power to change a whole school culture based on her demeanor.

Looking back on her career, Kathleen shares,

> You often think to yourself, "Should I apply for this job or not?" If you're asking the question, follow your gut instinct. If you see how you can impact the lives of students, take the opportunity and apply. If you have that kind of spirit about you and you're seen as responsible and trustworthy and not full of criticism about what's happening: "Let me see if I can help." This is how people start to see you as a leader. If you see how you can create an impact on the lives of students, give it a shot.

Unpacking Her Journey

- Kathleen is a problem solver able to diagnose a problem, develop a solution, and implement a new strategy or approach.
- She possesses characteristics of an inspirational leader who brings out the best in the individuals and teams around her.
- She has been willing to take risks by taking on leadership responsibility in challenging situations.

Take Action

After considering the different expectations of interviewees along the ladder of leadership, we invite you to practice preparing for the next level of interview in your leadership journey.

Strategies and Skills for Success

For Developing Leaders

Find a current job posting for a leadership position that you aspire to. Review the desired qualities and qualifications outlined in the job posting and identify the opportunities and challenges shared in the recruiting profile (Table 11.2).

To be prepared for the interview, complete the following steps:

- Develop five to seven questions that might be asked of a candidate for this position based on the job posting.
- Prepare a "headline" response to each question.
- Once you have the headlines, develop each story based on your skills and experiences.
- Provide relevant examples and evidence to support your responses.
- Practice delivering these responses aloud or on video and listen for your confidence.

Using the same job posting, do some additional research by visiting the school's website. Practice finding out everything you can from a website search:

- Learn more about their mission, vision, and values.

Table 11.2 Opportunities and Challenges. Use a simple chart with guiding questions to prepare for a real or imagined interview for a leadership role (Welch, 2022).

Desired quality or qualification	*Potential interview questions*	*Evidence based in personal experience*
What has the school identified as a desired quality or qualification for this leadership role?	What questions align with the desired quality or qualification?	What examples can I provide from my own leadership experiences and practice?

- Read additional documents that might be available online (e.g., strategic plan, student handbook).
- Identify additional key information to explore an alignment with your qualifications and to determine if there could be a fit for you.
- Brainstorm some specific questions you might (or would) want to ask in the interview process.

After going through this process, you might also want to role-play the interview process with a trusted colleague or mentor.

As you reflect on this experience, take a moment to consider your career positioning. Document your thinking from the interview practice, as well as your career positioning in your journal, or here in this book, so you can refer back to it later.

- What is your ultimate goal for your leadership journey?
- What might be the next logical step and where might that lead?

Scenarios

To put you in the head-of-school-interview frame of mind, we invite you to explore the following scenarios. You might want to document your thinking here in this book, in a separate document, or in your journal. After reflecting, you might want to review and discuss your ideas with a trusted colleague or mentor:

- In your head-of-school interview, you know you're going to be asked to actually demonstrate your capacity in a variety of environments. You arrive for the interview only to discover that your competitor is there as well and you'll be directly interacting with them throughout your visit. How do you maintain your "interview mindset" while interacting with your competition?
- In the head-of-school interview process, you're informed that if you make it to the top three and are invited to the school, you will be staying with a community member (instead of a hotel). You decide to go ahead with the interview. How do you manage the unrelenting 24-hour interview experience without having your own space to relax and decompress?

For Established Leaders

To prepare yourself to support aspiring leaders, we invite you to take a moment to reflect on your own past interview experiences:

- What were some of the most surprising experiences you encountered?
- What were ways that you felt either fairly or unfairly treated?

With that in mind, reflect on your own actions and practices as an employer:

- Where and when might you be able to ensure your practices are more equitable and inclusive?
- Where and when might you be able to put your own practices in place to check your own unconscious biases?

As appropriate, bring these ideas to your senior leadership team for discussion and potential implementation in your school setting.

For Schools or Organizations

We invite you to review your school's hiring process:

- What practices do you have in place to conduct a neutral hiring process?
- What questions are part of the standard interview process that might be exclusionary?
- What are the school's priorities (and possible biases) when advertising and conducting both internal and external candidate searches?
- What are the expectations of parents and the board for all leadership positions, and how do you address and adjust those expectations as needed?

After reflecting on this process, where could you improve the process to be more neutral? You might wish to consider systemic changes that will lead to building a more diverse team through more equitable hiring practices such as

- revising the first phase of applications, including the process for resume sorting, as well as the requirements for submitting a resume (e.g., requesting blind resumes)
- communicating your vision for equitable hiring practices to school stakeholders including the board
- providing diversity training for anyone involved in the hiring process, including the board
- considering the language used in job descriptions
- casting a wider net for advertising both internal and external candidate searches, including leveraging your internal network to find diverse candidates
- ensuring that you have a policy in place for recruiting and hiring diverse candidates

These actions present potential systemic changes that have the opportunity to cascade from the head-of-school interview process throughout all of the hiring practices at your organization. Next, as you proceed on your journey toward positions such as head of school, it's much more likely that you will need to conduct and master having difficult conversations, the subject of the following chapter.

References

Charles, A., Chandler, J., Neitzel, K., & Welch, D. (2021, August 11). *Promoting a gender-inclusive hiring process* [Blog post]. www.ecis.org/gender-inclusive-hiring/

Hunt, V., Layton, D., & Prince, S. (2015, January 1). Why diversity matters. *McKinsey and Company*. www.mckinsey.com/capabilities/people-and-organizational-performance/our-insights/why-diversity-matters

Magagna, J. (2020, December 23). Diversity, equity, and inclusion in recruiting. *TieOnline*. www.tieonline.com/article/2845/diversity-equity-and-inclusion-in-recruiting

Rock, D., & Grant, H. (2016, November 4). Why diverse teams are smarter. *Harvard Business Review*. https://hbr.org/2016/11/why-diverse-teams-are-smarter

Thompson, R. (2022, June 28). Inclusive hiring: Removing the bias in teacher hiring. *Teach Away*. www.teachaway.com/recruitment/blog/inclusive-hiring-removing-bias-teacher-hiring

Welch, D. (2022, February 16). The short guide to preparing for a headship interview. *TieOnline*. www.tieonline.com/article/3140/the-short-guide-to-preparing-for-a-headship-interview

12 | Strategies and Skills for Handling Difficult Conversations

> *We have credentials in how to teach, we don't have credentials about how to talk effectively with other adults. And here we are working with other adults.*
>
> —Jennifer Abrams, author, *Having Hard Conversations*

Handling conflict, even when it's a planned conversation, is rarely an easy task, even for experienced leaders. For most educators, dealing with conflict is not part of our training, and hopefully that's because it's a rare part of our experiences in schools, but it does happen.

When we're talking about difficult conversations in this book, we're talking about an intentional conversation about an uncomfortable or difficult topic or negative experience, where the goal is to share perspectives and experiences so that we can come to an agreement about how to move forward through mutual respect and understanding (not to persuade or "win"). This type of conversation is also referred to as a "hard conversation." In *Hard Conversations Unpacked* (2016), Jennifer Abrams describes a hard conversation as

> rang[ing] from a formal evaluation conference in which you tell someone they need to improve, to the briefest comment about behavior at a team meeting; from a colleague-to-colleague discussion in the parking lot, to the rollout of a district initiative that prompts resistance.
>
> occur[ing] between colleagues, with administrators, at team meetings, and with any adult connected to the school. The content can be teacher or administrator behavior, lack of follow-through, not meeting performance expectations, responding to a challenging communication, or about so many

other "goings on" that happen in schools. Whenever you feel uncomfortable or fearful, have second thoughts, or avoid saying something, you are circling a hard conversation.

(p. xi)

Engaging in difficult conversations and confrontation is an inevitable part of being a leader. Making time to practice in preparation for these unfortunately necessary engagements can help leaders or prospective leaders feel a little less intimidated when they do occur.

Reflections in the Research

One common challenge that confronts leaders is the increased and diverse interactions with a variety of colleagues (Bassett & Shaw, 2017; Irvine & Brundrett, 2019). Many leaders in school settings find that leading their colleagues is far different than leading children and young adults in their classrooms (Gurr & Drysdale, 2013; Irvine & Brundrett, 2019; Lipscombe et al., 2020). The skills of leading and managing children in a classroom do not seamlessly transfer to leading and managing adult professionals (Irvine & Brundrett, 2019). In the early stages of taking on a leadership role, female leaders might need help increasing their competence and confidence to navigate the various personnel issues with which they are confronted:

> Women often describe power as something that increases as it is shared. Therefore, it is not surprising that in order for many women to be comfortable with the notion of holding power, power needs to be conceptualized as something that is shared with others and that is not power over but, rather, power with.
> (Grogan and Shakeshaft, 2011, p. 7)

A female leader's ability to engage in difficult conversations within a professional community can be very dependent on her own cultural background, reliance on societal expectations, and upbringing. Individual histories of past interactions emphasize the need for female leaders to spend time on relational work that includes building relationships and a school culture that emphasizes trust, empathy, understanding, and listening (Garmston & Wellman, 2016; Ronnerman et al., 2017).

Leadership involves a high level of interacting and collaborating with colleagues (Irvine & Brundrett, 2019). Leaders inevitably find themselves mediating conflict and dealing with divisive colleagues (Bassett & Shaw, 2017). Ensuring that these interactions and collaborations are positive and productive is a key to leadership success (Irvine & Brundrett, 2019; McIntosh & Love, 2021). To lead professionals requires a level of proficiency in leading teams "through dialogue, reflection, and data" (Lipscombe et al., 2020, p. 11). Education leaders will need specific capabilities to support "learning conversations, engaging in reflective learning conversations, [and] giving and receiving feedback" (Lipscombe et al., 2020, p. 11).

Ten Strategies for Handling Difficult Conversations

Participants in the WWL interviews were asked, "Now that you've had extensive experience in a variety of leadership positions, how do you handle difficult conversations? What do you wish you knew about them earlier in your career?" Ten strategies were consistently highlighted. They are divided into two categories in what follows.

Five strategies emerged that help to build stamina and comfort level with difficult conversations so that you feel prepared and confident for the future. The other five strategies can be employed in the moment, during a confrontation or difficult conversation, to diffuse the situation and hopefully get to a point of compromise.

Building the Strength for Difficult Conversations

While we would prefer that confrontations remain rare in our education settings, they do happen. For many educators, they are not part of our training or our regular practice, so they can feel intimidating. The secret to feeling confident and capable is both understanding the process and practicing actions so that they become habits, leaving very few surprises to emerge.

1. Practice and Be Prepared

Melanie Vrba emphasizes the importance of practicing difficult conversations. She recognizes that "you have to have ones that go poorly (as well as ones that go well) so you can learn what to do and what not to do." Preparation is a key to success. Allowing the time and space for such conversations can ensure that they go well rather than ending in bitterness and distrust. Melanie suggests practicing in low-stakes situations, for example role-playing with a drama teacher, because they can really enliven the experience.

When Suzanna Jemsby started her leadership journey, she worked with a human resources director who allowed her to practice her first really big difficult conversation. They played it out in a theatrical way, which she found "so necessary." She says she felt as if she had thought through everything that could possibly happen, so that when the conversation actually came around, it was anticlimactic. After the meeting, she went straight to her computer and sent her interpretation of the meeting to the person she spoke to. She finds that providing documentation of the conversation is essential to ensure that all elements of the discussion are clear and recorded for both parties: "People deserve feedback, so we shouldn't shy away from conversation. It's important to do the follow-up." The follow-up provides an opportunity to confirm what was discussed and address any misunderstandings immediately.

Jennifer Tickle, falling back on previous experience as a theater director, says she views the job title and the desk as the props on her leadership "set." Although she finds these conversations difficult, she uses her props to recognize that people expect her to have difficult conversations. When reflecting back, she notes that even though the conversations were challenging, the feedback she receives is that the recipients are grateful to have had the discussion.

Prior to any potentially difficult conversation, Jasmeen Philen makes sure to do her research. She starts with the facts and speaks to all the parties involved. Preparation before the conversation ensures that she is prepared for all aspects of the conversation.

Michele Mattoon emphasizes that she does not shy away from difficult conversations since "the people who push your buttons are your greatest teachers because if you can figure out how to work with that person, then you're learning a lot, and that's part of the practice."

2. Observe and Be Observed

Rachel Hovington and Madeleine Heide stress the importance of both observing difficult conversations and being observed when they are leading difficult conversations to get feedback on their approach.

Rachel points out that "flattening the hierarchy is really important." Building trust means that there should be more people in the room to watch the conversation so you can have a thought partner afterward. There is always something to learn in every conversation, even for experienced leaders. Most of the phrases and approaches that Rachel uses during accountable conversations have come from great leaders in her career, and she reflects that she has improved in this area due to opportunities to observe others.

During more complex conversations, Madeleine also recommends having someone else present. An additional observer can help with logistics to plan and/or observe the conversation. An additional observer might also be required if a conversation has legal implications.

3. It's OK to Be Uncomfortable

Accountable conversations can be uncomfortable for everyone involved—for the person giving the feedback as well as the person receiving. However, when you have started to develop the skills to share difficult feedback in a "humane and growth-producing way," as Jennifer Abrams, author of *Having Hard Conversations* (2009) points out, you can move forward with the awareness that it is okay to be uncomfortable.

Recognizing that it will not be easy, and increasing your ability to deal with the discomfort, is a necessary part of the process. Jennifer recognizes that she started developing these skills by modeling and accepting feedback, which resulted in changes to her own behavior. She now has a "stronger stomach" and has learned that you "can be able to sit with more discomfort."

As you grow and develop your skills (perhaps applying strategies in the *Take Action* section later in this chapter), you will find that you can have confidence in the way you hold difficult conversations. The discomfort can shift from lack of confidence to the care and respect that you have for those with whom you are speaking.

4. Don't Wait

Katie Ham has recognized over time that you have to be honest and deal with situations in a timely manner rather than let things simmer: "As leaders, it's incumbent upon us to be honest and direct; everyone deserves the opportunity for growth. In having those difficult conversations, it's about being supportive and kind and doing it in a space where the other person feels comfortable, not vulnerable."

Similarly, Katie Koening recommends dealing with any issues that arise as soon as possible and not allowing yourself to create a laundry list: "When something happens that is disruptive, and I don't jump into it and it continues, I become frustrated both with what's happening and my lack of response. Try to focus on one thing and only then move on to the next thing—to go from item to item is not productive or helpful or being a kind human." Both women point out that people might need processing time and that giving all parties the space to come back to a conversation several days later can be very effective.

Katie Ham notes that going back to those conversations after some time away is essential for everyone's development. Katie Koening recognizes that issues will not necessarily be resolved after one conversation: "It's important to make sure they know that I care and I want this to go well and I want them to be successful. Sometimes things are better when they work themselves out." However difficult they might be, when faced head-on, these conversations can become opportunities that lead to productive growth.

5. Act in Accordance with Your Values

Renée Green began her career nervous about confrontation; this nervousness was connected to her awareness that others might be holding on to stereotypes about people who look like her. Although she has grown and evolved, and the world has changed a bit, Renée finds herself still very much aware of the stereotypes about Black women, constantly wondering to herself, "Am I smiling enough, being nice enough, being kind enough?" In spite of this, she feels she is now able to just say whatever it is that needs to be said with compassion and clarity.

Even though these conversations can be challenging on many levels, Renée observes that "we are a learning profession where we have tests and summatives and moments of high stakes. Why do we shun some of those moments and embrace others? It's all a part of the learning journey, and if you embrace it as such, it's really not as daunting. You can build a relationship even when it starts in a time of crisis."

Sawsan Jaber comes to any difficult conversation remembering that she has bigger issues within education that she wants to focus on, rather than worrying about any potentially intimidating individual conversation. This allows her to have the confidence to engage in individual conversations while keeping her emotions in check. She reminds herself that there is a wide variety of factors that shape the way people see and think. Overcoming differences through these often-challenging conversations is, for her, a first step toward accomplishing her goals as an educator.

Katie Wellbrook notes that integrity is crucial: "If you're going to have a difficult conversation, and you're holding them to a standard, you have to be meeting that standard. Hypocrisy is the best way to break down cultural credibility and trust in you as a leader. . . . You have to show up and do the thing you say you're going to do. If you don't do it, you have to apologize." Clarity and consistency in how you approach them can keep difficult conversations from growing even more difficult.

Strategies to Employ in the Moment

1. Recognize Inherited Power Dynamics

Many of the participants pointed out the importance of being aware of positional power and authority. Female leaders, with or without an official title, need to be aware when there's a perception that they have greater access to school leadership or are in a position of influence. Madeleine Heide recognizes the need to acknowledge power dynamics. She shares that "as a leader, you don't have to fight for that level of authority; you already have it. Therefore, the other person you are entering into the conversation with doesn't have it. You have to recognize that." Junlah Madalinski confirms that "if you don't recognize that power dynamic, whether unintentional or intentional, you leverage that power in a way that gets what you want out of that conversation." The fact that others see you as having power will affect your interactions whether you want it to or not.

Regardless of a leader's personal interactions with a teacher, Junlah also recognizes that there is often a history of interactions with previous administrators, and Rachel Hovington shares, "It depends who the individual is, what their journey is, their experience with leaders before, the kind of family they came from, the kind of recent experiences and long-term experiences they came from." She highlights that she always has the same outcome and expectations, but she approaches different situations differently, prioritizing being able to adapt her approach based on the context, for example being to be able to let things go or bring things forward depending on whom she is working with, as part of contextual leadership. Even though they weren't personally involved, current leaders often become responsible for solving the challenges of previous leaders in order to move forward. Past experiences and interactions can act as invisible participants during these kinds of hard conversations.

To ensure that power dynamics are addressed during any conversation (including difficult ones), Junlah advises, "Find ways to actively dismantle that power structure. You have to be committed to ensuring that regardless of how difficult that conversation is, the person feels listened to, understood and respected. If that happens, your job as an educational leader is done." Prioritizing relationship building up front can help to facilitate difficult conversations when they arise.

2. Be Direct

Grace McCallum points out the importance of dealing with any issues that arise as soon as possible, which ideally means during the actual conversation. She underscores the importance of getting to the point right away, without small talk. Starting a difficult conversation with small talk makes it harder to focus on the item at hand because you have "clouded the conversation with an emotional connection." For Grace, being clear is being kind, and she starts these conversations directly by stating something along the lines of "I wanted to meet with you today to talk about. . . . It might be uncomfortable for both of us, but we'll get through it," which gives both parties permission to feel the awkwardness and dive into challenging content.

Sheena Nabholz recognizes that "being able to look people in the eye and give the hard honest truth has become an act of compassion. The kindest thing you can do for somebody is tell them the truth." Following an intentional structure during a difficult conversation that includes compassion as you provide direct feedback enables the recipient to recognize an opportunity for growth. A framework for this, based on these interviews, is provided at the end of this chapter.

3. Actively Listen

Katrina Charles points out that the act of listening can often solve a problem on its own. In fact, she has found that people often know the answer to their issues already and that her role can often be to simply "let people have the opportunity to talk, to get it off their chest, and in the end, they realize they've solved their own problem." She believes that it is often just human connection that we are missing and that the key is to be genuinely listening.

Clarissa Sayson employs compassion and empathy to realize that not everything is as it might appear on the surface. Because people make decisions based on their values and beliefs, she explains, learning how to listen to another person in order to understand their perspective is a valuable skill. Rather than focusing on communicating their own thoughts, Clarissa suggests that leaders should consider how they can help the other person work through their own thinking.

When preparing for a difficult meeting, Arden Tyoschin reminds herself that she welcomes the opportunity to consider other ways of thinking. She is open-minded enough to listen to something that might make her think a different way, but she will not compromise her grounded beliefs in education. She enters meeting spaces ready to listen with genuine curiosity, looking for moments of "I never thought of it like that" and taking a new way of thinking away from the conversation.

Lynn Sawyer implements the same strategy. She notes that a best practice is to understand that "the people you're having a confrontation with also have a point of view. It will only help you if you can listen and truly understand their point of view." You need to be able to articulate their concerns back to them, state that it matters to you, and see what you can do to come together to find a solution. As mentioned previously, a framework for this, based on these interviews, is provided for you at the end of this chapter.

Caroline Brokvam also recognizes that active listening, including paraphrasing and mirroring body language, can often de-escalate or even solve a problem. Building up listening skills and compassion is important for female leaders in order to feel better prepared to solve the challenges that come to them in their roles. Caroline recommends coaching training for female leaders even if they do not intend to become a coach, pointing out that "you can't really solve someone else's problems, they have to come to that on their own." The skills that are developed through helping others work through their own thinking can be vital.

4. Slow Down the Conversation

One highly effective strategy that a female leader can implement immediately was described by Kathleen Naglee. She focuses on being a very good listener so she can slow down her reaction to confrontations. When someone is angry, she just repeats back what she is hearing, without implying her judgment. She echoes back, "You're telling me this . . . is this right?" This strategy provides immense relief to the person speaking because they feel that they have been heard.

Once the conversation is slowed down and the concerns of the speaker have been heard and articulated, Kam Chohan identifies that it is almost like a negotiation to get them aligned to where you want to be. She recognizes that "people need the same thing—to be valued, to be listened to. If you can reason and negotiate with them, they will see there's a different view of things." This approach takes time and can often go against our instinct to immediately try to offer solutions but is usually much more effective in the long run.

5. Separate the Person from the Action

Lola Aneke recognizes the importance of separating the behavior from the person. During a conversation, she does not address the person, she addresses the behavior. Nathalie Henderson also uses a similar approach, preferring to take the perspective that "it's not that you're right and I'm wrong. In this situation, these actions were not in the best interest of students."

Dr. Chaunté Garrett approaches a challenging conversation by recognizing that "my job is to serve and protect everyone." Creating clarity around the values of the organization enables a leader to address challenges and misalignment head on. As a result, conversations can focus on creating alignment with what we value.

Nneka Johnson leans into difficult conversations, saying, "We all need to be better. We all need to hold each other accountable for what we do. Difficult conversations don't scare me. People are human; it's just something we have to do. In leadership, you can't shy away from difficult conversations." She spends time building relationships so parents and teachers know she is coming from a place of empathy. Once you learn that any frustration is likely not directed at you personally, you can empathize, sympathize, and listen.

Are You Ready?

Handling confrontation, and leading accountable conversations, can feel so intimidating. But the good news is that they are skills that can be learned, and there are strategies that work in almost any situation.

Strategies and Skills for Handling Difficult Conversations

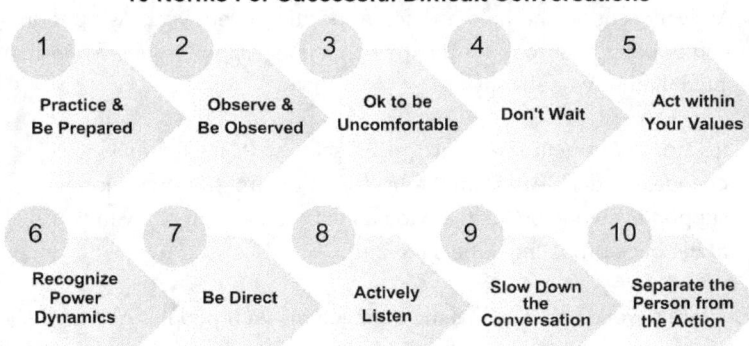

Figure 12.1 Ten Steps to Successful Difficult Conversations. A framework can help women leaders feel confident and focused as they enter difficult conversations with colleagues and followers.

Finding Her Path: Katrina Charles

Name: Katrina Charles
Role: International Baccalaureate Diploma Programme Coordinator
School: American School of Doha
Location: Doha, Qatar

Katrina Charles says she never saw herself as someone to step out to lead a team. Born in Trinidad and Tobago, she started her teacher training there and then moved to the United Kingdom for more formal training as an economics and business teacher. Reflecting back, she notes that she had very strong women in her department molding her during her years in the United Kingdom. The women who started and led the department taught her to always be proud about what you're doing and "if you're going to do something, do it to the best of your ability."

In a male-dominated school with very few women in leadership roles, she learned that if you don't have confidence and believe in yourself and what you're doing, you're not going to make your mark. This experience taught her that "you're a leader in your classroom, then you're a leader among your colleagues." She was trained for a dual role as a pastoral leader and a department leader, and then she took the leap into more senior leadership roles as a director of teaching and learning and later as an associate principal.

At every school, she held a different position every year. As opportunities came along, she took the next step, seizing opportunities when they presented themselves. She says,

> It's not about getting into it for the sake of it. It's for making a change. Leaders lead from the back, not the front. It's your job to support everyone on the team to be the best they can be, with you at the back propelling others forward.

Through this work, she was making connections with people. Although she didn't initially set out to be a school leader, she feels it happened by default because her perspective is that she has a voice and is willing to put herself forward "to represent the underrepresented."

Over time she realized that she was doing a good job and people had confidence in her and that colleagues were coming to see her privately about problems. She points out that that's often how it starts, saying "most of the time people want an ear to listen. They don't want you to solve their problem. They just want to know that somebody cares about what they're saying."

On her path to school leadership, Katrina also highlights the importance of two important member groups of a school community: parents and students. Effecting change for these two groups defines her purpose as a school leader. When students have confidence in what she's saying and doing and parents feel comfortable sharing feedback with her, she recognizes her leadership skills.

Over time, she realized at different schools that she could manage different personalities, and it was a skill that set her apart. When she noticed certain skills that she recognized in herself being identified time and again as leadership skills, she began to believe in herself. She says, "Internally, you believe in yourself, but it's good to get that external validation and trust." Hearing her mentors say, "Yes, you can do this" combined with all of those other experiences helped her gain the confidence that she could be a leader.

Katrina observes that

> as women, we always second-guess ourselves. A position comes up, and we immediately think about what we lack, whereas a man thinks about how great he can be. He is putting himself forward, thinking about what he *does* have. We need to bring the confidence men have; they don't often think to undermine themselves.

Unpacking Her Journey

- Katrina gained invaluable practical experience in a wide variety of leadership roles.
- She recognized a leadership skill in her ability to use her voice to put herself forward to represent the underrepresented.
- She is a very caring person who is a trusted listener and confidant.

Take Action

For Developing Leaders

In order to help you feel as prepared as possible for a difficult or accountable conversation, we encourage you to practice your skills first. This challenge requires you to work with a colleague with whom you feel safe being vulnerable:

Rehearse a difficult conversation. You can think of something that is happening in your context right now or an experience you have had in the past.

If nothing contextual comes to mind, below are three common scenarios that we have experienced that you might choose to rehearse.

After you've practiced, take a few moments to reflect; this can be on your own or with the colleague you rehearsed with:

- What made you feel calm and confident?
- Where did you lose focus?
- What phrases felt natural and easy to use?
- Where were you left at a loss for words?

Extension: Triad Role Play

As an extension of a peer-to-peer partner role play, you might want to try adding a third person. In a triad of trusted colleagues, conduct the role play of a difficult conversation with one colleague acting as an observer.

While the conversation is happening, the observer can act like a "remote control" and pause the role play to discuss choices and options. This gives you an opportunity to think through your choices at each step of the conversation.

Scenarios

To help you prepare for these kinds of potentially challenging interactions, we invite you to explore the following scenarios. You might want to document your thinking here in this book, in a separate document, or in your journal. After reflecting, you might want to review and discuss your ideas with a trusted colleague or mentor:

- A teacher is consistently just slightly bending the rules (coming in just as the bell rings, making negative comments in meetings, being short with other teachers). Nothing is explicitly wrong, but her attitude is impacting the mood of her team.
- Another leader you work with prefers a compliance/management approach rather than a transformative leadership approach. She has asked the instructional coaches to go into classrooms with a checklist of 10–12 things that should be "on display" in classrooms. This is not the vision for instructional coaching in your school. How do you approach the principal?
- An email exchange becomes passive-aggressive. You can either continue the back and forth via email, you can drop it and be mad about it, or you can step away from the computer and have a conversation. What do you do and why?

For Established Leaders

Difficult conversations can be one of the most intimidating parts of being a leader. When we do not have experience seeing them from both sides of the table, they can feel hazy and unclear. As an experienced leader, you might have concrete strategies that work for you and these conversations might no longer intimidate you. To help aspiring leaders be better prepared for the experience, you can

- invite an aspiring leader to sit in on a conversation or offer to reflect with them afterward
- share a story of conflict, including how you handled it and what you learned
- offer to share examples of the types of conflicts you deal with and offer to guide them through the thinking process

For Schools or Organizations

We invite you to consider the way confrontation is managed within your organization. Based on your personal experience, or stories from others,

- Is there some kind of consistency around leadership communication and methods of resolving conflict, or does each leader seem to employ a completely different style?
- Is there a structured conversation protocol for use at every leadership level?
- Have all educators, and in particular leaders, had training in conflict management in difficult conversations?

After reflecting on the current status of how confrontation is handled in your organization, are there opportunities to

- develop standards of practice for difficult conversations at every leadership level?
- provide training for both teachers and leaders on how to navigate conflict and confrontation, potentially including observation and reflection on real conversations?
- develop resources, including sentence stems or conversation structures, that can be used when needed (for anyone within the organization)?
- create a "rehearsal space" to be used for those who need to practice a conversation that might feel challenging for them?

Using structured conversations (e.g., protocols) is one frequently referenced way that leaders can practice and develop the skills necessary for handling difficult conversations with confidence and competence.

Conversation protocols help to logically scaffold difficult conversations in ways that can lead to satisfactory outcomes for all participants.

Navigating difficult conversations is just one of the stressful responsibilities of leadership. Our next chapter will look at how busy leaders prioritize and find focus in such a demanding and ever-changing role.

References

Bassett, M., & Shaw, N. (2017). Building the confidence of first-time middle leaders in New Zealand primary schools. *International Journal of Educational Management, 32*(5), 749–760. https://doi.org/10.1108/IJEM-05-2017-010

Garmston, R., & Wellman, B. (2016). *The adaptive school: A sourcebook for developing collaborative groups*. Rowman & Littlefield.

Grogan, M., & Shakeshaft, C. (2011). *Women in educational leadership*. Jossey-Bass.

Gurr, D., & Drysdale, L. (2013). Middle-level secondary school leaders: Potential, constraints and implications for leadership preparation and development. *Journal of Educational Administration, 51*(1), 55–71. https://doi.org/10.1108/09578231311129143

Irvine, P., & Brundrett, M. (2019). Negotiating the next step: The part that experience plays with middle leaders' development as they move into their new role. *Educational Management Administration & Leadership, 47*(1), 74–90. https://doi.org/10.1177/1741143217720457

Lipscombe, K., Grice, C., Tindall-Ford, S., & DeNobile, J. (2020). Middle leading in Australian schools: Professional standards, positions, and professional development. *School Leadership & Management*. https://doi.org/10.1080/13632434.2020.1731685

McIntosh, E., & Love, C. (2021). Leading from the middle. *Notosh*. https://learn.notosh.com/leadingfromthemiddlewhitepaper

Ronnerman, K., Grootenboer, P., & Edwards-Groves, C. (2017). The practice architectures of middle leading in early childhood education. *International Journal of Child Care and Education Policy, 11*(1), 1–20. https://doi.org/10.1186/s40723-017-0032-z

How Busy Leaders Prioritize and Find Focus

> *I schedule time in my calendar every week to spend time either by myself or with other colleagues (including students, teachers, parents) on tasks that are not urgent but absolutely important and transformational. These conversations have the potential to shift culture, improve learning, and improve our thinking about learning.*
>
> —Arden Tyoschin

Leadership is demanding. Not only are we constantly trying to make progress on our own goals for ourselves and for our organization, but we also have to simultaneously keep in mind the varying needs of the whole community of stakeholders. Balancing those competing priorities can quickly become overwhelming, especially if you don't have a strategy or system to deal with them.

In the WWL interviews, participants were asked how they deal with the many demands of their roles and what strategies they have developed to cope with these demands. This chapter highlights strategies that help these leaders manage their daily tasks and interactions.

Reflections in the Research

Education leadership is a complex endeavor. From avoiding initiative fatigue to dealing with the volatility, uncertainty, complexity, and ambiguity of the world in general and international schools specifically, education leaders need to find the daily workflow that will allow them to be most effective. As educators transition from roles as classroom teachers to school leaders, their daily schedules will look and feel drastically different (McGuire, 2021). Leaders are often tempted to do and be everything. Striking a balance in many areas is a key to being an effective leader. Finding a balance between long-term and short-term goals and the urgent and the important, and setting boundaries between the personal and the professional, are only a few of the areas leaders will address as they establish their productive habits and daily workflow to lead with impact.

Successful leaders decide where their efforts can have the most impact. Circles of concern, influence, and control (see Figure 13.1) are often used

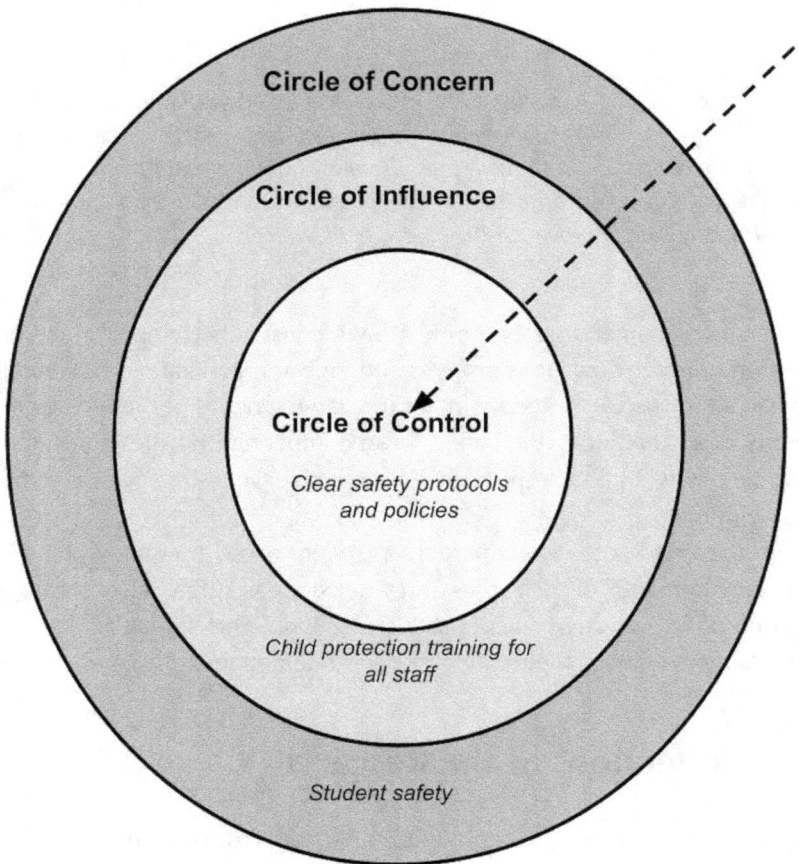

Figure 13.1 Circles of concern, influence, and control help education leaders prioritize tasks and decisions in a proactive manner (adapted from the work of Stephen Covey, 2020).

by busy leaders to guide decision making that will positively impact learning within their schools.

- The **circle of concern** includes issues that cause worry and concern but that we have no direct ability to control.
- The **circle of influence** encompasses the issues that we can realistically impact but maybe not directly.
- The **circle of control** includes actions, decisions, situations, and thoughts within our personal ability to control.

Education leaders can find and maintain focus when they regularly ask themselves two questions:

1. What is within my control in this situation?
2. What small, proactive, or positive action can I take in response?

Many school leaders keep a sharp eye on their school's vision as a constant reminder of what is a priority. By focusing on a shared vision, a leader and her staff can minimize feeling overwhelmed by all of the daily demands of leadership roles that often divert our attention (New Leaders, 2022). A shared vision can also facilitate the sharing and distribution of responsibilities among leaders at all levels in a school community.

The Urgent-Important Matrix (also known as the Eisenhower Matrix and the Covey Matrix) (see our adaptation of this graphic organizer in Chapter 10, Figure 10.1) is a timeless visual tool used by leaders to manage their time (Eisenhower, 1954; Covey, 2020; Andersen et al., 2010; Horn, 2021; Patterson, 2022). School leaders can use this type of simple framework to determine the importance and urgency of tasks in order to make decisions aligned with priorities.

Once priorities are determined, leaders often benefit from focusing on one thing at a time rather than multitasking. Focusing absolute attention on completing one task at a time can help leaders to complete tasks more quickly than restarting and refocusing multiple times. Whether managing calendars and email inboxes or planning and implementing large-scale projects, the real task is for leaders to know their personal work style and to leverage productivity tools and systems that will work best for them and their school community.

Strategies for Finding Focus

Shifting Between Macro and Micro Views

Many of our WWL participants talked about being realistic in terms of managing both large- and small-scale projects. Carla Marschall notes that "it's really important, when you're in a leadership position, not to have a knee-jerk reaction and get distracted by the 'daily fires.'" She advises leaders to "find a mechanism to think at the level of the balcony and level of the dance floor." Of course there's short-term stuff that you need to take care of right away that is just as important as strategic work, Carla explains, but you need to make sure to take incremental steps toward the larger goal on a daily basis as well.

Arden Tyoschin also points out the importance of making time for big-picture tasks. While leading through the COVID crisis, Arden learned to create time in her schedule for the "not urgent, but important." These are blocked-off times, either by herself or with others, that have the potential to result in transformational work, to shift culture, improve learning, and improve thinking about learning. On her school's leadership team, in Arden's description, they're seeing an increased impact because they're focusing on making time for the important but not urgent.

Recognize What's in Your Control

Abeer Shinnawi points out that "you're the one who has the control over what you can accomplish." She recognizes that you don't need to accomplish everything all at once, but you can chip away at tasks based on needs, time, physical or mental energy. Importantly, she has learned not to ruminate over what she could or should have done: "You can't go back and reverse the past; you have to learn from it and apply it to your next project."

Differentiating between what she can control and what's out of her hands has helped Beth Dressler free up "brain space" for other things. She says, "Sometimes the decision is made for you. I have a box in my brain and I just shut the box." In other words, she intentionally lets go of things that are out of her control so they no longer take mental energy.

How Busy Leaders Prioritize and Find Focus

Table 13.1 Weekly Calendar. Experienced women leaders make time to prioritize and plan ahead, including scheduling time for themselves to reflect on and plan for ongoing school-related projects. When looking ahead to the next week on a Friday afternoon, time slots that remain open during the upcoming week can become times for planning, reflection, and well-being.

WEEKLY PRIORITIES:
- Classroom visits with new teachers for informal feedback conversation
- Review professional learning action plan in preparation for full-day faculty inservice next month
- Support internal coordinators to launch self-study surveys and identify goals for standards committees

	Monday	*Tuesday*	*Wednesday*	*Thursday*	*Friday*
6:00	Meeting: Internal Coordinators Focus: Self-Study Surveys and Standards Committee Goals				
7:00					
8:00					Classroom visits
9:00	Classroom visits		Meeting: Senior Leadership		
10:00		Classroom visits		Professional Learning Planning	
11:00			Classroom visits		
12:00					Next Week's Bulletin Submissions Due
1:00		Meeting: Academic Leadership		Classroom visits	Organize Next Week's Bulletin
2:00				Classroom visits	
3:00			Early Release: Faculty Meetings/ Professional Development		• Reflect on this week • Look ahead to next week
4:00	Meeting: Professional Learning Committee				
5:00	Personal: GYM		Personal: GYM		Personal: GYM
6:00	Family: Dinner	Family: Dinner	Family: Dinner	Family: Dinner	Family: Dinner
7:00	Meeting: School Board				

Know Yourself and Schedule Accordingly

Knowing yourself, how you operate, and what you need in order to be productive was another key highlight of the WWL interviews. Carlene Hamley knows that she needs time to process things, so she builds that time into her schedule. Knowing who you are and what you need to get the job done means you can operate efficiently in any situation.

Carlene also points out how important it is to pay attention to your own body and recognize how you're feeling. If you're tired, stressed, and tense all the time, this could be a sign you need to pause and come back to a task or project: "It doesn't mean you failed, it just means you're re-calibrating. You can take a step away and re-energize, which will give you much more renewed energy to what you want to achieve. It's all about knowing who you are, how you react to things, and paying attention to that."

Firoozeh Dumas talks about how she manages her day to be most productive. She (seriously) jokes that she's "smarter in the morning," so she wakes up early and uses her quiet morning time to meditate and plan her day. She also takes this time to explicitly recognize the progress she has made on large projects through incremental, short-term steps. Although every day of her life is different, her number one priority is her child and her family. She says that "all the relationships in our life are like a garden; you have to tend to them." Over time, she has learned that she needs to be kind to herself too. Every day she makes a to-do list, which is often all about taking care of others, and "sometimes I just forget that I need to just be nice to myself." She's learned to make this more of a priority as she's gotten older.

Charlotte Diller also knows that she works best in the morning. A regular practice for Charlotte includes closing each day by noting the three to five items that she will focus on the next day. As a result, she is able to begin each day with a clear focus. When she has control over timing, she sets her meetings for the afternoons so she can be productive in the morning. She delegates tasks to others on her team when she recognizes that they possess a particular skill set better suited to a given task. As she explains it, she understands that she doesn't need to do everything herself, but she does need to support others.

Be Strategic

Katrina Charles believes that in order to make decisions, you have to have a strategic plan. Katrina says she likes to have a "live strategic plan that I can tweak weekly." She plans out her weeks with specific days for specific tasks, like certain days for meetings or for admin tasks. Because disorganization makes being an effective leader so hard, she notes that the need for organization can't be overemphasized.

Being strategic also includes working well with the people on your team. Suzanna Jemsby recommends setting clear expectations with your admin so that you have the time you need to be effective and efficient. As Suzanna walks to school, she sets calls and meetings, and she has a specific day of the week that's blocked out for thinking. Her recommendation is to "hire phenomenal people, become good at delegating, and you do less and less." To help become more efficient in your work, she says you need to figure out what it costs to run a meeting by looking at the salaries of all the people involved. If you have to have that meeting, make sure it's a $6,000 meeting if that's what it costs. Recognizing how much a meeting "costs" could help you think about time in general.

Create a 'To-Be' List, Not a 'To-Do' List

Angela Meiers highlights an important mindset shift that all leaders should make. Most of us, she points out, follow the default mentality of "If I have this, if I do this, then I'm going to be . . ." The problem with this, Angela continues, is that you can follow all of that but everything might still be unsatisfactory.

The option she recommends is thinking about "Who am I seeking to be? Why does my business exist? Who do I want to be for myself, my clients, my community?" When you are very clear on your responses, you can look at your to-do list, and if it does not serve your to-be list, your congruence is going to be off: "If you know who you want to be and you take actions every day to be that, I believe you will have an abundance of clarity, happiness and impact."

Angela observes that leadership is a risk that requires a constant state of self-awareness and reflection. She offers the reminder that "you can feel it in every bone in your body when you're not living your best life, not serving in the way that only you can serve. It's the balance of those two."

Strategies and Skills for Success

Finding Your Personal Process

This chapter has shared some prioritizing tips and approaches that came up during the WWL interviews, but keep in mind that every leader's situation is different, and you shouldn't feel like you need to start adopting all of these ideas right away in order to make progress. Gathering these and other similar examples for inspiration, and testing out different methods, can help you recognize what might work for you, but ultimately, you will find yourself creating your own system for staying focused and productive.

Finding Her Path: Suzanna Jemsby

Name:	Suzanna Jemsby
Role:	Head of School
School:	Washington International School
Location:	Washington, D.C., United States

Suzanna Jemsby says that her journey to leadership started when she was a student herself. She went to a traditional British school with many positions of responsibility for students, including titles like prefect, house captain, and head girl. Along with being captain of sports teams, that was where she realized she enjoyed being able to lead others and that laid the first stone on her path to leadership.

As a very young child, she knew she wanted to be a teacher. Once she became a teacher, she thought she could make a bigger impact from a position of leadership than from the classroom, and in her first teaching position, she sought additional responsibilities. As her career progressed and she moved between schools, she assumed more leadership responsibilities with every new role.

The first time she moved into a formal leadership role, she was encouraged to take on a role as a principal. Even though she didn't feel like the role was right for her, she went for the interview because she liked the head of school. When she got to the interview, she realized she had nothing to lose. She was up against two white men who had previously been principals. She realized that this was an opportunity to be "the most authentic me that I could be," which turned out to be a fit for the environment and the school.

During that interview process, she acknowledges that she was tempted to think about the leadership role rather than who she would be serving, the students. She had to run a morning meeting but didn't know the student body. When she looked out and caught the eye of a young woman in the back row, she realized she did know her, that "she had been at a previous international school with me." Everything became much easier because she could remember that these were students, and she knew the kinds of stories they had. At that moment, they went from being 300 anonymous students to being "Akiko and her friends."

When she runs leadership seminars for aspiring leaders of color, her advice is to be the most authentic person you can be right from the get go. If you can't feel right at home, you won't be happy, and that's no way to be a leader; you have to be able to be you.

Unpacking Her Journey

- Suzanna experienced leadership while still a student herself.
- She recognizes that her strength as a leader comes from being her authentic self.
- She remains focused on the students she serves, rather than the leadership role or title that she holds.

Take Action

For Developing Leaders

To help you bring perspective, and hopefully some space, to your daily life as a leader, we invite you to frame your perspective on priorities, projects, and goals.

Referencing Angela Meiers's practice of creating a to-be list, consider the following prompts:

- Who am I seeking to be?
- Why does my organization exist?
- Who do I want to be for myself, my clients, my community?

Reflecting on these three prompts,

- How can you present your vision of yourself as a leader in your daily actions?
- Where and when can you take action to move closer to becoming the leader you strive to be?
- How can you prioritize choices that move you closer to your goals?

We invite you to take this opportunity to consider daily actions that could move you closer to your to-be list.

Scenario

To bring this concept to life, we invite you to explore the following scenario. You might want to document your thinking here in this book, in a separate document, or in your journal. After reflecting, you might want to review and discuss your ideas with a trusted colleague or mentor.

Taking into consideration Kathleen Naglee's statement "the distraction is the job" (meaning it's essential to prioritize interactions with other humans when you're in a physical space with them), how would you schedule your day as a head of school? Include before and after the school day, as well as what happens during the day.

For Established Leaders

You are already in the very busy role of school leader. We invite you to take this opportunity to reimagine your daily actions, habits, and tasks in accordance with your bigger-picture goals. You might wish to map your thinking on the accompanying graphic (Figure 13.2).

Consider the following processes:

- **Finding Your Practice**: How do you work best? What times of day do you feel most productive? How can you take advantage of your personal rhythm within the constraints of your current work day?
- **Setting Your Goals**: What are some of the urgent daily tasks that you address in your day-to-day life as an educator? What are more long-term, future-focused tasks that you do or could bring to the forefront of your planning?

- **Making it Routine**: How can you pull these two things together to create a workflow routine that will align your personal workplace rhythm with your bigger picture goals and day-to-day tasks?

With all of this in mind, consider how you can bring attention to the future-focused tasks in your daily actions. Reframe your perspective to begin with the end in mind and make a habit of checking in on, and making progress toward, that idea or plan through daily or weekly tasks and reflection. Developing a process of reflective practice in order to revisit your big-picture goals throughout the year in alignment with your daily tasks

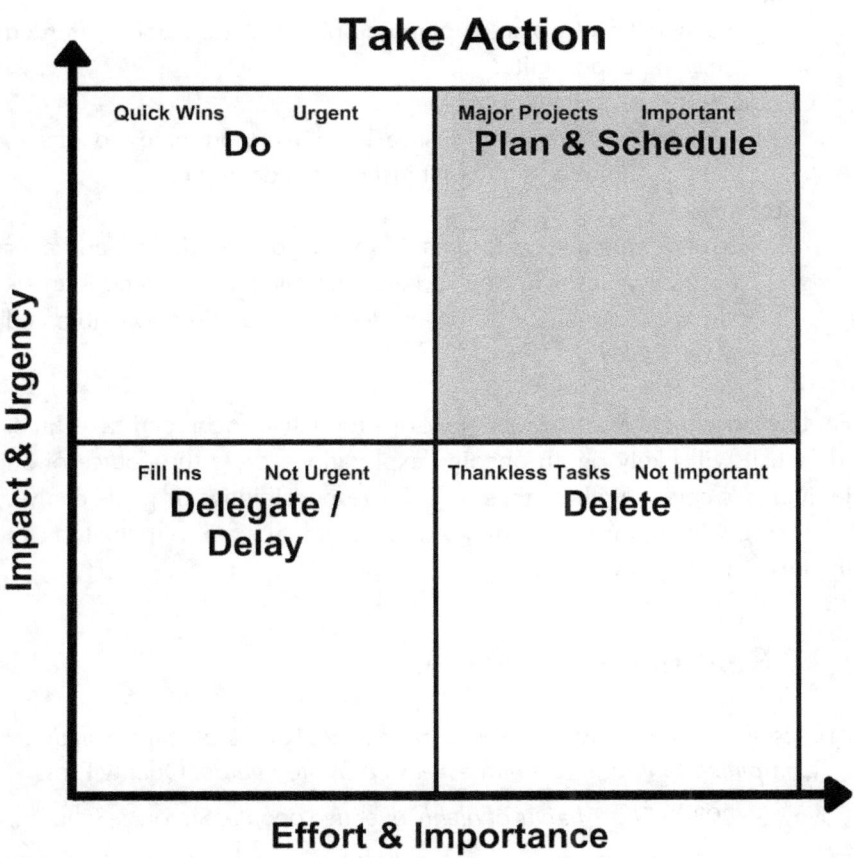

Figure 13.2 The Urgent-Important Matrix in action (adapted from Stephen Covey's visualization of the Eisenhower Principle and the Impact/Effort Matrix by Andersen, Fagerhaug, & Beltz).

will help you make consistent progress as well as adjust and revise your goals as needs change.

For Schools or Organizations

A school or organizational culture can create structures and identify opportunities for leaders to collaborate, organize, and plan.

How does your school/organization incorporate opportunities for leaders to

- Plan?
    Teachers have protected planning periods. Are leaders afforded the same opportunity?
- Collaborate?
    Leadership teams should have regular opportunities to ideate, plan, and think together, not just put out daily fires.
- Reflect?
    Consider organizing leadership retreats before, during, and after a school year for leaders to celebrate, plan, and reflect. Retreats can last for one day or longer, depending on time available and related goals.

Finding an effective process or flow of productive focus can take time. In fact, it will likely be an ongoing exploration across the course of an individual's career, with changes as your responsibilities or goals evolve. It's also very interwoven, in complex and individual ways, with the topic of the next chapter, well-being.

References

Andersen, B., Fagerhaug, T., & Beltz, M. (2010). *Root cause analysis: Simplified tools and techniques: A step-by-step guide*. Quality Press.

Covey, S. (2020). *The 7 habits of highly effective people*. Simon & Schuster.

Eisenhower, D. D. (1954). *Address at the Second Assembly of the World Council of Churches, Evanston, Illinois*. www.presidency.ucsb.edu/documents/address-the-second-assembly-the-world-council-churches-evanston-illinois

Horn, E. (2021, November 15). 10 tips and tools for school leaders. *Technotes*. https://blog.tcea.org/10-tips-tools-school-leaders/

McGuire, D. (2021, January 29). 7 tips to help Aps master time management. *Communicator, 44*(5). www.naesp.org/resource/7-tips-to-help-aps-master-time-management/

New Leaders. (2022, March 8). Six actions to keep moving your school's vision forward [Blog post]. *New Leaders, Inc*. www.newleaders.org/blog/blog-six-actions-to-keep-moving-your-schools-vision-forward

Patterson, C. (2022, January 11). Time to revisit time management for school leaders [Blog post]. *Network for Educator Effectiveness*. https://neeadvantage.com/blog/time-to-revisit-time-management-for-school-leaders/

 Finding a Space of Well-Being in a Busy Leadership Role

Feeding my soul means focusing on my creative side: from writing, to directing, to composing. Every year on my birthday I try something I've never done before . . . last year, I learned to swim. This year, I plan to climb a mountain. A small one!

—Mary Ashun

Finding a space of well-being in a busy leadership role is no easy feat. In addition to the high demands of a leadership position, many women leaders often face the additional prospect of motherhood. In this chapter, we'll explore the strategies shared by the Women Who Lead that they find effective for supporting their own health and well-being along with balancing parenting and a highly demanding leadership role.

Initially, in the WWL interviews, this question included the word "balance." Many women felt that the concept of balance promotes the double standard that only women are expected to perfectly balance all aspects of their lives including family and career, whereas men are, for example, allowed the freedom to just focus on work. Throughout the interviews, the question was adapted slightly to use the phrase "well-being." While the term might come up in some of the answers quoted in what follows, we do recognize the problems with "balance." What we are seeking to prioritize here is a healthy harmony that aligns with each individual's sense of health and well-being.

Because leaders have the potential to influence the well-being of the school community, this chapter focuses on actions you can take to support your well-being independently, essentially actions you can primarily do on your own, while the subsequent chapter identifies actions that you can take that involve others to help create an environment for yourself and your colleagues that supports well-being.

Reflections in the Research

The greatest bias women face might be the one against mothers, the maternal wall bias (Williams, 2021). When women become mothers, they are confronted with assumptions that they are somehow less competent and less committed to their jobs. Even when female leaders who take on motherhood turn out to be competent and committed, they can still face shame and judgment for pursuing aspirations beyond being a devoted mother.

Although men seem to be sharing more responsibilities within their family lives, women still shoulder a significant load due to a variety of assumed personal and professional roles (Klenke, 2018). Female educators might choose to remain in teaching roles because their work calendar (e.g., daily hours, holidays) is more in sync with those of their children, making childcare more manageable. However, the higher demands and expectations placed on school leaders more directly impact their self-care and well-being.

According to a 2022 Rand Corporation study, "Principal and teacher well-being is a matter of immediate concern for principals and teachers themselves and for the students they teach" (Steiner et al., 2020, p. 1). The study also found that learning environments suffer when educator wellness and mental health are deficient (Steiner et al., 2020). Administrator burnout is another threat that accompanies an unhealthy work–life imbalance. Female leaders, who tend to go above and beyond the expectations of their roles and responsibilities to reach their goals, should strive to protect and maintain the passion that brought them to choose education as their life's work. Regularly reminding themselves of their "why" is a frequently recommended practice for school leaders (Kafele, 2020).

Anyone who has traveled on an airplane is familiar with the safety instruction to "secure your own mask first before assisting others." In order to best serve their learning communities, school leaders must prioritize their own well-being. It is vital that leaders model balance and self-care for themselves, their families, and their colleagues. Setting boundaries such as decreasing email use outside of work hours can have a significant impact on well-being (Mahfouz et al., 2022). Wellness programs, exercise classes, mindfulness practice, regular in-person and virtual connections with family

Strategies and Skills for Success

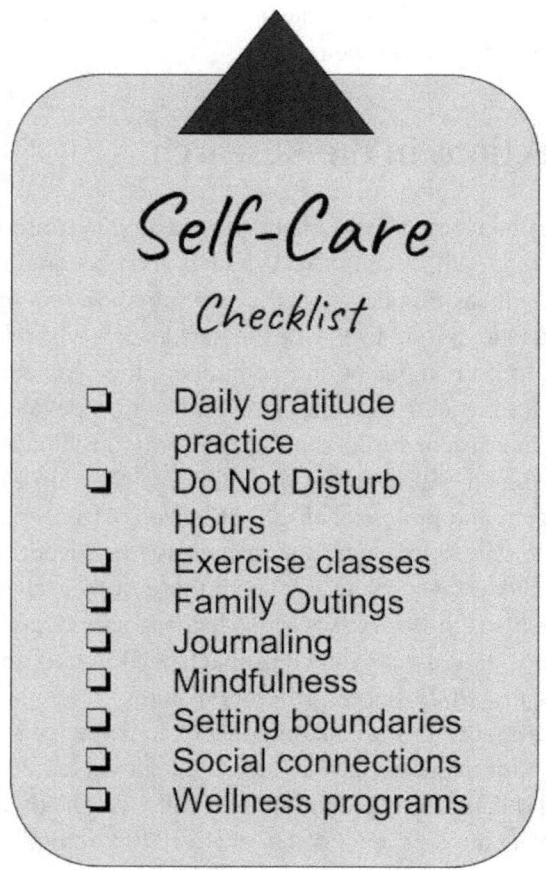

Figure 14.1 Self-Care Checklist. There are many ways that busy school leaders can define and practice self-care.

and friends, and daily journaling and gratitude habits are among the top self-care recommendations from practicing school leaders (Figure 14.1). Engaging with a coach or mentor can also support new practices and learning while reducing feelings of isolation.

Strategies for Well-Being: Making It Work

As many of the Women Who Lead interviewees point out, a leadership position can be all-encompassing. Community expectations can lead school leaders to feel pressure to work around the clock. This can become especially challenging when combined with the responsibilities of family life, and the extra mental burden traditionally placed on women to manage the household. The WWL interviewees highlighted several specific strategies developed throughout their leadership journey.

Love Your Work

Overall, the biggest theme that emerged regarding well-being was that our Women Who Lead truly love their jobs, and because they find so much satisfaction and fulfillment in their work, dedicating time to being a successful leader is worth it.

Arden Tyoschin believes that if "deep down you love the challenge and you love working with people and with students, it doesn't feel so much like it's a burden; it's something you embrace." Her love of creativity allows her to see being faced with a really difficult scenario as an opportunity to go through the creative process, which doesn't feel like a burden.

Similarly, while she does enjoy tai chi and reading in her spare time, one interviewee finds joy in the process of pursuing excellence as a leader: "A leader should be prepared to make some sacrifices, such as sleep, family life, social life and maybe your hobby." She believes that if you put it in the perspective that this is what you chose to do and this is what you enjoy doing, then you will do it well, and you will be able to find further enjoyment in managing it.

Identify Family Time

Beth Dressler shares how she prioritizes her family. She intentionally blocks family time on her calendar on certain mornings, evenings, and Sundays. She notes that these blocks of time become purposeful opportunities to focus on family connection.

Similarly, Clarissa Sayson notes that she tries to make sure to have family dinner time where everyone is present in the moment: "As my children get older, I'm trying to be more conscious of who my children are becoming and being available to them. It's really hard when I'm home and thinking about work, but I know that they're the most important people I need to focus on." Intentional strategies for focusing and prioritizing like these were frequently mentioned as helping several of the WWL interviewees create space for family time together without allowing work to creep in.

Find What Feeds Your Soul

Catriona Moran recognizes that when you become a leader, you have to define what balance means for you. Knowing that school leaders have a huge commitment to their school communities, Catriona offers the following reminder:

> We all need to find what feeds our souls. We're constantly giving to our organizations. We're constantly giving to other people. And they need us. They look to us for compassion, guidance and leadership. The constant giving means we need to replenish our soul.

Catriona does that through singing with a group. She finds that "music is a great equalizer; whatever culture I'm in, it allows me to engage with the local community in a way I would not otherwise be able to do." Every leader needs to find what this replenishing activity is for themselves.

Prioritize Your Health

Kathleen Naglee notes that leaders are in a position that often brings with it continuous high stress and must be careful not to let their health deteriorate. For Kathleen, eating healthy and lifting weights helps protect her from the emotional stress she takes on every day. She also tries to get to bed early every night. "Learning to stop is something we're all learning," she says, describing the collective journey toward less stress.

Sheena Nabholz shared her story of having a recent heart incident that, according to her doctor, was largely due to stress. She notes that she has consequently had to do a lot of learning "about how to take the job a little less seriously, and be a little kinder to myself when I've had enough." She has worked to build tools to manage stress, like walking, meditating, and knowing how to mentally disengage from work.

Know Yourself and Find Your Flow

Several women elaborated on their personal progress toward more balance and on what works for them. Dr. Nneka Johnson has converted her basement into a gym and can sometimes find herself still working out at midnight. She finds training is essential for her well-being. She's able to stay driven and motivated because she's always focused on the outcome and her goals.

Like others mentioned before, Elsa Donohue feels most balanced when she's doing what she loves, which is her work. She knows she needs to make time for movement every day but also that she doesn't have to be perfect every day. Just taking time to do some deep breathing can really help, she explains. As she has grown older, she has realized that balance might not be found in a specific period of time, like in a single day. If she can find a place of happiness and a flow sometime in the week, Elsa shares, that's enough.

Madeleine Heide finds that the "weight of the position" gets in her way and she hasn't found a way around that yet. She continues to find the energy required in her role due to her own self-efficacy: "You believe that you have something to offer. I believe that about myself, therefore I can keep going because I still have something that I want to make a difference."

Bridget Doogan highlights the importance of daily practices like mediation, gratitude, and nutrition. She recognizes that you have to be intentional about self-care so that you can bring your best self to work. She intentionally seeks spaces where she can be calm and creative to build daily practices that include creative productivity. These are not indulgences, she clarifies, but intentional practices designed to enable her to be successful and productive when it's time to work.

Caroline Brokvam has found that she needs time to "switch off" after talking all day. Listening to podcasts allows her to have that mental space without more screen time. Family time also helps her to intentionally not think about work. Whether it's exercise, meditation, or podcasts, it's clear that everyone should work toward finding their own individual mix of solutions in order to find a space of well-being.

Advocate for a Personal Life

Anita Chen shared her story of moving to Finland, away from her family, when her daughter was very young. She pointed out that Finnish society places a high priority on families, so she had very generous childcare leave. However, even with all of the support, she still felt like she was failing because she was struggling to juggle home and work, which had an impact on her mental well-being. This experience taught her the importance of being able to look after yourself and family before attending to school issues, which became one of her criteria when she began looking for her next job.

One interviewee noted that once you're in a leadership position, having a family can actually make it easier to draw distinctions between work and personal life. Katie Koenig explains that it's challenging to be a leader, no matter your gender. She points out that "it's hard to be a young single woman, because there's a lot of hustle in leadership, and it's really easy to say, 'I have to go home to my family,' and I don't get to say that. Having a life outside of that takes a lot of advocacy." Whatever their family situation, the reality is that leaders need to find ways to place effective boundaries between work and home life, and express them to others.

Take a Break

Many of our Women Who Lead also noted the importance of taking time to rest. Liz Kleinrock referenced Audre Lourde in recommending the importance of breaks: "The act of self-care is an act of rebellion. White supremacy wants you to be exhausted, burnt out and disorganized. If there's a day you need to stay offline, take it. Making sure you have people who are going to have your back and bring joy into your life, being mindful of who and what is giving from you and who and what is taking from you." Whether it's an extended length of time or just a few minutes in the day, intentionally taking time to give yourself a mental and/or physical rest is essential.

No One Size Fits All

There's no one way to find a space of well-being in a leadership role. Although, as so many of the Women Who Lead have said, when you love your job it doesn't feel like work, there are plenty of strategies you can apply to give yourself mental and physical space to do things outside of education (Table 14.1).

Table 14.1 Prioritizing Personal Well-Being. Busy women leaders can prioritize their well-being and set boundaries by identifying times as they plan for the upcoming week.

WEEKLY PRIORITIES:
• Classroom visits with new teachers for informal feedback conversation
• Review professional learning action plan in preparation for full-day faculty inservice next month
• Support internal coordinators to launch self-study surveys and identify goals for standards committees

	Monday	*Tuesday*	*Wednesday*	*Thursday*	*Friday*
6:00	• 10 minutes: Mindfulness practice • Review messages, email, and daily calendar	• 10 minutes: Mindfulness practice • Review messages, email, and daily calendar	• 10 minutes: Mindfulness practice • Review messages, email, and daily calendar	• 10 minutes: Mindfulness practice • Review messages, email, and daily calendar	• 10 minutes: Mindfulness practice • Review messages, email, and daily calendar
7:00	Meeting: Internal Coordinators Focus: Self-Study Surveys and Standards Committee Goals	Open Office Hour	Open Office Hour	Open Office Hour	Open Office Hour
8:00					Classroom visits
9:00	Classroom visits		Meeting: Senior Leadership		
10:00		Classroom visits		Professional Learning Planning	
11:00			Classroom visits		
12:00	Lunch:		Lunch: Grade 12 Class Representatives		Next Week's Bulletin Submissions Due
1:00		Meeting: Academic Leadership		Classroom visits	Organize Next Week's Bulletin
2:00				Classroom visits	
3:00	Open Office Hour	Open Office Hour	Early Release: Faculty Meetings/ Professional Development	Open Office Hour	• Reflect on this week • Look ahead to next week
4:00	Meeting: Professional Learning Committee	Open Office Hour			
5:00	Personal: GYM		Personal: GYM		Personal: GYM
6:00	Family: Dinner	Family: Dinner	Family: Dinner	Family: Dinner	Family: Dinner
7:00	Meeting: School Board	Family: Evening walk	Family: Evening walk	Family: Evening walk	Family: Evening walk
8:00					
9:00	Evening Do Not Disturb Settings Begin Until 6:30 a.m. (where possible)				

Finding Her Path: Dr. Mary Ashun

Name: Dr. Mary Ashun
Role: Principal
School: Ghana International School
Location: Accra, Ghana

Dr. Mary Ashun knew from a very early age that "it was in me to be a bit bossy and tell others what to do." As a child, she set up her own school when she was six years old. Dr. Ashun spent her childhood in both Ghana and the United Kingdom and eventually earned her PhD in biochemistry at the State University of New York at Buffalo. Her intent was to work in the field of biochemical research in part because she loved the investigative and inquiry process. When she was required to do community service in her fourth year of graduate school, she chose to teach science at a local private independent school due to what she refers to as "a great mix," her love of science and kids.

That's when she first thought she could be a teacher, but she was worried about supporting her family. She and her husband, a marine engineer, took out a map and asked themselves, "Where shall we live?" At that time, they decided to move to Canada, where they found a beautiful mix of England and the United States. She speaks passionately about her first experience as a high school teacher in Canada. This led her to commit to the teaching profession and earn a bachelor's of education, where her greatest takeaway was the belief that all children can learn and that they all learn in different ways. She taught at a variety of schools and then became a professor in order to multiply her impact by instructing teacher candidates to be great teachers. Her desire to work with kids again, coupled with her principal's certification, took her back to K–12 education as a school leader. Eventually a recruiter reached out to her to come to Ghana.

In her career teaching primary and secondary school, she was often the only teacher with a PhD and the only Black teacher. With every step in her career, elements of leadership have appeared to guide her journey, even in her very first year as a teacher. In that role, her principal often reached out to her for feedback because she had a strong academic preparation in her PhD program, she was a visible minority, and she was one of the youngest teachers. She didn't see this as leadership at the time; it was only when she began to be assigned to committees in her second school that she began to recognize that with her experiences, knowledge, and perspectives, she was a leader.

> **Unpacking Her Journey**
>
> - Mary's advanced degree and specialty set her apart as someone with a depth of knowledge that others sought to learn from.
> - She cares deeply about kids and recognizes that every student can learn in their own way.

 ## Take Action

For Developing Leaders

To help you prepare for the increasing demands of a leadership position, we invite you to think about how you might create space for well-being in your life.

Think of something that truly brings you joy (it could be outside of work) that you know will be non-negotiable when you step up into a leadership position. How will you ensure that you are making space and time for this activity, even when your days get so much fuller?

Scenarios

To help you reflect on your own space of well-being, we invite you to explore the following scenarios. You might want to document your thinking here in this book, in a separate document, or in your journal. After reflecting, you might want to review and discuss your ideas with a trusted colleague or mentor:

- Keeping in mind Sheena Nabholz's story about needing to reprioritize after a health problem, if you had a severe health incident during your tenure as a school leader, how would you be vulnerable with your staff to communicate your need to "slow down"?
- The school's board has been very explicit about adding a STEAM program. While you believe in this, you know that your math, design, and science departments are already over-committed. What are you going to do?

For Established Leaders

We invite you to take this opportunity to reflect on how you're creating space for well-being in your busy role. Reflect on your career journey. When you think back to before your tenure as a leader, were there activities that brought you joy, fulfillment and a sense of well-being (outside of school)? Are you still participating in these activities? If so, how do you make it work? If not, we invite you to consider ways to bring at least an element of these activities back into your life.

For Schools or Organizations

Instead of encouraging educators to practice self-care, minimizing workload is a real-time way schools can support employee well-being. Consider the complex nature of educator responsibilities and expectations and reflect on opportunities to de-implement (DeWitt, 2022):

- In your school or organization, where are there opportunities to remove ineffective practices?
    - Consider informal processes (e.g., reducing emails, meetings) and formal processes (e.g., shifting traditional grading practices to standards-based grading).
- How might a thoughtful process of de-implementation impact your school's culture? How might it impact student learning?

There has been an increased effort on the part of many organizations to take educator well-being into consideration in recent years, but there is still much work to be done. One surprisingly impactful way that individual leaders can make a difference is simply by setting an example of self-care and balanced priorities in the area of well-being, which is the focus of our next chapter.

References

DeWitt, P. (2022). *De-implementation: Creating the space to focus on what works*. Corwin Press, Inc.

Kafele, B. (2020, December 1). The mental balancing act for school leaders. *ASCD, 78*(4). www.ascd.org/el/articles/the-mental-balancing-act-for-school-leaders

Klenke, K. (2018). *Women in leadership: Contextual dynamics and boundaries* (2nd ed.). Emerald Publishing.

Mahfouz, J., King, K., & Yahya, D. (2022, September 6). Five ways to support the well-being of school leaders. *Greater Good Magazine.* https://greatergood.berkeley.edu/article/item/five_ways_to_support_the_well_being_of_school_leaders

Steiner, E., Doan, S., Woo, A., Gittens, A., Lawrence, R., Berdie, L., Wolfe, R., Greer, L., & Schwartz, H. (2020). *Restoring teacher and principal well-being is an essential step for rebuilding schools: Findings from the state of the American teacher and state of the American principal surveys* [Report]. Rand Corporation. www.rand.org/pubs/research_reports/RRA1108-4.html

Williams, J. (2021). *Bias interrupted: Creating inclusion for real and for good*. Harvard Business Review Press.

 Shaping a Culture of Well-Being and Leading by Example

As a leader, I realized the profound impact managing my own time and stress had on my team. My leadership team needed me to say that I wasn't taking on any new tasks after a long period of intense work, to make it OK for them to put themselves first for a while.

—Sheena Nabholz

We know how hard it is to find a space of well-being for ourselves as individuals. As leaders, not only do we have the challenge of managing time and priorities to find space for well-being, in a position that never truly stops, but we also have the responsibility to model strategies for well-being for others.

In the previous chapter, we explored the ways that the Women Who Lead have built strategies for refreshing, nourishing, and recharging independently. In this chapter, we'll focus on the ways that they are intentional in designing their days, their communication, and their work routines to ensure that there is time for, and clarity around, the ways that they find a sense of balance.

This chapter's title includes the phrase "leading by example" because the strategies here might be helpful not only for you as an individual leader but to also pass on and discuss in your organization with others. Everyone in your organization deserves to find space for well-being. Sharing and encouraging the practices described here could help others uncover new approaches as well.

While each of these practices is designed with the individual in mind, if you scale them up to an organizational level so that each member has the opportunity to prioritize, set routines and boundaries, and be intentional with their time, you'll be working toward creating an organization that puts wellness at the center instead of an expectation that "just happens" outside of work.

Reflections in the Research

Well-being is a familiar term among educators around the world and is defined as "the state of being happy, healthy, or prosperous" (Merriam-Webster, n.d.). The World Health Organization (2021) expands the definition of well-being to "encompass quality of life, as well as the ability of people and societies to contribute to the world in accordance with a sense of meaning and purpose" (p. 10). While the well-being of school leaders is critical, that of the teachers they lead is of equal importance when considering the overall health and wellness of a school community. Developing and maintaining a healthy work–life balance can help school leaders to center relationship-focused interactions rather than being problem focused or reactionary (Mahfouz et al., 2022). A leadership team that practices and models a healthy work–life balance is a key component to nurturing a culture of well-being where the community possesses a proactive style ready to effectively meet challenges that arise (Darling-Hammond & Cook-Harvey, 2018). When learning environments are more personalized, the wider community benefits, teachers experience a greater sense of efficacy, and parents feel welcome in the school community. When school leaders plan for and implement personalizing structures, student achievement and well-being improve (Darling-Hammond & Cook-Harvey, 2018).

McKinsey and Company's *Women in the Workplace 2022* report reveals that women leaders are the linchpins creating and demanding supportive and inclusive workplaces that the younger generation of women want and expect. The study also highlights that a significant majority of women under 30 "would be more interested in advancing if they saw senior leaders with the work–life balance they want" (McKinsey & Company, 2022, p. 16). Women leaders are striving to enhance the work culture, even in places where it's not yet well established.

While the culture of work often values being "busy" and experiencing "burnout," it should not be viewed as a badge of honor for school leaders. Prioritizing personal well-being is key for leaders to be able to effectively support a "system aimed at promoting a healthy school climate and student well-being" (Mahfouz et al., 2022, para. 21). As responsible individuals overseeing the success and well-being of all who enter the building, whether children or adults, school leaders must take care of themselves in order to fulfill their commitment to learning (Ball, 2023).

Demonstrating Positive Approaches to Well-Being

Leaders have the strongest influence in shaping school cultures and systems and have the potential to build sustainable school cultures where educators feel valued and supported within their professional roles and beyond. Through leading by example, leaders demonstrate that they value well-being—for themselves and others. This chapter offers six strategies to consider when building a school culture with wellness in mind.

Be a Role Model for Others

Dr. Chaunté Garrett recognizes the importance of being a role model in the area of getting rest, explaining that "if others can see me stop and rest and enjoy something, those opportunities also give them permission." During the pandemic, she realized she needed to be able to communicate to others that she had, for example, gone for a walk or had gone out for brunch. Being able to communicate self-care gives others permission to engage in similar practices that support their well-being.

As shared in Chapter 14, Sheena Nabholz has learned how to be kinder to herself, build tools to manage stress, and mentally disengage from work, after a recent heart incident largely due to stress, and the space she's created for herself has also cascaded down to her staff. She found that her colleagues also needed her to state her boundaries and priorities to make it OK for them to put themselves first. When she was able to share her story about the importance of taking care of her own health, her staff realized that they could do the same. She says, "They needed me to say that I wasn't taking on any new tasks to make it OK for them to put themselves first." Being a role model for self-care is a huge aspect of being a leader and building a culture of sustainability in your organization. Being able to be vulnerable, sharing the need to intentionally take space and time for your own health, sets the standard for the entire school community.

Be Intentional

Dr. Mary Ashun notes that making time for well-being must be intentional. When she started as a school leader, she had no balance, and she really struggled. Once she became intentional and set a timetable and communicated it, she was able to plan for self-care and creativity. Dr. Ashun is a writer (she's written 13 books, four plays, and lyrics for music), and every year she sets a goal to do something she's never done—on her next birthday she's climbing a mountain. She now plans for creativity time every week and makes it part of her routine.

Nathalie Henderson firmly believes in "me time." She recognizes that she needs frequent breaks, and she knows herself well enough to take them when she needs them. She finds energy in her other passions, having started two separate businesses (travel and leadership consulting). As with many of our Women Who Lead, Nathalie says, "It's not work to me because I enjoy it." Leaders shouldn't "shy away from help; take your me time, and don't do things you don't want to do because society says that you should do it," as she refreshingly explains her position on setting boundaries and following your instincts about where you should put your energy.

Prioritize

Bridget McNamer views productivity in two ways. From one perspective, "You need to prioritize because it's simply not possible to be all things to all people." From the second perspective, she recommends that you "promote yourself to key stakeholders. You need to think about yourself objectively; keep yourself in mind as you're planning. If you don't have a fuel tank that's full on your end, you're not going to be able to deliver for others."

Lola Aneke reminds herself that her productivity doesn't define her. Even if she doesn't finish what she expects, it's OK. To find this space of mental well-being about productivity, she believes in the power of the mind–body connection: "When you send negative energy or emotions, your body tells you you can't. When you tell yourself to take it easy, you can manage it." She recognizes that there are days when she's just not going to be as productive, and she uses self-talk to remind herself that she will catch up the next day.

Set Boundaries

Katrina Charles has recognized the importance of setting boundaries: "As leaders, we need to be very aware of what we do to set boundaries, so we model those boundaries. We set the tone for how we work. If the leader works around the clock, it sets the tone for everyone else." Once you set boundaries, others will respect them.

She highlights that "setting boundaries based on priorities is a difficult thing when everything appears to be a priority." The first step is to develop a relationship with your line manager to be very clear about exactly what needs to be done first so you can prioritize. Ultimately, you need to know what your limits are so that you can say no when needed.

Suzanna Jemsby sets very clear boundaries between work and home. Even in a high-stakes school in a high-stakes city, she has committed to herself that she will not burn out. She sets clear boundaries and communicates them to the team, and then she is disciplined about holding to them. Suzanna says, "Surround yourself with excellence, and you can do anything." She notes the importance of not personally taking the emotional burden for the whole school onto yourself.

Set Routines

Beth Dressler sets specific routines and priorities to find a space for mental well-being. For instance, she intentionally blocks out family time; at school, she blocks time in her calendar to be visible by visiting classrooms; and for herself, she blocks time to exercise. The combination of all of these routines allows her to find a groove for most of the year. At some times of the year, "It will be a sprint, and things might get out of whack," but, she explains, "You can find your groove again when you shift back down into marathon mode," into a less-frantic, long-distance pace.

Over the years, Carlene Hamley has learned that she needs exercise and sport to find a sense of balance. She needs to find that gap in the day where she can "get the endorphins going" and have quiet time in her brain so she can process. This time for physical movement also provides space for mental well-being. She also finds that having a goal helps her stay focused and purposeful in all the decisions that she makes.

Creating a Culture of Well-Being

Although the goals of the organization are always going to influence priorities for all members of staff, by thinking intentionally and critically about the importance of wellness, and the practices that can help empower others to seek a space of health and balance, we can begin to build a culture of well-being. Being a role model in your leadership position, and valuing the effort it can take to set priorities and respect boundaries, is a powerful first step in shifting things from a mindset that prioritizes work above all else to enabling everyone to bring their best self to work.

Finding Her Path: Nadine Richards

Name: Nadine Richards
Role: High School Principal
School: American School of Dubai
Location: Dubai, United Arab Emirates

Nadine Richards describes her path to school leadership as having happened differently than for most leaders. She started her career in criminal justice, wanting to advocate for those who didn't have a voice. She thought she was going to fulfill that mission as a lawyer.

While working in the District Attorney's office, she realized she wanted to make a difference in children's lives before they got into the justice system. She began working in the board of education's legal department, advocating for students with special needs. These opportunities gave her access to a lot of different perspectives and made her interested in having a more hands-on role in impacting children's lives, which led her to become a teacher.

As a teacher, she was always looking for opportunities to expand various dispositions in her students, including global citizenship, communication, and interpersonal skills. She noticed that her students saw themselves through her; they felt seen, valued, and heard. She took advantage of any opportunity to have a hands-on approach and volunteered to be class advisor and chaired several committees. Nadine credits her superintendent at the time, Dr. Weiss, for "giving me that little nudge and push" into leadership: "Dr. Weiss saw things I didn't even recognize in myself" that helped her to see her own leadership potential. Although her first official role after completing her leadership certification was as dean of students, she sees now that she was a leader long before applying for that position.

She realized she had the capacity to lead when she was in the classroom as a social studies teacher. She says,

> Female students in my classroom saw me as more than a teacher, they saw me as someone they could look up to. They valued what I said. They sought me out for advice and counseling. Some of those students are Facebook friends now, and they're thirty to thirty-five years old. They're doctors, lawyers, entrepreneurs, and parents. I am shocked every time I see or hear from them because they're just extraordinary. They taught me the importance of community and seeing the whole child, not just focusing on remembering content. I had fun with them. That's when I realized I was a leader, and even more so now when I see them become adults, parents, and professionals.

She truly believed in and embraced her leadership when she was an assistant principal. At the time, she was working with a university as a mentor to aspiring administrators, which is when she realized that this was something that was part of her calling and something she enjoyed doing. She notes that every one of the people she's had the opportunity to mentor have gone on to leadership positions. Only one chose not to go into admin, but the skills she learned allowed her to be a better leader in the job she was already in.

While in the United States, she continued her path to school leadership in roles as assistant principal and deputy principal before moving to Dubai. Again, it was a woman, former superintendent P'Simer, who demonstrated to her how one can lead strategically with empathy and compassion. This stayed with her. She began her international career as deputy superintendent and then as head of school in an American curriculum school with many Arab expats. She says she "welcomed the challenge [of moving overseas]. It didn't matter that I was in education for seventeen to eighteen years at that point. I learned more about education (operational and instructional leadership) than I had ten years before." Her experience led her to "rethink learning, the importance of social-emotional connections, and how they impact how we learn more than content."

While in Dubai, she developed her own consultancy focused on helping schools improve their leadership and teaching. As a consultant, she worked with a school that is part of the GEMS Education group, supporting them to earn accreditation with the New England Association of Schools and Colleges. Her final role as a school leader in Dubai was high school principal at the American School of Dubai prior to returning to the United States.

For Nadine, leadership has never been about titles. Leadership, to her, is about how she can make a difference; how she can empower people, learn more, and grow.

Unpacking Her Journey

- Nadine's passion to advocate for children defined her pathway as a school leader.
- Her focus on consulting and supporting school improvement leads to measurable results.

Take Action

For Developing Leaders

To be prepared for the increasing demands on your time as you move forward in your leadership journey, we invite you to reflect on your current role and consider how you might be able to bring an intentional focus to your professional life today.

Identify specific practices that resonated with you in this chapter that promote well-being that you can bring into your daily habits. Select at least one that you can try in the next few days. How can this small change have a positive impact on your daily life and the lives of others on your team?

After a few weeks of implementing this practice, take a moment to reflect on the outcome of this change. You might wish to share this opportunity to embrace a wellness practice with another aspiring leader in your school community for support and encouragement.

Strategies and Skills for Success

Scenario

To consider your impact as a leader on the culture of well-being in schools, we invite you to explore the following scenario. You might want to document your thinking here in this book, in a separate document, or in your journal. After reflecting, you might want to review and discuss your ideas with a trusted colleague or mentor.

Your team is stretched thin. Meetings are rushed, and team members are sensitive to every interaction. You can tell that many are close to the breaking point. How do you address this shared sense of overwhelm and bring attention to the fact that you are aware of stress levels? What potential practices can you bring to your team to help create a sense of well-being? How might you implement them?

For Established Leaders

As we saw in the stories from the Women Who Lead, shaping a culture of well-being requires self-reflection and intentional practice. To get a better understanding of where your school community is at right now, we invite you to conduct a "well-being check" (Figure 15.1). Consider this an opportunity to "take a pulse" of your school community to better understand the demands that are being put on them and how they are responding and coping with the level of workload they face.

For Schools or Organizations

Examine the ways in which your school's processes, structures, and systems encourage or discourage well-being. This could many aspects of the school's operation, and include items like

- increasing the variety of food options available on campus
- decreasing the lengths of required department meetings
- including activities like meditation or quiet time during in-school prep days
- increasing flexibility around leave requests
- decreasing demands on leaders on a daily basis

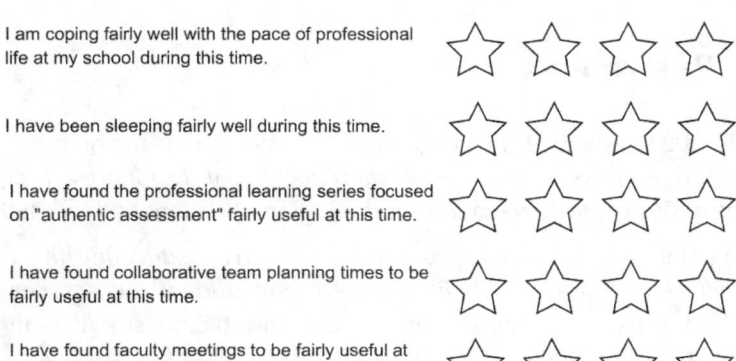

Figure 15.1 Checking in on Well-Being. Shaping a culture of well-being can include regular well-being surveys that teachers can complete anonymously. The data that emerges can help to inform school leaders about how their teachers are doing and where they might need additional support.

Perhaps start with a survey; an honest look at educators' well-being in your school (including leaders) would almost inevitably improve both teaching and learning in countless ways!

Of course, lasting and sustainable organizational change can be incredibly difficult without widespread cooperation, whether the focus is on well-being or the broader topics of equality and support for women leaders that this book has focused on. Women in education can't do it all on their own; they need the support of champions, mentors, and other allies as they work toward change. The next chapter briefly outlines some suggestions for sharing with school leaders so that they recognize what they need to do and understand some strategies for how to begin doing it.

References

Ball, T. (2023, January 24). Navigating new waters: Focusing on principals' health and well-being. *Regional Educational Laboratory Program.* https://ies.ed.gov/ncee/rel/Products/Region/midatlantic/Blog/106973

Darling-Hammond, L., & Cook-Harvey, C. (2018). *Educating the whole child: Improving school climate to support student success.* Learning Policy Institute. https://learningpolicyinstitute.org/sites/default/files/product-files/Educating_Whole_Child_REPORT.pdf

Mahfouz, J., King, K., & Yahya, D. (2022, September 6). Five ways to support the well-being of school leaders. *Greater Good Magazine.* https://greatergood.berkeley.edu/article/item/five_ways_to_support_the_well-being_of_school_leaders

McKinsey & Company. (2022). Women in the workplace 2022 [Special report]. *McKinsey & Company.* www.mckinsey.com/featured-insights/diversity-and-inclusion/women-in-the-workplace#/

Merriam-Webster. (n.d.). Well-being. *Merriam-Webster.com.* www.merriam-webster.com/dictionary/well-being

World Health Organization (WHO). (2021). Health promotion glossary of terms 2021. *World Health Organization.* www.who.int/publications/i/item/9789240038349

16 Next Steps
Moving Toward Whole-School Change

Even in my journey, I have had the experience of being excluded. I am now intentional about aligning myself with allies who are doing the work to confront these exclusionary practices, so that large, influential organizations can recognize the changes that need to be made.
—Dominique Blue

Now that you have explored the stories of our Women Who Lead throughout this book, and you have hopefully taken the opportunity to reflect and take action with each chapter, we hope you are feeling more prepared in your leadership journey. Regardless of your current position, we know from the research and the stories in this book that women leaders in schools need more support. Now that you know some of the experiences of real women leaders and understand how cultures, histories, and systems shape the pathways to leadership, we encourage you to apply everything you've learned to create and demand a more equitable experience for yourself and all women who lead.

As you go through this process and consider the action steps outlined in this chapter, we hope that you will start a conversation to share these strategies with all of the leaders in your school community, including men who lead. In the international school context, where women hold only around a quarter of the head-of-school positions (Diversity Collaborative, 2021), men who lead are key partners in effecting change. With this in mind, the strategies shared here are geared toward current school leaders, including men, who want to take steps toward developing more inclusive environments for women leaders.

DOI: 10.4324/9781003426110-19

Strategies and Skills for Success

The following strategies are designed to be shared with current school leaders who want to do something to help. However, the ideas apply to anyone and everyone; we all need to examine our personal beliefs and shift our perspectives as we work to create more equitable and inclusive school communities, and this chapter offers the opportunity to reflect on our established behavior patterns so that we can do so.

Reflections in the Research

Attending a workshop, taking a course, or reading a book is often only an early stage of a learning process. The real challenge is incorporating new learning into our daily workflow rather than just filing the resources away in a drawer or a digital folder. Learning only truly transforms us when it changes our perspectives and leads to action. Now is the time to take action.

To put new learning into practice and build it into our workflow, it's essential to create a simple action plan that will lead to implementing the learnings that have resonated with you throughout this book. If you have been documenting your thoughts and noted interesting perspectives in a notebook or journal, you might start by reviewing ideas and prioritizing your actions.

McKinsey and Company (Christensen et al., 2021) recommend a simple 3 × 3 × 3 approach to setting clear and achievable development goals: three goals, three months, and three people (Table 16.1). Focusing on no more than three development goals at any given time can allow for the necessary level of intentionality as you incorporate new practices. Identifying

Table 16.1 A 3 × 3 × 3 Goal-Setting Template. Focusing on three short-term goals over a three-month period that includes three supportive individuals can lead to the successful development and integration of new skills and habits.

	WHAT are three short-term developmental goals I will achieve?	WHEN will check-ins occur/goal be accomplished?	WHO will provide support and monitor progress?
1			
2			
3			

interconnected goals can help to broaden and reinforce the skills and competencies you're trying to develop. Setting a three-month time frame creates a natural checkpoint as you work toward achieving longer-term goals; three months requires greater specificity while following the natural quarterly rhythms of a school year. Finally, involve three other people to support your development to serve as accountability partners, resources, mentors, and cheerleaders to celebrate and reinforce your efforts.

There are many formulas and templates available to support and document goal setting and action planning. Using a SMART goal formula can help set specific parameters for each action. Goals that are set to be specific, measurable, achievable, relevant, and time-bound are more attainable and more likely to be met. A simple table layout or spreadsheet can provide a framework for organizing the details of each action that will be taken (Table 16.2). Consider what activities will support reaching an overarching goal. Identify success criteria for each activity and set a reasonable deadline for completion. Documenting your progress can provide evidence of your growth, which can be motivational for your process.

You valued your personal development as a woman leader, and/or the development of other women, which likely led you to purchase this book. Hopefully you now feel the need to take action and make progress more urgently. So now what? How can you bring this work to your school/organization? Once again, we turn to the WWL participants. Throughout the course of their interviews, the participants highlighted specific strategies over and over again. Here we have woven them together to outline a six-step process. The strategies discussed in what follows were specifically formulated to guide current school leaders; if you're not currently in a formal leadership position, consider ways of sharing them with women leaders you know.

Table 16.2 Action Plan Template. A basic action planning table template that can guide the process of applying new learning.

Activity	Responsible	Completion date	Resources required	Indicators of success	Status Complete✓

What Can School Leaders Do to Help?

1. Don't Center Yourself

This is not about how you feel, or what you need, or what you want to do. It's about listening, providing space for others, and doing the work internally to shift your own mindset and deal with your internal biases. If you are not a person of color, you can promote equity in ways that do not center your personal perspective, or through the actions you take, rather than raising your own voice.

2. Amplify the Voices of Others

As an individual, you can start by amplifying the voices of those from underrepresented groups, who too often go unheard. Create space for others who might not have a forum to speak out or an established audience to listen to them. Maybe this is giving space in your leader's newsletter to someone who doesn't normally get an audience, featuring work in a staff meeting, or providing an opportunity for community stakeholders to hear an alternate perspective.

3. Speak Out

When you hear racist or sexist comments or witness biased behavior, speak out. This is especially essential for men in leadership. Among groups of men, during hiring practices, in meetings, whenever you see this behavior, call it out and clarify that it's wrong. When men criticize racist and sexist behavior around other men, it makes a bigger impact than you might imagine. When women share their experiences with you, listen to them and give credence to their experiences. Find ways to help women be heard at levels where any necessary action can be taken. Rationally state, again and again, what needs to change to create a more equitable environment.

4. Encourage Aspiring Leaders

If there are women you see as potential leaders, give them a metaphorical "tap on the shoulder" to encourage them to take on informal and formal leadership. The WWL stories shared in this book reveal that this is how many were encouraged to start on their own pathway to leadership. Naming and sharing leadership traits that you observe in others can be an epiphany for them, especially for women. When you take the time to notice, identify, and articulate these traits, you are helping women build the confidence they need to take their next step.

5. Do the Work

Make it a priority to do equity work. You can start by learning on your own to build your capacity for doing this work with others. Assemble committees with diverse membership to create policies that inform and promote anti-biased and antiracist practices. As an established school leader, you can provide opportunities for professional learning for staff and the extended school community. You can recruit your board and parent community to do the work, too. You might want to hire an expert in this area to facilitate conversations, or you might have members of staff who can lead this work. Making learning and growth a priority includes protecting time and providing access for all.

6. Put Policies in Place

As you build your understanding and school-wide capacity, ensure that policies support practices to reduce unconscious bias in hiring (for example, accepting blind CVs without photos). Make it a point to hire people from a wider variety of backgrounds. When you look at your school's website, or that of a new school you are considering, note the visual impact of the images of the leadership team. If the images include only white men, let that lead to a deeper conversation about the unconscious bias informing hiring practices. Overall, normalize seeing women, people of color, non-native speakers of English, and LGBTQ+ people in leadership positions. Give them a seat at the table.

Take Your Next Step Forward

While this list is far from exhaustive, these are solutions that were raised time and again during the WWL interviews. These are actions that many schools and school leaders still need to embrace. If you are a school leader, it is likely that you have someone on your staff right now who has concrete ideas about how your school can take on more equitable practices. Engage with these members of your school community and take the right first step for your organization. If you need a community to reach out to, connect with our Women Who Lead. They have all had to confront these challenges to get to where they are.

Find more ways to connect with us, the Women Who Lead, and other growing and aspiring leaders on the book website.

Finding Our Path (While Writing this Book!): Closing Thoughts from the Authors

As we are wrapping up our time with you in this book, we are reflecting on the ways that the act of writing this book is allowing us to see ourselves as leaders in ways that we hadn't before.

Kim's Thoughts

As I shared in the introduction, hearing all of these stories, and seeing the ways they connect, called me to action. While I had always wanted to write a book, I never felt I had words valuable enough to share. This book gave me a purpose and an opportunity to become an advocate for the women I work with and for the stories I held.

Knowing that I was the only person who could share these stories in this way, because I was the only one who had heard them all, but also recognizing that these are not my personal stories, was a challenging journey. The thought "Who am I to be sharing these stories?" kept creeping into my mind. But after so many conversations with aspiring leaders in the Women Who Lead course, I started to see myself as the courier for these words.

After being encouraged by other guests on the #coachbetter podcast (thank you Rania Saeb) and the support of many of the women mentioned in this chapter (in particular Madeleine Heide, Joellen Killion, Nneka Johnson, and Clarissa Sayson), as well as fellow author Jayson Richardson, I finally begin to see myself as an author, too. While it still feels hard to write those words, bringing together these stories and sharing them in a way that is approachable and comprehensible to others and connecting with research has changed my self-perception. While these might not be my stories, the research is, and that research deserves to be shared.

Writing this book has helped me realize that I have a perspective that is unique and worth sharing. It has even helped me recognize my voice in my primary area of expertise, instructional coaching in international schools. I found myself frustrated by a specific problem in the international school community early in this writing process, and started thinking, "Why isn't anyone else doing this?" and almost immediately realized, "I can do this work, I have a voice, and I can make an impact." By thinking of myself as a writer and author, I have been able to prioritize time to write for other publications, to clarify my own thinking and focus on spreading the work I believe in to a wider audience. In writing this book, I have found my voice.

Christina's Thoughts

During the writing of this book, I found myself in an ongoing search for a new school leadership role, one that had not been going very well for longer than I care to admit. I found strength in the experiences of the various pathways to leadership that were revealed in each woman's interview. While reading the stories of women leaders, listening to their interviews, and diving into research related to the challenges faced by women in leadership across sectors, I suppose it was inevitable that I would gain important insights. What I didn't expect was how the voices of the Women Who Lead would provide advice, guidance, and moral support as I was finding my path back to school leadership. The negative thoughts of the impostor that once sat on my shoulder were replaced by the stories of the WWL participants and the research that underpins and explains their experiences. Every story was like a motivational talk that helped me to name and confront my own internal challenges and reminded me of my own ability to lead.

One common theme throughout many of the observations and reflections of the WWL interviews is women leaders attributing their success to "luck," "serendipity," or "being in the right place at the right time." These are all-too-frequent attributions to chance, when, in fact, all of these women leaders have put in the effort to learn, develop, and practice skills and competencies that led to leadership roles and responsibilities.

Like the WWL interview participants, I have been out here steadily developing competencies, engaging in practical experiences, acquiring knowledge, and building skills. I have been tapped on the shoulder by other women in leadership roles who invited me into a space where I was able to see myself as a leader. In fact, it's safe to say that it has only ever been other women who have suggested and extended invitations to leadership experiences that have come to fruition for me.

> The act of researching and writing this book has been a transformational journey. I hope that the reflections in the research will serve to ground the reality of the experiences of the WWL participants. May the established leaders who engage with the content of this book find themselves changing in ways that increase their support for the women who lead around them. May the developing leaders who engage with the content of this book also find themselves changing in ways that will allow them to begin, or continue, shaping their personal pathway to school leadership.

Although we have only shared a little of our own stories here in this book, the act of writing has helped us see ourselves as advocates for women, and for ourselves. Being able to connect the stories in this book to the experiences of women we know, we are intentionally supporting the next generation of women leaders.

Now that we have shared these stories with you, we look forward to our next book that might include YOUR story.

Take Action

For Developing Leaders

As you are navigating your own leadership journey, hopefully you now recognize ways that you could have been better supported, or ways that you wish your leaders represented your vision of leadership. While these experiences are fresh in your mind, we invite you to consider the following question:

> What does it mean to be a successful woman who leads?

When you describe this ideal woman leader, how can you bring her characteristics into your practice to become the leader you wish to be and to support others on the pathway behind you? Once you have this idea clear in your mind, envision yourself as the leader you wish to be. Describe yourself in the future, as if you are already there. How does future-you lead?

For Established Leaders

We hope that there have been some "aha moments" for you the established leader in this book, as well as some opportunities to reshape your thinking about your own leadership. Being able to define what you believe in, and clearly describing that vision to others, is a foundational step in becoming the leader you wish to be. To frame your developing perspective on leadership, we invite you to write your leadership manifesto.

As an example, Joellen Killion mentioned that she lives by the following creed:

> *Excellence can be achieved if you . . .*
> *. . . care more than others think is wise*
> *. . . risk more than others think is safe*
> *. . . dream more than others think is practical*
> *. . . expect more than others think is possible*

These simple statements are clear, concise, and actionable—and they provide great insight into Joellen Killion's goals for leadership and life.

Take the time to clearly define what you believe about leadership and develop one coherent statement, your "leadership vision." Your statement should be unique to you and should articulate your leadership vision to the world:

- How would you articulate your own leadership manifesto?
- What do you want others to think about when they hear your name?

Once you've completed your manifesto, please pay it forward and invite a developing leader to read this book and consider their potential for leadership. Remember how powerful a simple nudge can be? Nudge another educator who might not even realize how much potential they have!

For Schools or Organizations

Examine how your school's practices, policies, structures, etc. might favor a particular type of leader (e.g., cis-gender, middle-aged, man, white).

- What actions could your school community take to influence a more inclusive leadership pool at your school?

- How could your school community engage in a more expansive conversation to create a more inclusive definition around what it means to lead at your school?

The challenges faced by women who aspire to leadership in education can seem impossible to overcome, and it is only through broader support from current leaders that true change will take place. If you are in any position to help move your organization move forward, even slightly, take the strategies listed in the previous chapter (and the dozens of women's stories told throughout the whole book) as your call to action!

References

Christensen, L., Gittleson, J., & Smith, M. (2021, April 19). Intentional learning in practice: A 3x3x3 approach. *McKinsey & Company*. www.mckinsey.com/capabilities/people-and-organizational-performance/our-insights/intentional-learning-in-practice-a-3x3x3-approach

Diversity Collaborative. (2021). *Determining the diversity baseline in international schools* [Report]. https://www.iss.edu/wp-content/uploads/DC-Baseline-Analysis-2021.pdf

Appendix A

Women Who Lead Interview Participants

Table A.1 Women Who Lead Interview Participants. All information based on participant details at time of interview during 2020.

Last name	First name	Professional role	School/ organization	Location
Abrams	Jennifer	Author	Author	California, USA
Aneke	Lola	CEO, Cadet Academy	Cadet Academy	Abuja, Nigeria
Ashun	Mary	Principal of School	Ghana International School	Accra, Ghana
Bell	Sanée	Principal	Public School, Texas	Texas, USA
Bland	Mel	Founding Principal	Te Uho o te Nikau Primary School	Auckland, New Zealand
Bloom	Katrina	Elementary School Assistant Principal	American International School Abu Dhabi	Abu Dhabi, United Arab Emirates
Blue	Dominique	Middle School Dean	Basis International School, Guangzhou	Guangzhou, China

Appendix A

Table A.1 (Continued)

Last name	First name	Professional role	School/organization	Location
Botbyl	Christina	Curriculum Director	American International School Kuwait	Kuwait
Brokvam	Caroline	Director	American School of Antananarivo	Antananarivo, Madagascar
Caldwell	Rachel	Head of School	Pechersk School International Kyiv	Kyiv, Ukraine
Cave	Emily	Head of School	NCIC Immersion School, China	China
Charles	Katrina	IB Diploma Programme Coordinator	American School of Doha	Doha, Qatar
Chen	Anita	Director of Technology	International School of Helsinki	Helsinki, Finland
Chohan	Kam	CEO	Educational Collaborative for International Schools	United Kingdom
Chow	Sandra	Director of Innovative Learning	Keystone Academy	Beijing, China
Diller	Charlotte	Director of Technology	International School Kuala Lumpur	Kuala Lumpur, Malaysia
Donohue	Elsa	Head of School	Vientiane International School	Vientiane, Laos
Doogan	Bridget	Director of Professional Learning	Near East South Asia Council of Overseas School	Bahrain
Dressler	Beth	Deputy Head of School	Dresden International School	Dresden, Germany
Dumas	Firoozeh	Author	Author	California, USA

Appendix A

Last name	First name	Professional role	School/organization	Location
Garrett	Chaunté	Superintendent	Charter school	North Carolina, USA
Glass	Shaina	Tech Applications Coordinator	Public school in Houston	Texas, USA
Green	Renée	Dean of Student Life	Singapore American School	Singapore
Ham	Katie	Upper School Principal	Nanjing International School	Nanjing, China
Hamley	Carlene	Director of School Development	Shekou International School	Shenzhen, China
Heide	Madeleine	Head of School	Asociación Escuelas Lincoln American International School	Buenos Aires, Argentina
Henderson	Nathalie	Chief Schools Officer	Indianapolis Public Schools	Indiana, USA
Hovington	Rachel	Head of School	International School of Hannover	Hannover, Germany
Jaber	Sawsan	Founder & Consultant, HS Teacher	Education Unfiltered Public school	Illinois, USA
Jemsby	Suzanna	Head of School	Washington International School	Washington, D.C., USA
Johnson	Chanel	Math & Science Specialist	Public school	Texas, USA
Johnson	Nneka	Director of Innovation	International School of Dakar	Dakar, Senegal
Killion	Joellen	Senior Advisor	Learning Forward	Colorado, USA

(*Continued*)

Appendix A

Table A.1 (Continued)

Last name	First name	Professional role	School/organization	Location
Kleinrock	Liz	AntiBias AntiRacist Educator In Progress	Teach & Transform	California, USA
Koenig	Katie	Elementary School Principal	Rabat American School	Rabat, Morocco
Kuhns	Michelle	Education Consultant and Leadership Coach	Balanced Professional Learning	USA
Leong	Fay	Director of Educational Programs, Pudong Campus	Shanghai American School	Shanghai, China
Madalinski	Junlah	Elementary and Middle School Principal	Schutz American School	Alexandria, Egypt
Madrid	Rebekah	Middle School Vice Principal	Yokohama International School	Yokohama, Japan
Maiers	Angela	CEO	You Matter	Colorado, USA
Marschall	Carla	Director of Teaching and Learning	United World College Southeast Asia	Singapore
Mattoon	Michele	Executive Director	National School Reform Faculty	Indiana, USA
McCallum	Grace	Elementary School Principal	Frankfurt International School	Frankfurt, Germany
McNamer	Bridget	Chief Navigation Officer	Sidecar Counsel	USA
Medved	Marta	Head of School	Western Academy of Beijing	Beijing, China

Appendix A

Last name	First name	Professional role	School/ organization	Location
Moran	Catriona	Head of School	Saigon South International School	Ho Chi Minh City, Vietnam
Nabholz	Sheena	Head of School	Lincoln Community School	Accra, Ghana
Nachef	Rashida	Director of High School System	Institute of Applied Technology	Abu Dhabi, United Arab Emirates
Naglee	Kathleen	Head of School	International School of Helsinki	Helsinki, Finland
Philen	Jasmeen	Elementary School Assistant Principal	International School Manila	Taguig City, Philippines
Remington	Michelle	Director	The KAUST School	Kingdom of Saudi Arabia
Reynolds	Fiona	Deputy Head of School	American School of Bombay	Mumbai, India
Richards	Nadine	High School Principal	American School of Dubai	Dubai, United Arab Emirates
Robinson	Erin	Middle School Principal	United World College Southeast Asia	Singapore
Sargent-Beasley	Emily	Head of Campus, Pudong	Shanghai American School	Shanghai, China
Sawyer	Lynn	Educational Consultant	Sawyer Educational Consulting	Nevada, USA
Sayson	Clarissa	Elementary School Principal	International School Beijing	Beijing, China
Schmidt	Nicole	Principal	American International School Johannesburg	Johannesburg, South Africa

(*Continued*)

Appendix A

Table A.1 (Continued)

Last name	First name	Professional role	School/ organization	Location
Shinnawi	Abeer	Founder & Consultant	Altair Education Consulting	Maryland, USA
Shoman	Nina	Assistant Dean of Learning Enrichment and Readiness	Moraine Valley Community College	Illinois, USA
Silva	Daniela	Director of Technology	Colegio Franklin Delano Roosevelt, The American School of Lima	Lima, Peru
Thompson	Jane	Head of School	American School of Paris	Saint-Cloud, France
Tickle	Jennifer	Secondary Principal	Dresden International School	Dresden, Germany
Tyler	Tambi	Head of School	The Colorado Springs School	Colorado, USA
Tyoschin	Arden	Head of School	Harare International School	Harare, Zimbabwe
Varney	Helen	Principal	Target Roads School	Auckland, New Zealand
Vrba	Melanie	High School Principal	Western Academy Beijing	Beijing, China
Waudby	Tara	Head of School	Riffa Views International School	Bahrain
Welch	Deb	CEO	Academy of International School Heads	USA
Wellbrook	Katie	Assistant Principal for Academics	Suzhou Singapore International School	Suzhou, China

Appendix B

WWL Interview Questions

1. Please tell us your name and your role. Please tell us about your journey into leadership.
2. Can you pinpoint the moment in your career when you realized "I am a leader" or "I have the capacity to lead"?
3. What are the unique challenges women face in pursuing a leadership position? (for example imposter syndrome, double standards for men vs women). Do you have a personal story from your experience you can share?
4. What did you learn in the interview process? How do you get your foot in the door? How is a leadership interview different than others we might be more familiar with?
5. How do you handle confrontation (difficult conversations) differently now at this point in your career as compared to at the start of it?
6. Please tell us a bit about how you find balance in your life, as a leader. How do you manage everything—being a parent, a leader, etc.? For example, do you have a hobby that's not directly related to your job but helps support your job?
7. As a leader, what decision-making process do you go through to determine what priorities enter your headspace and what don't? What advice do you have for others when it comes to finding your focus or priorities?
8. Which one or two other women have done the most to mentor you, and can you share a specific piece of wisdom you learned

Appendix B

from them? How important is mentorship to women in leadership? Do you have a personal story of mentorship you can share with us?
9. What's the emerging skill that you think female leaders will need? Which skill do you think is going to be the most important for women leaders coming up in the next two to three years and why?
10. At Eduro we think of ourselves as relentless learners, and we believe fully that it is so important to keep finding new authors, speakers, podcasts, and other resources to push our thinking. Which resources are currently stretching your thinking? Please share the name of a female author who inspires you (or a specific book written by a woman). *Table 14.1* (Continued)